2020

中国法治建设年度报告

（中英文）

中国法学会 编

中国长安出版传媒

前　言

2020年是中华人民共和国历史上极不平凡的一年。面对错综复杂的国际形势、艰巨繁重的国内改革发展稳定任务特别是新冠肺炎疫情严重冲击，在以习近平同志为核心的党中央坚强领导下，全国各族人民顽强拼搏，疫情防控取得重大战略成果，在全球主要经济体中唯一实现经济正增长，脱贫攻坚战取得全面胜利，决胜全面建成小康社会取得决定性成就，交出一份人民满意、世界瞩目、可以载入史册的答卷。2020年也是中国法治建设具有里程碑意义的重要一年：这一年，中央全面依法治国工作会议召开，明确了习近平法治思想在全面依法治国中的指导地位；这一年，十三届全国人大三次会议表决通过《中华人民共和国民法典》，开创国家法典编纂立法的先河；这一年，中共中央印发《法治中国建设规划（2020—2025年）》《法治社会建设实施纲要（2020—2025年）》，明确了法治中国建设、法治社会建设的路线图和施工图；这一年，全国政法机关充分发挥职能作用，全力做好疫情防控工作、护航脱贫攻坚，助力续写经济快速发展和社会长期稳定"两大奇迹"新篇章；这一年，法治政府建设取得新成效，政法领域全面深化改革取得新突破，扫黑除恶专项斗争圆满收官，司法为民、公正司法水平明显提高，平安中国、法治中国建设迈上新台阶，法治宣传、法学教育和法学研究取得新成绩。2020年，中国法治建设取得新的重大进展，必将激励全国人民以更加昂扬的姿态奋进在全面依法治国的伟大征程上！

目 录

坚定不移走中国特色社会主义法治道路
为全面建设社会主义现代化国家提供
有力法治保障 …………………………… 习近平（ 1 ）

一、关于全国人大及其常委会的立法工作
　　和监督工作 ………………………………………（ 1 ）
二、关于依法行政 …………………………………（ 19 ）
三、关于政法领域改革 ……………………………（ 26 ）
四、关于审判、检察、公安和司法行政工作 ……（ 35 ）
五、关于人权法治保障 ……………………………（ 57 ）
六、关于知识产权保护 ……………………………（ 68 ）
七、关于生态文明法治建设 ………………………（ 77 ）
八、关于法治宣传、法学教育和法学研究 ………（ 87 ）
九、关于国际交流与国际合作 ……………………（ 96 ）
结束语 ………………………………………………（108）
附　录 ………………………………………………（110）

Contents

Preface ·· (117)
Unswervingly Follow the Socialist Legal Path with
   Chinese Characteristics to Provide a Strong Legal
   Guarantee for Building a Modern Socialist Country
   in All Respects ······················· Xi Jinping (120)

I. The Legislative and Supervisory Work of the
   National People's Congress and Its Standing
   Committee ·· (150)
II. Law – Based Government Administration ········ (183)
III. Judicial and Law Enforcement Reform ········ (196)
IV. Judicial, Procuratorial, Public Security and
   Judicial Administrative Work ················ (213)
V. Legal Protection of Human Rights ············· (254)
VI. Protection of Intellectual Property Rights ······ (272)
VII. Building the Rule of Law in Ecological
   Civilization ·· (288)

VIII. Legal Communication, Legal Education,
     and Legal Research ·················· (307)
IX. International Exchanges and Cooperation ········ (323)
Conclusion ································· (342)
Appendixes ································· (345)

坚定不移走中国特色社会主义法治道路 为全面建设社会主义现代化国家 提供有力法治保障[1]

习近平

这次中央全面依法治国工作会议的主要任务是，总结经验，分析形势，明确任务，对当前和今后一个时期全面依法治国工作作出部署，动员全党全国全社会齐心协力，为深入推进全面依法治国、加快建设中国特色社会主义法治体系、建设社会主义法治国家而奋斗。

我们党历来重视法治建设。在新民主主义革命时期，我们党就制定了《中华苏维埃共和国宪法大纲》以及大量法律法令，创造了"马锡五审判方式"。新中国成立后，在社会主义革命、社会主义建设时期，我们党领导人民制定了"五四宪法"和国家机构组织法、选举法、婚姻法等一系列重要法律法规，建立起社会主义法制框

---

[1] 这是习近平总书记2020年11月16日在中央全面依法治国工作会议上讲话的主要部分。来源：《求是》2021年第5期。

架体系，确立了社会主义司法制度。进入改革开放历史新时期，我们党提出"有法可依、有法必依、执法必严、违法必究"的方针，强调依法治国是党领导人民治理国家的基本方略、依法执政是党治国理政的基本方式，不断推进社会主义法治建设。

党的十八大以来，党中央明确提出全面依法治国，并将其纳入"四个全面"战略布局予以有力推进。党的十八届四中全会专门进行研究，作出关于全面推进依法治国若干重大问题的决定。党的十九大召开后，党中央组建中央全面依法治国委员会，从全局和战略高度对全面依法治国又作出一系列重大决策部署，推动我国社会主义法治建设发生历史性变革、取得历史性成就。我们把"中国共产党领导是中国特色社会主义最本质的特征"写入宪法，完善党领导立法、保证执法、支持司法、带头守法制度，党对全面依法治国的领导更加坚强有力。我们完善顶层设计，统筹推进法律规范、法治实施、法治监督、法治保障和党内法规体系建设，全面依法治国总体格局基本形成。我们推进重要领域立法，深化法治领域改革，推进法治政府建设，建立国家监察机构，改革完善司法体制，加强全民普法，深化依法治军，推进法治专门队伍建设，坚决维护社会公平正义，依法纠正一批冤错案件，全面依法治国实践取得重大进展。

当前和今后一个时期，推进全面依法治国，要全面贯彻落实党的十九大和十九届二中、三中、四中、五中全会精神，围绕建设中国特色社会主义法治体系、建设社会主义法治国家的总目标，坚持党的领导、人民当家作主、依法治国有机统一，以解决法治领域突出问题为着力点，坚定不移走中国特色社会主义法治道路，在法治轨道上推进国家治理体系和治理能力现代化，为全面建设社会主义现代化国家、实现中华民族伟大复兴的中国梦提供有力法治保障。要重点抓好以下工作。

第一，坚持党对全面依法治国的领导。党的领导是推进全面依法治国的根本保证。我们党是世界最大的执政党，领导着世界上人口最多的国家，如何掌好权、执好政，如何更好把14亿人民组织起来、动员起来全面建设社会主义现代化国家，是一个始终需要高度重视的重大课题。历史是最好的教科书，也是最好的清醒剂。我们党领导社会主义法治建设，既有成功经验，也有失误教训。特别是十年内乱期间，法制遭到严重破坏，党和人民付出了沉重代价。"文化大革命"结束后，邓小平同志把这个问题提到关系党和国家前途命运的高度，强调"必须加强法制。必须使民主制度化、法律化"。正反两方面的经验告诉我们，国际国内环境越是复杂，改革开放和社会主义现代化建设任务越是繁重，越要运用法治思维和法治手段巩固执政地位、改善执政方式、提高执政能力，保证党和国家长治久安。

全党同志都必须清醒认识到，全面依法治国决不是要削弱党的领导，而是要加强和改善党的领导。要健全党领导全面依法治国的制度和工作机制，推进党的领导制度化、法治化，通过法治保障党的路线方针政策有效实施。要坚持依法治国和依规治党有机统一，确保党既依据宪法法律治国理政，又依据党内法规管党治党、从严治党。

2015年，我在中央政治局常委会听取最高人民法院和最高人民检察院党组工作汇报、在省部级主要领导干部学习贯彻党的十八届四中全会精神全面推进依法治国专题研讨班开班式等场合都明确指出，"党大还是法大"是一个政治陷阱，是一个伪命题；对这个问题，我们不能含糊其辞、语焉不详，要明确予以回答。党的领导和依法治国不是对立的，而是统一的。我国法律充分体现了党和人民意志，我们党依法办事，这个关系是相互统一的关系。全党同志必须牢记，党的领导是我国社会主义法治之魂，是我国法治同西方资本主义国家法治最大的区别。离开了党的领导，全面依法治国就难以有效推进，社会主义法治国家就建不起来。

当然，我们说不存在"党大还是法大"的问题，是把党作为一个执政整体、就党的执政地位和领导地位而言的，具体到每个党政组织、每个领导干部，就必须服从和遵守宪法法律。有些事情要提交党委把握，但这种把握不是私情插手，不是包庇性的干预，而是一种政治性、程序性、职责性的把握。这个界线一定要划分清楚。

第二，坚持以人民为中心。全面依法治国最广泛、最深厚的基础是人民，必须坚持为了人民、依靠人民。要把体现人民利益、反映人民愿望、维护人民权益、增进人民福祉落实到全面依法治国各领域全过程，保证人民在党的领导下通过各种途径和形式管理国家事务、管理经济文化事业、管理社会事务，保证人民依法享有广泛的权利和自由、承担应尽的义务。

推进全面依法治国，根本目的是依法保障人民权益。随着我国经济社会持续发展和人民生活水平不断提高，人民群众对民主、法治、公平、正义、安全、环境等方面的要求日益增长，要积极回应人民群众新要求新期待，坚持问题导向、目标导向，树立辩证思维和全局观念，系统研究谋划和解决法治领域人民群众反映强烈的突出问题，不断增强人民群众获得感、幸福感、安全感，用法治保障人民安居乐业。

第三，坚持中国特色社会主义法治道路。我说过，我们要坚持的中国特色社会主义法治道路，本质上是中国特色社会主义道路在法治领域的具体体现；我们要发展的中国特色社会主义法治理论，本质上是中国特色社会主义理论体系在法治问题上的理论成果；我们要建设的中国特色社会主义法治体系，本质上是中国特色社会主义制度的法律表现形式。我们既要立足当前，运用法治思维和法治方式解决经济社会发展面临的深层次问题；又要着眼长远，筑法治之基、行法治之力、积法治之势，促进各方面制度更加成熟更加定型，为党和国家事业发展提供长期性的制度保障。

自古以来，我国形成了世界法制史上独树一帜的中华法系，积淀了深厚的法律文化。中华法系形成于秦朝，到隋唐时期逐步成熟，《唐律疏议》是代表性的法典，清末以后中华法系影响日渐衰微。与大陆法系、英美法系、伊斯兰法系等不同，中华法系是在我国特定历史条件下形成的，显示了中华民族的伟大创造力和中华法制文明的深厚底蕴。中华法系凝聚了中华民族的精神和智慧，有很多优秀的思想和理念值得我们传承。出礼入刑、隆礼重法的治国策略，民惟邦本、本固邦宁的民本理念，天下无讼、以和为贵的价值追求，德主刑辅、明德慎罚的慎刑思想，援法断罪、罚当其罪的平等观念，保护鳏寡孤独、老幼妇残的恤刑原则，等等，都彰显了中华优秀传统法律文化的智慧。近代以后，不少人试图在中国照搬西方法治模式，但最终都归于失败。历史和现实告诉我们，只有传承中华优秀传统法律文化，从我国革命、建设、改革的实践中探索适合自己的法治道路，同时借鉴国外法治有益成果，才能为全面建设社会主义现代化国家、实现中华民族伟大复兴夯实法治基础。

有一点要明确，我们推进全面依法治国，决不照搬别国模式和做法，决不走西方所谓"宪政"、"三权鼎立"、"司法独立"的路子。实践证明，我国政治制度和法治体系是适合我国国情和实际的制度，具有显著优越性。在这个问题上，我们要有自信、有底气、有定力。事实教育了我们的人民群众，人民群众越来越自信。

面对突如其来的疫情，我们始终坚持坚定信心、同舟共济、科学防治、精准施策的总要求。2月5日，我就主持召开中央全面依法治国委员会第三次会议，在疫情防控关键时刻专门部署依法防控疫情工作，我特别强调，疫情防控越是到了最吃劲的时候，越要坚持依法防控，在法治轨道上统筹推进各项防控工作。各地区各部门从立法、执法、司法、普法、守法各环节全面发力，严格按照法定权限和程序实施区域封锁、病人隔离、交通管控、遗体处置等措施，严厉打击妨害疫情防控的违法犯罪行为，依法化解涉疫矛盾纠纷，为疫情防控取得重大战略成果提供了有力法治保障。

第四，坚持依宪治国、依宪执政。宪法是国家的根本法，具有最高的法律效力。党领导人民制定宪法法律，领导人民实施宪法法律，党自身要在宪法法律范围内活动。全国各族人民、一切国家机关和武装力量、各政党和各社会团体、各企业事业组织，都必须以宪法为根本的活动准则，都负有维护宪法尊严、保证宪法实施的职责。任何组织和个人都不得有超越宪法法律的特权，一切违反宪法法律的行为都必须予以追究。

党的十八届四中全会明确提出，坚持依法治国首先要坚持依宪治国，坚持依法执政首先要坚持依宪执政。我们讲依宪治国、依宪执政，同西方所谓"宪政"有着本质区别，不能把二者混为一谈。坚持依宪治国、依宪执政，就包括坚持宪法确定的中国共产党领导地位不动摇，坚持宪法确定的人民民主专政的国体和人民代表大会制度的政体不动摇。

维护国家法治统一，是一个严肃的政治问题。我国是单一制国家，维护国家法治统一至关重要。2015年立法法修改，赋予设区的市地方立法权，地方立法工作有了积极进展，总体情况是好的，但有的地方也存在违背上位法规定、立法"放水"等问题，影响很不好。要加强宪法实施和监督，推进合宪性审查工作，对一切违反宪法法律的法规、规范性文件必须坚决予以纠正和撤销。同时，地方立法要有地方特色，需要几条就定几条，能用三五条解决问题就不要搞"鸿篇巨制"，关键是吃透党中央精神，从地方实际出发，解决突出问题。

第五，坚持在法治轨道上推进国家治理体系和治理能力现代化。法治是国家治理体系和治理能力的重要依托。只有全面依法治国才能有效保障国家治理体系的系统性、规范性、协调性，才能最大限度凝聚社会共识。

新中国成立70多年来，我国之所以创造出经济快速发展、社会长期稳定"两大奇迹"，同我们不断推进社会主义法治建设有着十分紧密的关系。这次应对新冠肺炎疫情，我们坚持在法治轨道上统筹推进疫情防控和经济社会发展工作，依法维护社会大局稳定，有序推进复工复产，我国疫情防控取得重大战略成果，我国将成为今年全球唯一恢复经济正增长的主要经济体。在统筹推进伟大斗争、伟大工程、伟大事业、伟大梦想的实践中，在全面建设社会主义现代化国家新征程上，我们要更加重视法治、厉行法治，更好发挥法治固根本、稳预期、利长远的保障作用，坚持依法应对重大挑战、抵御重大风险、克服重大阻力、解决重大矛盾。

第六，坚持建设中国特色社会主义法治体系。中国特色社会主义法治体系是推进全面依法治国的总抓手。要加快形成完备的法律规范体系、高效的法治实施体系、严密的法治监督体系、有力的法治保障体系，形成完善的党内法规体系。要坚持依法治国和以德治国相结合，实现法治和德治相辅相成、相得益彰。

"治国无其法则乱，守法而不变则衰。"要加快完善中国特色社会主义法律体系，使之更加科学完备、统一权威。党的十八大以来，全国人大及其常委会通过宪法修正案，制定法律48件，修改法律203件次，作出法律解释9件，通过有关法律问题和重大问题的决定79件次。

截至目前，现行有效法律282件、行政法规608件，地方性法规12,000余件。民法典为其他领域立法法典化提供了很好的范例，要总结编纂民法典的经验，适时推动条件成熟的立法领域法典编纂工作。要研究丰富立法形式，可以搞一些"大块头"，也要搞一些"小快灵"，增强立法的针对性、适用性、可操作性。

要积极推进国家安全、科技创新、公共卫生、生物安全、生态文明、防范风险、涉外法治等重要领域立法，健全国家治理急需的法律制度、满足人民日益增长的美好生活需要必备的法律制度，填补空白点、补强薄弱点。数字经济、互联网金融、人工智能、大数据、云计算等新技术新应用快速发展，催生一系列新业态新模式，但相关法律制度还存在时间差、空白区。网络犯罪已成为危害我国国家政治安全、网络安全、社会安全、经济安全等的重要风险之一。

第七，坚持依法治国、依法执政、依法行政共同推进，法治国家、法治政府、法治社会一体建设。全面依法治国是一个系统工程，要整体谋划，更加注重系统性、整体性、协同性。依法治国、依法执政、依法行政是一个有机整体，关键在于党要坚持依法执政、各级政府要坚持依法行政。法治国家、法治政府、法治社会相辅相成，法治国家是法治建设的目标，法治政府是建设法治国家的重点，法治社会是构筑法治国家的基础。

我多次强调，推进全面依法治国，法治政府建设是重点任务和主体工程，对法治国家、法治社会建设具有示范带动作用，要率先突破。现在，法治政府建设还有一些难啃的硬骨头，依法行政观念不牢固、行政决策合法性审查走形式等问题还没有根本解决。要用法治给行政权力定规矩、划界限，规范行政决策程序，健全政府守信践诺机制，提高依法行政水平。要根据新发展阶段的特点，围绕推动高质量发展、构建新发展格局，加快转变政府职能，加快打造市场化、法治化、国际化营商环境，打破行业垄断和地方保护，打通经济循环堵点，推动形成全国统一、公平竞争、规范有序的市场体系。

行政执法工作面广量大，一头连着政府，一头连着群众，直接关系群众对党和政府的信任、对法治的信心。要推进严格规范公正文明执法，提高司法公信力。近年来，我们整治执法不规范、乱作为等问题，取得很大成效。同时，一些地方运动式、"一刀切"执法问题仍时有发生，执法不作为问题突出。强调严格执法，让违法者敬法畏法，但绝不是暴力执法、过激执法，要让执法既有力度又有温度。要加强省市县乡四级全覆盖的行政执法协调监督工作体系建设，强化全方位、全流程监督，提高执法质量。

全民守法是法治社会的基础工程。普法工作要紧跟时代，在针对性和实效性上下功夫，落实"谁执法谁普法"普法责任制，特别是要加强青少年法治教育，不断提升全体公民法治意识和法治素养，使法治成为社会共识和基本准则。要强化依法治理，培育全社会办事依法、遇事找法、解决问题用法、化解矛盾靠法的法治环境。

古人说："消未起之患、治未病之疾，医之于无事之前。"法治建设既要抓末端、治已病，更要抓前端、治未病。我国国情决定了我们不能成为"诉讼大国"。我国有14亿人口，大大小小的事都要打官司，那必然不堪重负！要推动更多法治力量向引导和疏导端用力，完善预防性法律制度，坚持和发展新时代"枫桥经验"，完善社会矛盾纠纷多元预防调处化解综合机制，更加重视基层基础工作，充分发挥共建共治共享在基层的作用，推进市域社会治理现代化，促进社会和谐稳定。

第八，坚持全面推进科学立法、严格执法、公正司法、全民守法。要继续推进法治领域改革，解决好立法、执法、司法、守法等领域的突出矛盾和问题。

公平正义是司法的灵魂和生命。要深化司法责任制综合配套改革，加强司法制约监督，完善人员分类管理，健全司法职业保障，规范司法权力运行，提高司法办案质量和效率。要健全社会公平正义法治保障制度，努力让人民群众在每一个司法案件中感受到公平正义。要继续完善公益诉讼制度，有效维护社会公共利益。党的十八大以来，党中央确定的一些重大改革事项，健全纪检监察机关、公安机关、检察机关、审判机关、司法行政机关各司其职，侦查权、检察权、审判权、执行权相互配合的体制机制等，要紧盯不放，真正一抓到底，抓出实效。

近年来，司法腐败案件集中暴露出权力制约监督不到位问题。一些人通过金钱开路，几乎成了法外之人，背后有政法系统几十名干部为其"打招呼"、"开路条"，监督形同虚设。要加快构建规范高效的制约监督体系，坚决破除"关系网"、斩断"利益链"，让"猫腻"、"暗门"无处遁形。

2018年1月起，为期3年的扫黑除恶专项斗争在全国展开。扫黑除恶专项斗争把打击黑恶势力和"打伞破网"一体推进，清除了一批害群之马。近3年来打掉的涉黑组织相当于前10年的总和，对黑恶势力形成了强大震慑。要继续依法打击破坏社会秩序的违法犯罪行为，特别是要推动扫黑除恶常态化，持之以恒、坚定不移打击黑恶势力及其保护伞，让城乡更安宁、群众更安乐。

第九，坚持统筹推进国内法治和涉外法治。法治是国家核心竞争力的重要内容。当前，世界百年未有之大变局加速演变，和平与发展仍然是时代主题，但国际环境不稳定性不确定性明显上升，新冠肺炎疫情大流行影响广泛深远。我国不断发展壮大，日益走近世界舞台中央。要加快涉外法治工作战略布局，协调推进国内治理和国际治理，更好维护国家主权、安全、发展利益。要加快形成系统完备的涉外法律法规体系，提升涉外执法司法效能。要引导企业、公民在走出去过程中更加自觉地遵守当地法律法规和风俗习惯，运用法治和规则维护自身合法权益。要注重培育一批国际一流的仲裁机构、律师事务所，把涉外法治保障和服务工作做得更有成效。

我们要坚定维护以联合国为核心的国际体系，坚定维护以国际法为基础的国际秩序，坚定维护以联合国宪章宗旨和原则为基础的国际法基本原则和国际关系基本准则。对不公正不合理、不符合国际格局演变大势的国际规则、国际机制，要提出改革方案，推动全球治理变革，推动构建人类命运共同体。

第十，坚持建设德才兼备的高素质法治工作队伍。全面推进依法治国，首先要把专门队伍建设好。要加强理想信念教育，深入开展社会主义核心价值观和社会主义法治理念教育，推进法治专门队伍革命化、正规化、专业化、职业化，确保做到忠于党、忠于国家、忠于人民、忠于法律。

对法治专门队伍的管理必须坚持更严标准、更高要求。一些执法司法人员手握重器而不自重，贪赃枉法、徇私枉法，办"金钱案"、"权力案"、"人情案"，严重损害法治权威。要制定完善铁规禁令、纪律规定，用制度管好关键人、管到关键处、管住关键事。要坚决清查贪赃枉法、对党不忠诚不老实的人，深查执法司法腐败。最近，政法系统开展队伍教育整顿试点工作，查处了一批害群之马，得到广大群众好评。要巩固和扩大试点工作成果，坚持零容忍，敢于刀刃向内、刮骨疗毒。

法律服务队伍是全面依法治国的重要力量。总体而言，这支队伍是好的，但也存在不少问题，有的热衷于"扬名逐利"，行为不端、诚信缺失、形象不佳；极个别法律从业人员政治意识淡薄，甚至恶意攻击我国政治制度和法治制度。要把拥护中国共产党领导、拥护我国社会主义法治作为法律服务人员从业的基本要求，加强教育、管理、引导，引导法律服务工作者坚持正确政治方向，依法依规诚信执业，认真履行社会责任，满腔热忱投入社会主义法治国家建设。要推进法学院校改革发展，提高人才培养质量。要加大涉外法学教育力度，重点做好涉外执法司法和法律服务人才培养、国际组织法律人才培养推送工作，更好服务对外工作大局。

第十一，坚持抓住领导干部这个"关键少数"。领导干部具体行使党的执政权和国家立法权、行政权、监察权、司法权，是全面依法治国的关键。各级领导干部要坚决贯彻落实党中央关于全面依法治国的重大决策部署，带头尊崇法治、敬畏法律，了解法律、掌握法律，不断提高运用法治思维和法治方式深化改革、推动发展、化解矛盾、维护稳定、应对风险的能力，做尊法学法守法用法的模范。要把法治素养和依法履职情况纳入考核评价干部的重要内容，让尊法学法守法用法成为领导干部自觉行为和必备素质。

同志们！深入推进全面依法治国，必须坚持党的集中统一领导。各级党委和政府要加强对法治建设的组织领导，重大部署、重要任务、重点工作要抓在手上，确保落到实处。要深入贯彻党的十九届五中全会精神，将"十四五"时期经济社会发展和法治建设同步谋划、同步部署、同步推进。党中央即将印发法治中国建设规划和法治社会建设实施纲要，新的法治政府建设实施纲要也将很快出台，各级党委和政府要抓紧抓实抓好。各条战线各个部门要强化法治观念，严格依法办事，不断提高各领域工作法治化水平。法治工作部门要全面履职尽责。中央依法治国办要履行统筹协调、督促检查、推动落实的职责，及时发现问题，推动研究解决。要力戒形式主义、官僚主义，确保全面依法治国各项任务真正落到实处。

推进全面依法治国是国家治理的一场深刻变革，必须以科学理论为指导，加强理论思维，从理论上回答为什么要全面依法治国、怎样全面依法治国这个重大时代课题，不断从理论和实践的结合上取得新成果，总结好、运用好党关于新时代加强法治建设的思想理论成果，更好指导全面依法治国各项工作。

一、关于全国人大及其常委会的立法工作和监督工作

2020年，中国全国人大及其常委会共制定法律9件，修改法律12件，通过有关法律问题和重大问题的决定12件。截至2020年12月底，中国现行有效的法律共283件。2020年5月28日，十三届全国人大三次会议通过《中华人民共和国民法典》。该法自2021年1月1日起施行。《中华人民共和国婚姻法》《中华人民共和国继承法》《中华人民共和国民法通则》《中华人民共和国收养法》《中华人民共和国担保法》《中华人民共和国合同法》《中华人民共和国物权法》《中华人民共和国侵权责任法》《中华人民共和国民法总则》同时废止。据此，2021年1月1日，现行有效法律最新统计数字为274件。

（一）通过立法实施宪法规定的重要制度

——召集全国人民代表大会会议，是宪法规定的全国人大常委会的职权。根据新冠肺炎疫情形势和防控工作需要，2月，全国人大常委会作出《关于推迟召开第

十三届全国人民代表大会第三次会议的决定》，这是改革开放40多年来首次推迟召开全国人大会议。这一决定，符合宪法原则和精神，符合有关法律规定，有利于贯彻落实党中央统筹推进疫情防控和经济社会发展工作的重大决策部署，有利于维护人民生命安全和身体健康，有利于保证大会聚焦主题、顺利完成任务。4月，又适时作出《关于第十三届全国人民代表大会第三次会议召开时间的决定》，决定大会于2020年5月22日在北京召开。

——授予国家勋章和荣誉称号是宪法规定的重要制度。在抗击新冠肺炎疫情斗争取得重大战略成果之际，根据宪法和国家勋章和国家荣誉称号法，8月，全国人大常委会作出关于授予在抗击新冠肺炎疫情斗争中作出杰出贡献的人士国家勋章和国家荣誉称号的决定，国家主席签署主席令，授予钟南山"共和国勋章"，授予张伯礼、张定宇、陈薇"人民英雄"国家荣誉称号，隆重表彰抗疫斗争中作出杰出贡献的功勋模范人物，弘扬他们忠诚、担当、奉献的崇高品质。

——坚决维护宪法和香港基本法确定的香港特别行政区宪制秩序，加强香港特别行政区维护国家安全立法。根据宪法和香港特别行政区基本法，十三届全国人大三次会议作出《关于建立健全香港特别行政区维护国家安全的法律制度和执行机制的决定》。6月，全国人大常委会制定香港特别行政区维护国家安全法并决定将该法律列入香港特别行政区基本法附件三，由香港特别行政区在当地公布实施。8月，全国人大常委会通过《关于香港特别行政区第六届立法会继续履行职责的决定》，妥善解决因疫情推迟选举情况下立法机关空缺问题。11月，全国人大常委会作出《关于香港特别行政区立法会议员资格问题的决定》，对香港立法会议员的法定要求和资格条件作出清晰界定，确保以爱国者为主体的港人治港。这一系列立法举措，为坚持和完善"一国两制"制度体系，维护国家主权、安全、发展利益，保障香港长治久安和长期繁荣稳定提供了宪制依据和法治保障。

——选举法是保障公民行使选举权和被选举权，依法产生各级人大代表的重要法律。针对各地基层行政区划撤乡并镇改设街道、基层人大代表数量逐年减少的实际情况，10月，全国人大常委会修改选举法。修改后的该法，适当增加县乡两级人大代表名额的基数，将不设区的市、市辖区、县、自治县的人大代表名额基数从120名提高至140名，将乡、民族乡、镇的人大代表名额基数从40名提高至45名，并明确重新确定代表名额的报备等，有利于更好保障人民当家作主权利，进一步夯实人民代表大会制度基础。

——完善国家象征和标志法律制度，维护国家权威与尊严。10月，全国人大常委会修改国旗法、国徽法，进一步规范国旗、国徽及其图案的悬挂和使用，有利于强化公民国家观念，弘扬爱国主义精神，培育和践行社会主义核心价值观，为实现中华民族伟大复兴凝聚精神力量。

——深化国家监察体制改革，强化对所有公职人员的监督和管理。6月，全国人大常委会审议通过公职人员政务处分法。该法将监察法的原则规定具体化，把法定对象全面纳入处分范围，使政务处分匹配党纪处分、衔接刑事处罚；明确实施政务处分的主体、处分事由、权限和程序，被处分人员维护合法权益的救济途径等，有利于处分决定机关、单位强化法治观念、程序意识，推进政务处分法治化、规范化，促进公职人员依法履职、秉公用权、廉洁从政从业。

（二）加强重点领域立法

——完成民法典编纂。民法典是中华人民共和国第一部以法典命名的法律，以法典化方式确认、巩固和发展了改革开放以来所取得的民事法治建设成果，开创了中国法典编纂立法的先河，具有里程碑意义。2017年3月，十二届全国人大五次会议审议通过民法典总则；2018年12月，2019年4月、6月、8月、10月，十三届全国人大常委会对民法典各分编草案进行拆分审议，对全部6个分编草案进行二审，对各方面比较关注的人格权、婚姻家庭、侵权责任3个分编草案进行三审。在此基础上，将民法典总则与经过审议和修改完善的各分编草案合并，形成民法典草案。2019年12月，全国人大常委会审议民法典草案并作出决定，将民法典草案提请十三届全国人大三次会议审议。2020年5月28日，十三届全国人大三次会议审议通过《中华人民共和国民法典》。民法典共7编、1260条，各编依次为总则、物权、合同、人格权、婚姻家庭、继承、侵权责任，以及附则，进一步完善了我国民商事领域基本法律制度和行为规则，为各类民商事活动提供了基本遵循，对坚持和完善社会主义基本经济制度、推动高质量发展，增进人民福祉、维护最广大人民根本利益，具有十分重要的意义。

——强化公共卫生法治保障相关立法。

为了全面禁止和惩治非法野生动物交易行为，革除滥食野生动物的陋习。2月，全国人大常委会制定《关于全面禁止非法野生动物交易、革除滥食野生动物陋习、切实保障人民群众生命健康安全的决定》。该决定聚焦滥食野生动物的突出问题，明确全面禁止食用野生动物，加强对非食用性利用野生动物的管理，严格禁止非法野生动物交易等，为维护公共安全和生态安全，保障人民群众生命健康安全提供有力立法保障。

针对抗疫实践中暴露的法治短板和防范应对公共卫生风险方面的不足，4月，全国人大常委会听取审议强化公共卫生法治保障立法修法工作有关情况和工作计划的报告。这是全国人大常委会首次制定专项立法工作计划，首次听取专门领域立法工作情况报告。专项立法修法工作计划统筹考虑提出需要制定修改的法律，其中包括拟在2020—2021年制定修改的法律17件，拟综合统筹、适时制定修改的相关法律13件，以及其他需制定修改的相关法律，为依法防控新冠肺炎疫情、完善和强化公共卫生法治保障体系提供法律支撑。

——完善国家安全领域立法。

制定生物安全法。生物安全法是生物安全领域的基础性法律。10月，全国人大常委会审议通过生物安全法。该法贯彻落实总体国家安全观，统筹发展和安全，建立健全国家生物安全领导体制机制，构建科学完备的生物安全风险防控制度，对生物安全风险监测、评估、预警、应对等作出具体安排，专章规定重大新发突发传染病、动植物疫情防控措施，着力提高我国生物安全治理能力，有利于保障人民生命安全和身体健康，维护生物安全和生态安全，促进生物产业有序健康发展。

制定出口管制法。出口管制法是统领出口管制工作的法律。10月，全国人大常委会审议通过出口管制法。该法立足更好履行防扩散等国际义务，在总结实践经验、参考国际通行制度的基础上，对出口管制清单、出口许可、最终用户和最终用途管理等基本制度作了规定，为做好新时期出口管制工作提供了有力法治保障。

——完善市场经济领域立法。

制定城市维护建设税法和契税法。8月，全国人大常委会审议通过城市维护建设税法和契税法。落实税收法定原则，按照税制平移思路，保持现行税制框架和税负水平总体不变，将相关暂行条例上升为法律。至此，现行18个税种中已有11个实现税收法定。

修改专利法和著作权法。加强知识产权保护，推动我国科技创新和文化繁荣发展，10月，全国人大常委会修改专利法，增加诚实信用原则，新设专利权期限补偿制度和药品专利纠纷早期解决机制，延长外观设计专利权保护期，加强对专利权人合法权益的保护，加大对专利侵权行为的惩治力度；明确单位对职务发明创造的处置权，加强专利化服务，新设专利开放许可制度，促进专利实施和运用；新设外观设计专利申请国内优先权制度等，明确授予局部外观设计专利权，完善专利授权制度，激励科技创新。11月，全国人大常委会修改著作权法，适应网络化、数字化技术发展应用形式，完善作品的定义和类型，对视听作品的著作权进行分类保护，对有关著作权出质、职务表演、诉前保全措施等作出规定，引入惩罚性赔偿制度，大幅提高法定赔偿额上限，加强法律衔接，为著作权人合法权益保障提供了有力法律武器。

——完善社会、民生领域立法。

制定退役军人保障法。退役军人保障法是关于退役军人保障工作的基础性、系统性、综合性法律。11月，全国人大常委会审议通过退役军人保障法。该法突出保障法定位，衔接国家和军队有关政策和体制改革，明确加强退伍军人保障体系建设，细化安置工作、待遇确定等原则，明确退役军人保障服务内容及退役军人工作主管部门职责，增强退役军人教育培训措施的针对性等，为加强退役军人保障工作、维护退役军人合法权益提供了法律保障。

修订未成年人保护法。10月，全国人大常委会对未成年人保护法作出修订。这次修订，强化了家庭、学校、社会、政府、司法等方面保护措施，健全未成年人保护工作协调机制，突出司法机关保护未成年人职责，建立侵害未成年人案件强制报告制度，完善有关网络保护措施，增加关于教育惩戒权的规定等，压实法律责任，保障未成年人合法权益，促进未成年人全面发展。

修订预防未成年人犯罪法。12月，全国人大常委会修订预防未成年人犯罪法。这次修订，明确实施分级预防，细化教育矫治措施，强化家庭监护责任，充实学校管教责任，夯实国家机关保护责任，发挥群团组织优势，推动社会广泛参与，为预防未成年人犯罪工作提供了有力法治保障。

——完善生态环境领域立法。制定长江保护法。12月,全国人大常委会审议通过长江保护法,这是我国首部保护长江全流域生态系统、推进长江经济带绿色高质量发展的专门法律。该法以习近平生态文明思想为指导,坚持生态优先、绿色发展,将"共抓大保护、不搞大开发"的理念确立为法律原则,建立健全长江保护的各项制度措施,加强长江流域生态环境保护和修复,促进资源高效合理利用,保障生态安全,用法治守护长江母亲河,实现人与自然和谐共生。

——完善军事领域立法。

修订国防法。12月,全国人大常委会修订国防法。作为国防领域的基本法,该法贯彻习近平强军思想,巩固国防和军队改革成果,对国防领导体制、武装力量任务、安全防卫政策、国防科研生产、国防动员制度等一系列重大问题作出规定,对完善中国特色军事法规制度体系具有重要意义,奠定了强军卫国的法制基石。

修订人民武装警察法。6月,全国人大常委会修订人民武装警察法。该法贯彻习近平强军思想,紧紧围绕武警部队领导指挥体制调整和使命任务拓展的改革需要,全面体现改革成果,规范和保障武警部队履行职责使命,符合武警部队的新体制新职能新要求,维护国家安全和社会稳定。

——审议通过刑法修正案(十一)。12月,全国人大常委会审议通过刑法修正案（十一）。此次修改，涉及47个条文，加大对安全生产犯罪的预防惩治，完善惩治食品药品犯罪的规定、破坏金融秩序和有关妨害社会管理秩序犯罪的规定，完善未成年人犯罪规定，加强企业产权和知识产权的刑法保护，强化公共卫生领域的刑事法治保障，对社会关注的冒名顶替入刑、抢控公交车方向盘入刑、高空抛物入刑、加重非法集资犯罪处罚、法定最低刑事责任年龄下调等问题作出直接回应。

2020年，全国人大常委会还修订了固体废物污染环境防治法、档案法，审议了乡村振兴促进法、数据安全法、个人信息保护法、海警法、海南自由贸易港法、反食品浪费法、反有组织犯罪法、监察官法、军人地位和权益保障法草案，以及动物防疫法、行政处罚法、野生动物保护法、海上交通安全法、兵役法、军事设施保护法修订草案等。其中，全国人民代表大会组织法、全国人民代表大会议事规则修正草案经两次常委会会议审议后决定提请十三届全国人大四次会议审议通过。

（三）为相关领域深化改革、扩大开放提供法律依据和法治保障

——贯彻党中央关于支持海南深化改革开放的战略部署，作出关于授权国务院在中国（海南）自由贸易试验区暂时调整适用有关法律规定的决定，用法治方式支

持海南建设自由贸易试验区和中国特色自由贸易港。为推进中国特色自由贸易港建设,加大知识产权保护力度,营造良好营商环境,12月,作出关于设立海南自由贸易港知识产权法院的决定。

——作出关于加强国有资产管理情况监督的决定,把握人大国有资产监督定位,围绕国有资产管理情况报告制度,完善报告、审议、整改问责、公开等环节工作机制,更好发挥人大在国有资产管理情况监督和国有资产治理方面的重要作用。

——作出关于授权国务院在粤港澳大湾区内地九市开展香港法律执业者和澳门执业律师取得内地执业资质和从事律师职业试点工作的决定,有利于发挥港澳法律人才的专业优势,促进粤港澳大湾区建设,推动香港、澳门更好融入国家发展大局。

(四) 持续推进科学立法、民主立法、依法立法

全国人大常委会进一步落实和完善科学立法、民主立法、依法立法体制机制,不断提高立法质量和效率,扎实做好立法及相关工作。一是加强对立法工作的组织协调,充分发挥人大在立法工作中的主导作用。二是坚持法律草案向社会公开征求意见。全年共有42件次法律草案通过中国人大网向社会公开征求意见,共收到306,090人提出的1,351,869条意见。三是强化代表对立

法工作的深度参与，更加注重发挥专门从事法律工作的代表以及近年来提出过相关议案、建议的代表在立法工作中的作用。四是加强基层立法联系点建设。增设6个基层立法联系点，修改完善基层立法联系点工作规则，指导联系点健全制度机制。全年共有民法典、刑法修正案（十一）、反食品浪费法等18件法律草案征求10个联系点意见，已经反馈意见建议1300余条，使立法工作更加接地气、察民情。五是加强对地方立法工作的联系指导。召开第二十六次全国地方立法工作座谈会，举办首次全国人大备案审查工作经验交流会暨备案审查工作培训班。

（五）关于全国人大常委会的监督工作

2020年全国人大常委会紧紧围绕党和国家工作大局，依法行使宪法法律赋予的监督权，坚持寓支持于监督之中，有序开展工作监督和法律监督，健全监督工作制度机制，创新监督方式，增强监督实效，保证党中央决策部署落到实处，保证法律有效实施、权力正确行使。

——检查法律实施情况。2020年，全国人大常委会检查了《关于全面禁止非法野生动物交易、革除滥食野生动物陋习、切实保障人民群众生命健康安全的决定》、野生动物保护法、农业机械化促进法、土壤污染防治法、慈善法、反不正当竞争法、公共文化服务保障法等1个决定和6部法律实施情况，并结合审议土壤污染防治法执法检查报告开展专题询问。

对《关于全面禁止非法野生动物交易、革除滥食野生动物陋习、切实保障人民群众生命健康安全的决定》、野生动物保护法，重点检查了依法打击滥食及非法猎捕交易、加强野生动物及其栖息地保护、完善配套法规规章和相关名录、执法监管及法律责任落实、人工繁育野生动物处置、养殖户转产转型等情况，推动形成科学健康文明的生活方式。对农业机械化促进法，重点检查了科研开发制度规范实施、质量保障法律责任落实、先进适用农机推广、社会化服务组织规范化管理、扶持政策落实、配套法规制定等情况，推动提高农业生产力水平。对土壤污染防治法，重点检查了土壤污染普查、调查、监测、预防，法规标准体系建设，农用地和建设用地安全利用，土壤污染风险管控和修复，以及专项资金等保障和监督制度落实情况，这是全国人大常委会连续第三年开展生态环保领域执法检查，运用法治方式助力污染防治攻坚战和生态文明建设。对慈善法，重点检查了慈善组织依法开展活动、规范募捐、财产信托和管理、捐赠人权利保护和义务履行、慈善服务发展、信息公开、推进慈善创新等情况，推动慈善事业依法健康有序发展。对反不正当竞争法，重点检查了普法宣传、法规制度建设、工作协调机制建立和作用发挥、对各类不正当竞争行为的查处等情况,针对网络不正当竞争等突出问题开展专项检查。对公共文化服务保障法,重点检查了有关标准、制度建立和执行,基础设施建设和利用,数字化和网络建设,公共文化服务组织、管理、提供、保障工作中政府责任落实等情况,推动公共文化事业发展,满足人民日益增长的美好生活需要。

在开展执法检查和专题询问过程中,全国人大常委会组成人员分别就完善法律制度、推动法律实施、加强和改进相关工作等提出了意见和建议。国务院和有关部门高度重视这些意见和建议,提出并采取了一系列改进和落实的工作措施。

——听取和审议专项工作报告,开展专题询问和专题调研。2020年,全国人大常委会加强对"一府一委两院"的监督,共听取和审议国务院、国家监察委员会、最高人民法院、最高人民检察院18个专项工作报告,开展2次专题询问、6项专题调研。

助力打好三大攻坚战。听取审议国务院关于年度环境状况和环境保护目标完成情况与研究处理水污染防治法执法检查报告及审议意见情况的报告,围绕全国人大常委会关于全面加强生态环境保护依法推动打好污染防治攻坚战的决议落实情况进行专题调研并听取审议调研报告,推动环境质量持续改善,助力打好污染防治攻坚战。听取审议国务院关于脱贫攻坚工作情况的报告、关于财政农业农村资金分配和使用情况的报告，坚持农业农村优先发展，支持打好脱贫攻坚战。

推动经济高质量发展。听取审议计划执行情况的报告，推动国务院和有关方面坚持稳中求进工作总基调，更好统筹疫情防控和经济社会发展工作，扎实做好"六稳"工作，全面落实"六保"任务，努力完成全年经济社会发展目标任务。对国民经济和社会发展第十四个五年规划纲要编制工作若干重要问题开展专题调研，形成22份调研报告，为党中央决策和国务院编制工作提供了重要参考，也为全国人大四次会议审查批准"十四五"规划纲要作了必要准备。听取审议国务院关于贯彻落实创新驱动发展战略推进科学技术进步法实施情况的报告，推动国务院及有关部门强化基础研究和关键核心技术攻关，深化新一轮科技体制改革，推进产业链和创新链融合发展。听取审议国务院关于农村集体产权制度改革情况的报告，推动形成农村集体经济新的实现形式和运行机制，维护农民合法权益，助力乡村全面振兴。听取审议国务院关于股票发行注册制改革有关工作情况的报告，推动国务院在充分预估并有效防范风险的基础上，积极稳妥推进注册制改革，提高金融服务实体经济能力。围绕政府投资基金管理与改革进行专题调研，进一步明晰政府投资基金的功能定位，完善制度、健全机制，更好服务国家战略。

促进民生社会事业发展。开展珍惜粮食、反对浪费情况专题调研，这是今年增加安排的监督工作项目，推动建立健全保障粮食安全、制止餐饮浪费的长效机制，增强节约意识，在全社会营造浪费可耻、节约为荣的氛围。开展社会保险制度改革和社会保险法实施情况专题调研，推动健全覆盖全民、城乡统筹、权责清晰、保障适度、可持续的多层次社会保障体系。开展民族团结进步创建工作情况专题调研，推动铸牢中华民族共同体意识。

加强对执法、监察、司法工作的监督。听取审议国务院关于公安机关执法规范化建设工作情况的报告，促进严格规范公正文明执法，提升执法工作的法治化水平和执法公信力。贯彻实施监察法，首次听取审议国家监察委员会关于开展反腐败国际追逃追赃工作情况的报告，推动健全追逃追赃领导体制、协调机制和法治体系。听取审议最高人民法院关于加强民事审判工作情况的报告，推动审判机关加强民事权益保护，为经济社会发展提供有力的司法服务和保障。听取审议最高人民检察院关于适用认罪认罚从宽制度情况的报告，推动提升诉讼效率，节约司法资源，快速化解社会矛盾，实现司法公正与效率有机统一。

——加强人大预算决算审查监督和国有资产监督

工作。

听取审议中央决算报告、审计工作报告、预算执行情况报告，审查批准 2020 年中央决算，听取审议审计查出问题整改情况报告并开展专题询问，推动积极的财政政策更加积极有为，提高资金使用效益，确保疫情防控、惠企利民等政策落到实处。持续推进人大预算审查监督重点拓展改革，研究制定关于加强中央预算审查监督的决定，制定关于加强地方人大对政府债务审查监督的指导意见，加大全口径审查、全过程监管力度，建立听取政府预算绩效评价情况及相关部门重要政策和重点资金绩效情况通报机制，增强审查监督的针对性和实效性。

结合审议国务院关于加强国有资产管理情况的综合报告，听取审议国务院关于 2019 年度财政部履行出资人职责和资产监管职责企业国有资产管理情况、国资系统监管企业国有资产管理情况的两个专项报告，推动深化国资国企改革，确保国有资本保值增值。总结实践经验，作出关于加强国有资产管理情况监督的决定，进一步完善报告机制和相关工作制度，增强监督刚性，推进人大国有资产管理监督深化拓展、提质增效。推进国资联网监督工作，基本实现全国县级以上地方建立国有资产管理情况报告制度全覆盖。

——做好规范性文件备案审查工作。按照"有件必备、有备必审、有错必纠"的要求，加大备案审查工作力度，督促纠正了一批与宪法法律不符的规范性文件，切实维护国家法治统一。全年共收到报送备案的行政法规、地方性法规、司法解释、特别行政区法律等1310件，进行逐件审查，区分不同情况作出处理。配合疫情防控、民法典实施、优化营商环境等，组织开展5个方面的专项审查和集中清理，发现需要修改或废止的规范性文件3372件，督促有关方面及时纠正。扎实开展依申请审查和移送审查，共收到公民、组织提出的审查建议5146件，对属于常委会审查范围的3378件逐一进行研究，提出处理意见，向审查建议人作了反馈；对不属于常委会审查范围的，依照规定分别移送有关机关处理。研究审查通过备案审查衔接联动机制移送的地方性法规58件，督促制定机关修改或废止27件。持续推进备案审查制度和能力建设，建成国家法律法规数据库（一期）。推动地方各级人大常委会普遍建立向常委会报告备案审查工作情况制度，逐步实现全覆盖的要求。

二、关于依法行政

2020年，中国政府坚持依法全面履行职能，深入推进法治政府建设，为统筹推进疫情防控和经济社会发展提供坚强法治保障和优质法律服务，法治政府建设各项工作取得新成效、实现新发展。

（一）国务院立法工作

2020年，国务院提请全国人大常委会审议法律议案9件，制定行政法规4部，修改行政法规33部，废止行政法规11部。国务院提请全国人大常委会审议批准的条约和国务院核准的条约18件。

——制定《农作物病虫害防治条例》。为明确农作物病虫害防治责任，规范防治规程和防治方式，鼓励专业化、绿色防控，3月，国务院公布《农作物病虫害防治条例》，自2020年5月1日起施行。条例对各级人民政府及其有关部门、农业生产经营者的防治责任作出明确规定，进一步完善农作物病虫害监测预报、农作物病虫害预防控制等制度，强化农作物病虫害应急处置，为农作物病虫害防治工作提供有力的法律保障。

——制定《保障中小企业款项支付条例》。为建立防范化解拖欠中小企业款项长效机制,进一步落实《中小企业促进法》关于国家机关、事业单位和大型企业不得违约拖欠中小企业的货物、工程、服务款项的规定,7月,国务院公布《保障中小企业款项支付条例》,自2020年9月1日起施行。条例从规范机关、事业单位和大型企业付款期限、明确检验验收要求、禁止变相拖欠、规范保证金收取和结算、公示拖欠款项信息、建立健全投诉和监督评价机制、明确迟延支付责任等方面作出规定,保障中小企业款项得到及时支付,缓解中小企业资金压力,切实保护中小企业合法权益。

——制定《政府督查工作条例》。为落实党中央关于统筹规范督查检查考核工作的要求,加强和规范政府督查工作,更好推动党中央、国务院决策部署的贯彻落实,12月,国务院公布《政府督查工作条例》,自2021年2月1日起施行。条例将近年来各级政府督查工作的成熟经验做法制度化,明确政府督查定位,规范政府督查程序,为政府督查工作提供法律规范和制度保障。

——修订《中华人民共和国预算法实施条例》。为体现深化财税体制改革的成果,细化明确预算法有关规定,8月,国务院修订《中华人民共和国预算法实施条例》,自2020年10月1日起施行。修订后的条例将预算法实施后出台的国务院关于深化预算管理制度改革等有关规定法治化，对授权国务院规定的事项作出具体规定，并根据近年来的实践对预算收支范围、转移支付、地方政府债务等事项作出相应规定。

——修订《企业名称登记管理规定》。为进一步释放企业名称资源，突出企业登记机关的服务职能，12月，国务院修订《企业名称登记管理规定》，自2021年3月1日起施行。修订后的条例充分尊重企业自主选择企业名称权利，明确企业名称自主申报的行为规范，简化企业名称登记流程，降低企业开办成本，强化事中事后监管，维护企业合法权益和良好市场秩序。

2020年，国务院还制定了《化妆品监督管理条例》，修改了《行政执法机关移送涉嫌犯罪案件的规定》《国家科学技术奖励条例》《城市供水条例》《城市房地产开发经营管理条例》《人工影响天气管理条例》《广播电视管理条例》《护士条例》《旅馆业治安管理办法》《实施国际著作权条约的规定》等行政法规。

(二) 依法行政工作

——开展法治政府建设督察工作。在2019年法治政府建设督察基础上，2020年继续开展党政主要负责人履行推进法治建设第一责任人职责及法治政府建设督察。由中央依法治国办牵头，会同24家中央国家机关组成督察组，由省部级领导带队对上海、内蒙古、黑龙江、江苏、山东、广西、海南、青海 8 个省份进行实地督察，深入 32 个市州、68 个县区，与领导干部、执法办案人员个别谈话 589 人次，访谈律师、民营企业家、群众 1073 人次，发现并推动整改各类问题，有效传导了压力、压实了责任。

——开展法治政府建设示范创建活动。完成第一批全国法治政府建设示范创建评估、命名工作，经过省级初审、第三方评估、人民群众满意度测评、实地核查、社会公示等环节，评选出 40 个综合示范地区和 24 个单项示范项目。组织开展示范地区和项目宣传交流活动，在《法治日报》开设"法治政府建设示范地区和项目巡礼"专栏，集中展播示范地区、示范项目的成绩和经验，有效发挥先进典型标杆引领、辐射带动作用，推动法治政府建设水平整体提升。

——积极开展行政法规专项清理工作。围绕实行高水平对外开放，一揽子修改 22 部、废止 1 部与外商投资法不符的行政法规；围绕推进"放管服"改革，一揽子修改 7 部、废止 10 部行政法规；围绕民法典贯彻实施，组织开展与民法典内容相关的行政法规、规章和行政规范性文件清理工作。

——建立并向社会公开现行有效行政法规库。对中华人民共和国成立以来国务院制定的行政法规进行全面梳理，核校现行有效的行政法规目录和标准文本，向社会公开发布，为社会公众提供了"看得见、找得着、用得上"的公共产品。

——加强法规规章备案审查工作。2020年各地方、各部门报送国务院备案的法规规章共2071件，依法逐件进行审查，对2046件予以备案登记，25件暂缓备案登记。对存在问题的法规规章均按照法定权限和程序作出处理。全国人大常委会办公厅、司法部联合印发《关于规范有序开展地方性法规统一报备工作的通知》，完成报备平台一体化建设。司法部成立法规规章备案审查专家委员会，进一步提高备案审查规范化、科学化和专业化水平。

——在疫情防控工作中推进依法行政。司法部印发《关于推动严格规范公正文明执法 为疫情防控工作提供有力法治保障的意见》，推动各级行政执法机关依法惩处各类抗拒疫情防控措施的行为，加强行政执法监督，及时处理疫情防控中的执法不作为、乱作为、过度执法等问题。

——提升行政执法规范化水平。开展行政执法"三项制度"专项监督行动，推动实现"三项制度"市县执法单位全覆盖。实施全国统一行政执法证件标准样式，加强证件管理，明确行政执法证件的制发机关、工作职责、编号规则等内容，从源头上解决证件样式标准不统一、重复发证、多头发证的问题。开展行政规范性文件合法性审核机制落实情况专项监督行动,督促指导各地区各部门改进工作。进一步完善行政执法和刑事司法衔接机制,修改《行政执法机关移送涉嫌犯罪案件的规定》。加快"全国行政执法综合管理监督信息系统"建设和推广应用,已初步实现与各省(区、市)的数据联通。

——推进行政裁决工作。国务院有关部门开展行政裁决示范点建设,建立行政裁决重点领域部门的示范建设联系机制。持续开展行政裁决事项清理工作,印发《国务院部门行政裁决清单》(第二批)。

——全面推行证明事项告知承诺制。自2019年试点以来,18个地区和部门试行告知承诺制的证明事项涉及户籍管理、市场主体准营、资格考试、社会保险、社会救助等60多个方面,共2000多项,切实方便了群众和企业办事,改善了营商环境。在总结试点经验基础上,国务院办公厅印发《关于全面推行证明事项和涉企经营许可事项告知承诺制的指导意见》,在全国部署推广。

——加强行政复议与应诉工作。2020年,全国各级行政复议机关共办结行政复议案件21.1万件。针对办案中发现的共性违法问题,下发行政复议意见书4726份,办结的立案受理案件中,作出撤销、变更、确认违法和责令履行决定等纠错决定2.6万件,直接纠错率为14.6%。全国行政机关负责人出庭率为41.8%,全国行政机关平均败诉率为 17.8%。国务院共审结行政复议案件 2693 件，其中，国务院行政复议裁决案件纠错率为 11.8%，国务院行政复议监督案件纠错率为 19.2%。通过个案纠错及下发意见书、建议书等方式，积极化解行政争议，促进依法行政，推动法治政府建设。深入推进行政复议体制机制改革，贯彻落实中央全面依法治国委员会《行政复议体制改革方案》，通过建立台账、调研督导、召开专题视频推进会等方式全力推动改革方案落实落地。加快复议法修订工作，加强行政复议工作规范化、信息化、专业化建设。

三、关于政法领域改革

2020年,中国政法领域改革聚焦人民群众反映强烈的突出问题,加快推进执法司法制约监督体系改革和建设工作,全面提升执法司法公信力,各项工作取得新突破。

(一) 加快构建执法司法制约监督体系

——召开会议专门部署。1月,中央政法工作会议在北京召开,会议部署以政法领域全面深化改革为牵引,破解政法工作面临的新情况新问题,全面提升政法工作现代化水平。深入破除政法领域体制性、机制性、政策性改革的堵点,针对放权后监督管理不到位问题,进一步完善政法系统司法监督政策措施,加强政法单位内部监督和问责,最大限度压减权力设租寻租空间。8月,中央政法委召开政法领域全面深化改革推进会,深入学习贯彻习近平总书记重要讲话精神,就加快构建上下贯通、内外结合、系统完备、规范高效的执法司法制约监督体系,确保执法司法公正廉洁、高效权威,明确下一步改革方向和重点。中央政法委全体会议、中央司法体制改革领导小组会议也就加快推进执法司法制约监督制度机制建设提出明确要求。中央政法各单位召开专题会议，部署贯彻落实政法领域全面深化改革推进会精神。

——加强制约监督制度建设。中央政法委研究制定《关于加强政法领域执法司法制约监督制度机制建设的意见》，从健全完善党对政法工作绝对领导的监督体系、政法机关制约监督体系、执法司法权力运行制约监督机制、政法领域服务管理行为监督体系、政法队伍管理监督制度、智能化制约监督体系等方面提出一系列改革举措。中央政法单位分别从完善四级法院审级职能定位、加强检察机关法律监督、推进公安执法监督管理机制改革、加强国家安全机关执法制约监督、深化公证体制机制改革等方面研究制定文件，完善政法系统内部制约监督机制。

——开展改革评估督查。全面评估党的十八届三中全会以来党中央部署的改革任务，系统梳理重大理论成果、制度成果、实践成果，总结改革经验，排查短板问题，研究意见建议，形成《党的十八届三中全会以来政法领域全面深化改革总结评估报告》。中央政法委组织开展政法领域改革专项督查，聚焦加强执法司法制约监督等重点内容，详细了解改革举措落实落地情况，深入剖析影响改革创新和推动落实的体制机制问题，提出改进完善的政策建议。

（二）进一步优化政法机构职能体系

——理顺党委政法委职能。深入贯彻落实《中国共产党政法工作条例》（以下简称《条例》），中央政法委组织开展《条例》贯彻落实情况督查，健全党领导新时代政法工作的体制机制，中央政法单位和各省区市制定了《条例》实施细则或办法。党委政法委与党委、政法单位之间，各级党委政法委之间关系进一步理顺，党对政法工作的政治领导、思想领导、组织领导制度机制进一步健全。完善党委政法委综合协调政法工作机制，建立平安中国建设工作协调机制。目前，全国18个省区市已经实现乡镇政法委员配备全覆盖。

——完善法院检察院组织体系。设立北京金融法院、海南自由贸易港知识产权法院，提升专业化办案水平和服务经济社会发展大局的能力。最高人民法院研究制定《关于完善四级法院审级职能定位的改革方案》，推动优化四级法院职权配置、案件管辖和机构设置。深化最高人民法院巡回法庭审判机制改革，加强知识产权法庭和国际商事法庭建设。全国检察机关机构职能实现系统性、整体性重构，刑事、民事、行政、公益诉讼"四大检察""十大业务"检察工作新格局已经形成。

——完善公安机关机构职能体系。完成30万原公安现役机构编制人员划转、干部转改定级，行业公安机关管理体制调整扎实推进。推动执法办案、监督管理、服务保障"一站式"办案模式建设，目前全国已建成执法办案管理中心2100余个，实现刑事案件集中办理、全流程全要素监督管理。

——深化法学会改革。5月，中共中央办公厅印发实施《关于进一步加强法学会建设的意见》，为切实保持和增强法学会的政治性、先进性、群众性，进一步加强法学会建设提供了遵循。中国法学会深入贯彻落实《中国法学会改革方案》，指导32个省级法学会制定印发改革方案，基本实现省市县三级法学会组织全覆盖。

(三) 深化司法责任制综合配套改革

——加快建立权责一致的司法权运行新机制。3月，中共中央办公厅印发实施《关于深化司法责任制综合配套改革的意见》，从完善分类管理、规范权力运行、加强监督管理、健全职业保障、提升办案效能等方面系统作出规定，推进司法责任制全面落地。最高人民法院印发《关于深化司法责任制综合配套改革的实施意见》，督促指导各级人民法院落实《关于完善人民法院审判权力和责任清单的指导意见》，进一步健全完善审判权力运行机制。最高人民检察院制定《人民检察院司法责任追究条例》，明确检察官及其他人员承担司法责任的范围、程序和形式，促进形成司法办案内部监督有效闭环。目前，法官检察官办案主体地位基本确立，全国法院98%以上案件的裁判文书由独任法官、合议庭直接签发，全国检察院90%以上的案件由承办检察官直接作出决定。

——加快完善法官检察官员额动态调整、员额退出和惩戒机制。最高人民法院制定《法官员额退出办法（试行）》及《省级以下人民法院法官员额动态调整指导意见（试行）》，推进完善法官员额动态调整机制，落实员额退出机制。最高人民法院研究制定《法官惩戒工作程序规定（试行）》《最高人民法院法官惩戒委员会章程》，筹备设立最高人民法院法官惩戒委员会，推动全面设立省级法官惩戒委员会，法官惩戒制度逐步进入实质化运行；最高人民检察院研究制定《检察官惩戒委员会章程》《检察官惩戒工作程序规定》，推动法院检察院加快完善惩戒制度，落实审判责任追究机制。

——建立健全法官检察官业绩考评制度。最高人民法院研究制定关于健全法官考核工作机制的指导性文件；最高人民检察院印发《检察机关案件质量主要评价指标》，建立以"案—件比"为核心的案件质量评价指标体系，进一步健全绩效考核制度。领导干部入额办案基本实现常态化，一批绩效考核不达标、违纪违法办案人员受到退出员额、追责等处理。

——统筹推进省以下地方法院检察院经费保障机制改革。最高人民法院会同财政部印发《人民法院诉讼费退付管理暂行办法》等5份文件，完善财物统管配套机制。推动规范省以下地方法院检察院财物省级统管模式，督导各地结合实际抓紧完善相关政策和方案，法院检察院依法独立公正行使职权的经费保障机制日益健全。

(四) 深化诉讼制度改革

——深入推进诉源治理。中央政法委研究制定《关于加强诉源治理 推动矛盾纠纷源头化解的意见》，坚持和发展新时代"枫桥经验"，把非诉讼纠纷解决机制挺在前面，推动更多法治力量向引导和疏导端用力，加强矛盾纠纷源头预防、前端化解、关口把控，完善预防性法律制度，从源头上减少诉讼增量。

——深化诉讼制度改革。继续深入推进以审判为中心的刑事诉讼制度改革，"两高三部"印发了《关于规范量刑程序若干问题的意见（试行）》《法律援助值班律师工作办法》。完善司法鉴定人出庭作证机制，加强和规范补充侦查工作，对重大案件侦查终结前开展讯问合法性核查。深化推进认罪认罚从宽制度实施，始终坚持宽严相济刑事政策、罪责刑相适应原则以及证据裁判原则，确保认罪认罚案件办理实现政治效果、法律效果和社会效果的统一。

——推进民事诉讼程序繁简分流改革试点。根据中央部署和全国人大常委会授权，最高人民法院印发民事诉讼程序繁简分流改革试点方案和实施办法，在15个省份、20座城市的305家法院启动改革试点工作，健全试点工作组织领导、工作联席会议、政策文件审核、试点工作月报、数据汇总评估、政策宣传解读等6项机制，印发试点问答口径、文书样式、数据指标体系等5个配套性文件，改革效果逐步显现，司法质量、效率进一步提升，司法资源配置更加合理优化，人民群众对公平正义的获得感不断增强，试点工作取得阶段性成效。

——完善刑罚执行制度。深入贯彻落实习近平总书记有关刑罚执行中突出问题的重要批示精神，全面分析研究减刑、假释、暂予监外执行产生违规违法问题在制度机制层面的短板弱项和风险漏洞，有针对性地研究提出健全完善减刑、假释、暂予监外执行制度机制的意见建议。推动实施《中华人民共和国社区矫正法》，持续推进刑罚执行一体化建设，不断健全罪犯管理与教育改造并重、专业力量和社会力量协同机制。

（五）完善政法公共服务体制机制

——提供更加便捷诉讼服务。最高人民法院制定下发一站式建设总体框架意见及21个专门规范，全国

98%的法院建设诉讼服务大厅，98%的法院开通诉讼服务网，95%的法院开通12368诉讼服务热线，95%的法院实现网上立案。疫情期间，全国法院网上开庭同比增幅超过450%，实现"线上庭审不打烊、抗疫和审判两不误"。中国裁判文书网公布的裁判文书达1亿950万篇，中国庭审公开网累计直播突破1000万场，已分别成为全球最大的裁判文书公开和政务视频直播网站。

——积极稳妥推进拓展公益诉讼案件范围。最高人民法院、最高人民检察院联合修订《关于检察公益诉讼案件适用法律若干问题的解释》，最高人民法院修订《关于审理环境民事公益诉讼案件适用法律若干问题的解释》，规范环境公益案件办理程序和法律适用规则。最高人民检察院部署积极办理群众反映强烈的安全生产、公共卫生、生物安全、妇女儿童及残疾人权益保护、网络侵害、扶贫、文物和文化遗产保护等领域公益损害案件；印发《关于积极稳妥拓展公益诉讼案件范围的指导意见》，严格把握新领域案件立案条件，强化程序保障；制发销售假冒伪劣口罩、军地协作、文物和文化遗产保护等领域公益诉讼典型案例。

——完善政法公共服务体系。司法行政机关加快公共法律服务体系建设，健全统一司法鉴定管理体制，建立实施国家统一法律职业资格考试制度，公共法律服务网络初步实现全业务、全时空覆盖，公共法律服务机构、人员总数达到历史最高水平。

——深化公安、司法行政"放管服"改革。推出新冠肺炎疫情防控期间治安管理便民利企15项措施、依法打击食药环和知识产权领域犯罪保障疫情防控期间复工复产10项措施，全力保障复工复产。出台《关于进一步深化"放管服"改革推进审批服务便民化的实施意见》等文件，加大证明事项清理力度。

四、关于审判、检察、公安和司法行政工作

（一）审判工作

2020年，最高人民法院受理案件39,347件，审结35,773件；地方各级人民法院受理案件3080.5万件，审结、执结2870.5万件，结案标的额7.1万亿元。

——刑事审判工作。2020年，各级法院共审结一审刑事案件111.6万件，判处罪犯152.7万人。依法严惩各种渗透颠覆破坏、暴力恐怖、民族分裂、宗教极端犯罪，坚定维护国家政权安全、制度安全。依法审结严重暴力犯罪案件4.7万件。深入推进禁毒斗争，审结毒品犯罪案件6.8万件。维护防疫秩序，依法审结涉疫犯罪案件5474件6443人。完成扫黑除恶专项斗争审判执行任务，专项斗争以来，依法审结涉黑涉恶犯罪案件33,053件226,495人。依法严惩贪污贿赂等腐败犯罪，审结贪污贿赂、渎职等案件2.2万件2.6万人；积极配合反腐败国际追逃追赃工作，依法审理追逃追赃、没收违法所得等案件316件，裁定没收"红通人员"姚锦旗等164人违法所得11.5亿元。严惩网络犯罪，依法审结

电信网络诈骗、网络传销、网络赌博、网络黑客、网络谣言、网络暴力等犯罪案件3.3万件。依法审结集资诈骗等涉众型经济犯罪案件1.5万件，涉及金额2.9万亿元。

——民事商事审判工作。2020年，各级法院共审结一审民商事案件1330.6万件，其中涉及教育、就业、医疗、住房、社会保障等民生案件134.7万件。审结婚姻家庭案件164.9万件，签发人身安全保护令2169份。会同全国妇联等单位深化家事审判改革，完善家事调解、家事调查、心理辅导等制度。审结一审环境资源案件25.3万件、环境公益诉讼案件3557件。依法审结破产案件10,132件，涉及债权1.2万亿元。依法审结一审涉外民商事案件18,163件。

——行政审判、国家赔偿工作。2020年，各级法院共审结一审行政案件26.6万件，服务"放管服"改革，助推法治政府和政务诚信建设。审结国家赔偿案件1.8万件。

——立案信访和审判监督工作。2020年，各级法院按照审判监督程序再审改判刑事案件1818件。坚持罪刑法定、疑罪从无、证据裁判，依法宣告656名公诉案件被告人和384名自诉案件被告人无罪。普遍建立一站式多元解纷机制，全面应用人民法院调解平台，诉前调解成功民事案件424万件。基本建成一站式诉讼服务中心，诉讼服务中心速裁、快审案件693.3万件。全国法院实现跨域立案服务全覆盖，累计提供跨域立案服务8.2万件。

(二) 执行工作

2020年，全国法院咬住青山不放松，不断巩固"基本解决执行难"成果，进一步健全解决执行难长效机制，全力以赴办好案、持之以恒抓质效，执行数据指标全面向好。受理执行案件1059.2万件，执结995.8万件，执行到位金额1.9万亿元，同比分别上升1.7%、4.3%和8.1%。整体呈现新收、结案、到位金额均上升，旧存、未结案均下降的"三升两降"态势，实现了执行工作良性循环状态和"3＋1"核心指标高标准运行常态化，在疫情、贸易摩擦等严峻形势下让更多的真金白银通过执行工作装到了老百姓的口袋里。

——党领导下的综合治理执行难工作格局进一步深化。落实中央全面依法治国委员会2019年1号文件，推动各地出台具体实施意见和任务分解方案，努力从源头上解决执行难问题。落实平安建设考评办法，压实相关部门协助执行责任。推动各有关部门尽快完成与国家"互联网＋监管"系统及全国信用信息共享平台联合惩戒系统的联通对接和信息共享。天津建立"司法裁判执行联动中心"，由市委政法委牵头，执行联动重点成员单位派员到天津高院执行局驻点办公，直接参与联动中心工作，研究解决重大问题；与公安系统合作的"涉机动车网上办案系统"上线，当地机动车执行从原来的"以日计算"缩短为"以分钟计算"。新疆喀什地区建立村镇协同执行机制，由县委政法委牵头并按月通报，各乡镇成立协同执行工作专班，常态化带案下乡，基层治理格局进一步完善，民族边疆地区对社会主义法治的认同进一步增强。江西省委政法委牵头召开综合治理执行难工作会议，建立健全执行联动长效工作机制，实现党委政法委领导执行联动工作的常态化、实体化运行。

——执行工作服务营商环境改善、社会诚信体系建设、新发展格局构建等方面的作用更加凸显。集中开展"发挥执行职能，做好'六稳'工作，落实'六保'任务"专项执行行动，为统筹推进常态化疫情防控和经济社会发展工作提供有力司法服务和保障。建立涉黑恶和职务犯罪案件刑事涉财产执行案件台账，加强部门协调，开通"绿色通道"，积极推动涉黑恶案件和职务犯罪案件涉财产执行工作，确保"打财断血"要求落实到位，坚决不让黑恶分子得到任何好处，彰显党中央巩固扫黑除恶和反腐败斗争压倒性胜利的坚强决心。北京高院与市财政局签署会议纪要，共同规范刑事涉案财物上缴工作。广东法院部署开展涉黑恶案件财产刑执行"雷霆行动",确保"案件一个不少""财产一笔不漏",强势"打财断血",力促"黑财清底",取得明显成效。充分发挥执行职能作用,积极应对国际国内形势发生的深刻变化,不断激发市场主体活力,营造激励企业家干事创业的浓厚氛围。福建高院建立"执破直通"机制,打通执行、破产程序的衔接堵点,推动市场出清,优化营商环境。山东法院开展查封土地和海域使用权专项清理,通过司法拍卖、执行和解等方式,释放土地资源4.6万亩、海域使用权3888公顷,依法释放生产要素,推动改善投资环境。新疆法院针对农牧区被执行人财产多为牛羊牲畜、苗木果脯等生产生活资料,财产变现具有季节性、周期性的特殊情况,把强制督促和柔性管理相结合,积极引导当事人达成和解协议,实现债权人和债务人的"双赢"。

——信息化、智能化助推执行能力持续提高。进一步推动执行工作与现代技术深度融合,提升执行信息化系统的集约化、精细化、智能化水平。借助区块链技术研发"终本智能巡查系统",在部分法院试用。扩大网络查控覆盖面,把被执行人出入境记录、税务登记信息、保险理财产品等纳入其中。积极推进与中国邮政EMS的跨域送达工作,通过文书电子推送、异地打印封装、同城送达的方式,减少成本,提高效率,助力节能减排和"美丽中国"建设。最高人民法院下发通知,进一步规范司法网拍辅助工作。与相关行业协会联合下发委托评估工作规范，推广使用网络询价评估系统，提升评估的科学性、精准性。疫情期间，执行信息化、智能化成果得到充分检验，网络查控系统平稳运行，线上事项委托数量增长近40%，移动执行平台作用凸显，确保了执行工作"不停摆"。司法网拍工作继续保持良好势头，网拍数量越来越多，拍卖金额越来越大，拍卖效果越来越好，保持"零投诉"。推进执行指挥中心实体化运行，依托执行指挥管理平台，完善执行关键节点的可视化监管和自动化预警，健全对下督办、分级分时督办等工作机制，实现对"案、人、事"的全流程、全方位管理。积极推进执行管理由专网向互联网延伸拓展，全面部署应用移动执行平台，加快推进应急响应系统建设，充分发挥"智慧执行"APP的监督管理和服务保障作用，研究将"智慧执行"APP拓展到代表端、委员端、当事人端和协助执行单位端，让代表、委员和人民群众更加全面理解执行、参与执行。江苏法院积极研发物联网查封财产监管系统、物联网电子封条和物联网称重系统，实现对被执行财产的"智"监管、"活"查封和"快"处置，有效提高法院查封财产的安全性，减少了被执行人规避执行情形。

——依法规范善意文明的执行生态进一步强化。建立健全"一案双查"工作机制，由执行部门和监察部门联合查处违法违规执行以及管理责任落实不到位等问题。借助全国执行申诉信访和督导案件系统，加强对信访案件、人大代表、政协委员关注案件等重点案件的监督管理。基本完成全国法院"一案一账号"案款管理机制建设，进一步规范案款管理，提高发放效率。最高人民法院会同最高人民检察院出台意见，建立全国执行与法律监督工作平台，加强和规范人民检察院对执行工作的法律监督。进一步消除消极执行、选择性执行、乱执行的存在空间，坚决肃清执行中人情案、关系案、金钱案，树立执行的权威和公信力。广东法院全面实施执行事务集约、繁简分流、团队办案三项机制，大幅度提高了执行质效。加强执行领域司法解释工作，建立完善以操作规程为核心的执行行为规范体系。精准采取失信惩戒、限制消费措施，将信用惩戒聚焦到打击少数规避、抗拒执行等违法失信行为上来。推进善意文明执行，建立失信名单分级分类管理和信用修复机制，让失信惩戒、限制消费更有针对性更可预期，让"诚信而不幸"的经营者、创业者有"东山再起"的机会。江西高院、宁波中院建立失信被执行人信用承诺和信用修复机制，针对性和操作性强，具有示范意义。广州互联网法院联合共青团广州市委员会，启动"湾区有爱　网护青春"工程，采取"线上＋线下""修复＋表彰""分级＋分类"多项措施，多元帮扶，信用激励，推动对青年被执行人善意执行。禁止超标的查封和乱查封，能"活封"的决不"死封"，尽最大努力保障企业财产效用发挥和正常运营。发挥司法网拍优势，加快财产变价流程，适当选择灵活变价方式，防止查封财产贱卖。疫情期间，最高人民法院出台做好执行工作相关事项的通知、做好不动产续封和银行存款续冻工作的通知、依法妥善办理涉新冠肺炎疫情执行案件若干问题的指导意见等多份司法文件，确保执行工作平稳有序开展，千方百计帮助中小微企业和困难主体纾困解难、渡过难关。收集近300个服务保障疫情防控和复工复产的执行案例，挑选出13个典型案例予以公布，起到示范指导作用。湖南法院开展工程机械案件集中执行行动，服务制造业健康发展。

——群众关心的突出问题得到进一步解决。常态化开展涉民生案件专项执行行动，贯彻涉民生案件"三优先"原则，加强与政府部门的沟通协调，积极争取政策支持，将符合条件的当事人纳入社会保障、脱贫攻坚范围进行司法救助或社会救助。元旦、春节前后集中开展涉民生案件执行行动，发放涉民生案款254亿元，增强了人民群众的获得感。充分认识耕地保护工作的极端重要性，运用司法手段遏制乱占耕地现象，支持地方政府及有关部门依法打击各类违法占用耕地行为，为守住耕地红线、筑牢粮食安全屏障保驾护航。持续加大涉党政机关和国有企业拖欠民营企业中小企业债务案件执行力度，加强与当地清欠工作负责机构沟通，细化工作措施，保障胜诉民营企业中小企业及时实现权益，营造法治化营商环境。山东法院加大党政机关、大型企业拖欠中小微企业账款执行力度，特别是联合发改委等重要党政部门对拖欠企业账款的党政机关实行"纳入失信名单预通知"制度，效果明显。内蒙古、浙江、湖北等高院结合自身实际，出台一系列司法政策文件，为中小微企业生存发展提供有力支持和保障。江西高院组织开展"落锤有声"解决执行难系列主题活动，吉林高院组织开展"执行工作进万家 执行局长走进直播间"主题活动，用鲜活的案例进行普法诚信教育，为综合治理执行难营造更加良好的舆论环境和社会氛围。江苏高院出台实质化解办理执行信访案件的指导意见，实行执行局长负责制，坚持实质性办理原则，重在解决实际问题，切实维护人民群众合法权益。

(三) 检察工作

2020年，全国检察机关共办理各类案件301万件，同比下降19.4%。其中，受理的审查逮捕、审查起诉、申诉案件同比分别下降30.6%、12.4%和46.1%；主动履职的公益诉讼、诉讼监督案件同比分别上升19.2%和9.6%。

——依法履行批捕起诉等职能。2020年，全国检察机关全年共批准逮捕各类犯罪嫌疑人770,561人、提起公诉1,572,971人。坚决维护国家安全和社会安定，严厉打击境内外敌对势力渗透颠覆分裂破坏活动。高压严惩杀人、抢劫等严重暴力犯罪，起诉5.7万人。突出惩治盗窃、诈骗、抢夺等多发性侵财犯罪，起诉35万人。依法惩治黄赌毒犯罪，起诉21.2万人。及时出台系列司法政策，指导依法追诉妨害疫情防控犯罪，批捕涉疫犯罪7227人，起诉1.1万人。推动扫黑除恶专项斗争取得全面胜利，2018年以来，共批捕涉黑涉恶犯罪14.9万人，起诉23万人。积极参与网络治理，起诉网络犯罪14.2万人。继续推进反腐败斗争，受理各级监委移送职务犯罪19,760人，已起诉15,346人，不起诉662人，对赵正永等12名原省部级干部提起公诉。深入落实认罪认罚从宽制度，对依法可不批捕和犯罪情节轻微、不需要判处刑罚的，不批捕8.8万人，不起诉20.2万人；捕后认罪认罚可不继续羁押的，建议释放或变更强制措施2.5万人。

——服务保障经济社会高质量发展。助力决战脱贫攻坚，救助3.2万人4.2亿元。助力污染防治攻坚，起诉破坏生态环境资源犯罪5.1万人，办理相关公益诉讼案件8.4万件。从严追诉金融诈骗、破坏金融管理秩序犯罪，起诉4.1万人。严惩洗钱行为，起诉洗钱犯罪707人，是2019年的4.7倍。协同国家版权局等对49起重大侵权盗版案挂牌督办，起诉侵犯知识产权犯罪1.2万人。制定专门规范服务自贸区建设，支持海南自贸港建设。出台21项举措支持粤港澳大湾区发展。与上海合作组织成员国和金砖国家检察机关召开视频会议，共商疫情防控常态化背景下惩防跨国犯罪，完善跨境司法协助机制。

——强化诉讼活动法律监督。2020年，督促侦查机关依法立案2.2万件，监督撤案2.4万件；依法当捕、应诉而未移送的，追加逮捕2万人，追加起诉2.9万人；对不构成犯罪或证据不足的不批捕13.8万人，不起诉4.1万人。对认为确有错误的刑事裁判提出抗诉8903件；提出民事抗诉4994件，提出再审检察建议9900件；对认为确有错误的行政裁判提出抗诉182件，提出再审检察建议198件，是2019年的2.4倍。全国检察机关监督纠正减刑、假释、暂予监外执行不当5.1万人次，对民事执行活动中的违法情形提出检察建议3.7万件，对行政执行活动中的违法情形提出检察建议2.5万件。持续深化专项监督，纠正虚假诉讼10,090件，对涉嫌犯罪的起诉1352人；针对一些行政诉讼程序空转，有效化解行政争议6304件。有序拓展公益诉讼检察，立案办理公益诉讼案件151,260件。保障律师依法执业，监督纠正执法司法机关阻碍律师行使诉讼权利958件。

——坚持检察为民增进民生福祉。起诉制售有毒有害食品、假药劣药等犯罪 8268 人，办理食品药品安全领域公益诉讼案件 2.7 万件。办理涉窨井盖刑事犯罪 106 件、公益诉讼 424 件。坚持和发展新时代"枫桥经验"，集中办理信访积案 2.5 万件。守护未成年人安全健康成长，从严追诉性侵、虐待未成年人和拐卖儿童等犯罪 5.7 万人。坚决维护国防利益和军人军属合法权益，起诉破坏军事设施、破坏军婚等涉军犯罪 381 人。坚决严惩任何伤医扰医犯罪，起诉 496 人。

（四）司法解释与案例指导工作

2020 年，最高人民法院和最高人民检察院联合出台司法解释 2 件，最高人民法院单独出台司法解释 26 件，其中刑事司法解释 2 件，民事司法解释 20 件，行政司法解释 2 件，其他司法解释 4 件。最高人民检察院单独出台司法解释 3 件，最高人民法院发布指导性案例 17 个，最高人民检察院发布指导性案例 34 个。这些司法解释和指导性案例为法律的正确实施发挥了积极作用。

——对正确处理刑事司法工作中重大复杂问题予以指导。3 月，最高人民法院、最高人民检察院联合发布《关于适用〈中华人民共和国刑法〉第三百四十四条有关问题的批复》，指导全国司法机关依法适用非法采伐国家重点保护植物罪，确保罪责刑相适应。9 月，最高人民法院、最高人民检察院联合发布《最高人民法院、最高人民检察院关于办理侵犯知识产权刑事案件具体应用法律若干问题的解释（三）》，依法惩治侵犯知识产权犯罪，维护社会主义市场经济秩序。

——对妥善处理经济社会发展和民生领域的新情况、新问题予以指导。7月，最高人民法院发布《关于证券纠纷代表人诉讼若干问题的规定》，完善证券集体诉讼制度，有效惩治证券违法违规行为，保护投资者合法权益。9月，最高人民法院发布《关于涉网络知识产权侵权纠纷几个法律适用问题的批复》；11月，最高人民法院发布《关于知识产权民事诉讼证据的若干规定》，保障和便利当事人依法行使诉讼权利，保证人民法院公正、及时审理知识产权民事案件。12月，最高人民法院公布《关于审理食品安全民事纠纷案件适用法律若干问题的解释（一）》，指导人民法院正确审理食品安全民事纠纷案件，保障公众身体健康和生命安全。根据《中华人民共和国民法典》等法律规定，结合审判实际，对目前有效的591件司法解释、139个指导性案例进行清理，有序推进新司法解释制定，确保民法典统一正确实施。

——对妥善处理行政诉讼领域的新情况、新问题予以指导。6月，最高人民法院公布《关于行政机关负责人出庭应诉若干问题的规定》，进一步规范行政机关负责人出庭应诉活动，促进实质性化解行政争议。9月，最高人民法院公布《关于审理专利授权确权行政案件适用法律若干问题的规定（一）》，指导人民法院正确审理专利授权确权行政案件。

——对妥善处理涉外商事海事纠纷予以指导。6月，最高人民法院发布《关于依法妥善审理涉新冠肺炎疫情民事案件若干问题的指导意见（三）》，依法妥善审理涉新冠肺炎疫情涉外商事海事纠纷等案件，平等保护中外当事人合法权益；9月，出台《关于人民法院服务保障进一步扩大对外开放的指导意见》，为更高水平对外开放提供司法服务和保障；12月，发布《商事仲裁司法审查年度报告（2019年）》，推进非诉纠纷解决机制建设。2020年，最高人民法院评选并发布8个维护船员合法权益典型案例和11个全国海事审判典型案例。

（五）公安工作

2020年，中共中央决定设立人民警察节，隆重举行中国人民警察警旗授旗仪式，习近平总书记亲自授旗并发表重要训词，极大地激发了全警铸警魂、守初心、担使命的奋进动力，为推进新时代法治公安建设提供了根本遵循，指明了前进方向。

——依法有力抗击新冠肺炎疫情。疫情发生后，各地公安机关严格落实防控措施，迅速组织开展疫区封控、秩序维护等工作，加强航空、海港、陆路口岸管控，及时调整出入境政策，构筑疫情防控坚固防线。公安部会同"两高"等部门出台指导意见，为依法惩处涉疫违法犯罪提供及时有效的法律依据。各级公安机关规范防疫期间执法办案，准确把握执法尺度，依法严厉打击伤医扰序、制售假劣防疫物资、制售假疫苗、破坏野生动物资源等涉疫情违法犯罪，有效防范执法风险和疫情防控风险。围绕统筹推进疫情防控和经济社会发展，先后推出一系列便民利企新举措，有效服务"六稳""六保"工作。

——依法严厉打击突出违法犯罪。全国公安机关坚持依法严打方针不动摇，为期三年的扫黑除恶专项斗争取得决定性胜利，共移送起诉黑社会性质组织3392个，恶势力犯罪集团1.1万个，强化反恐防恐措施，保持全国暴恐案事件零发生。开展命案积案攻坚行动，侦破命案积案6270起，全国现行命案破案率99.8%。部署开展新一轮打击整治枪爆违法犯罪专项行动，全国153个城市同步集中销毁非法枪爆物品。针对人民群众反映强烈的突出问题，组织开展打击整治，侦破电信网络诈骗刑事案件32.2万起、食药环知领域刑事案件7.5万起，抓获跨境赌博及相关犯罪嫌疑人7.5万名、外逃经济犯罪嫌疑人596名，深入开展"净边"专项行动，深化"三非"外国人治理。依法严厉打击妨害国（边）境管理、长江流域非法捕捞、侵犯公民个人信息、非法集资、新型毒品等各类违法犯罪活动，全面落实社会面治安防控措施，不断增强人民群众安全感。2020年，全国刑事案件立案数比2019年下降1.8%，其中，八类主要案件下降8.7%；治安案件发现受理数同比下降10.4%；较大道路交通事故、监所安全事故同比分别下降24%、60%。

——不断提升社会管理服务水平。坚持和发展新时代"枫桥经验"，开展"百万警进千万家"活动，摸排化解各类矛盾纠纷，消除安全隐患。深化社会治安防控体系建设，开展公务用枪专项排查整治，强化民用枪弹信息化监管，加强爆炸物品基础管控，开展"示范城市"创建和"护校安园""平安医院"建设活动，进一步提高维护社会治安能力水平。圆满完成全国"两会"、北京服贸会、上海进博会、深圳特区建立40周年庆祝大会等一系列重大活动安保任务。紧盯解决好群众"急难愁盼"问题，推出高质量便民服务举措，上线公安部"互联网+政务服务"平台，首次实现全国公安政务服务"一张网"，为群众提供900余项公安服务事项。深入推进居民身份证异地受理制度，推动开具户籍类证明和5项户口迁移业务"跨省通办"。全面实施非现场交通违法行为异地处理，跨省异地处理交通违法522万起。全面应用交管互联网服务平台和交管"12123"手机APP，互联网用户达3.6亿，提供网上服务24亿次，实施港澳居民来往内地通行证在内地换发补发新政，推动港澳居民、海外华侨持出入境证件享受交通、教育、医疗等9个领域35项服务便利落实落地。

——执法规范化建设向纵深推进。深入贯彻习近平总书记关于推进严格规范公正文明执法的重要指示精神，持之以恒深化执法规范化建设。8月，全国人大常委会专门听取和审议了公安机关执法规范化建设情况的汇报，对公安机关执法规范化建设成效给予充分肯定。积极推动治安管理处罚、道路交通安全、反有组织犯罪、网络犯罪防治、出入境管理等领域法律制修订工作。积极推进执法办案管理中心建设，全国建成执法办案管理中心2167个，28个省区市出台了建设标准、工作规范和管理运行制度。组织开展全国公安机关网上执法巡查和刑事案件受立案突出问题专项督察，整改执法办案突出问题。不断加强和改进看守所执法管理，依法保障和服务律师会见。广泛开展实战大练兵，提升全警法治素养和执法能力。继续落实执法资格等级考试制度，全国累计有180.5万名在职民警取得基本级执法资格，6万名在职民警取得高级执法资格。

（六）司法行政工作

——监狱工作。2020年，全国监狱安全稳定形势持续向好，连续2年无罪犯脱逃。推动罪犯文化教育和职业技能培训纳入地方政府规划。进一步健全监狱减刑、假释、暂予监外执行制度体系，全国已有600余所监狱建成减刑假释信息化办案平台，全面深化狱务公开，深入推进依法治监，不断提高监狱执法公信力。强化新冠肺炎疫情防控措施，推进监狱纳入地方联防联控机制，全国99.3%的监狱实现零感染，确诊病例全部治愈。

——社区矫正工作。认真学习宣传贯彻《中华人民共和国社区矫正法》，制定《中华人民共和国社区矫正法实施办法》，依法健全社区矫正体制机制，加强社区矫正机构和队伍建设，积极引导社会力量参与，加快构建监禁刑与非监禁刑相互衔接、统一协调的刑罚执行体系，不断提高社区矫正工作规范化、精细化、信息化水平。截至2020年年底，全国全年新接收社区矫正对象53万人，办理解除矫正55.8万人，现有社区矫正对象64.5万人。全国已累计接收社区矫正对象537.1万人，累计解除472.6万人，在矫期间再犯罪率一直处于0.2%左右的较低水平。各地社区矫正机构全年共完成调查评估案件275.3万件，对违法违规的社区矫正对象给予警告30,061人次，提请治安管理处罚1820人次，撤销缓刑3272人，撤销假释61人，对暂予监外执行罪犯收监1399人。

——司法行政戒毒工作。全力推动建立统一的司法行政戒毒工作基本模式，出台康复训练工作指南，完善统一模式运行制度规范,部署开展考核验收工作。深化教育戒治"个十百千"工程,推进优势教育戒治项目提档升级,加强康复训练专业化建设。组织开展"戒毒场所医疗工作巩固攻坚年"活动,积极参加医联体、医共体和专科联盟建设,全面提升场所医疗工作能力和水平。优化戒毒场所建设,推进"智慧戒毒"建设,深入开展戒毒工作理论研究和对外宣传,着力提升戒毒干警履职能力。截至2020年年底,全国共有司法行政戒毒场所381个,累计收治近157万人,全国司法行政戒毒场所实现新冠病毒零感染,安全稳定再创历史佳绩。

——公共法律服务体系建设。推进公共法律服务实体、热线、网络三大平台融合发展,进一步提升群众知晓率、首选率、满意率。建立健全政府购买法律服务机制,强化公共法律服务经费保障。截至2020年年底,已建成省、地(市)、县(区)、乡(镇)、村五级公共法律服务实体平台56.6万个。

——律师工作。印发《企业复工复产律师公益法律服务指南》,开展民营企业"法治体检"专项活动,组织编写疫情防控和企业复工复产律师公益法律服务指导案例,引导律师积极服务疫情防控和经济社会发展。疫情期间,各地组建公益法律服务团、律师专业服务团等3300多个,为党委政府疫情防控决策提供合法性审查、法律论证等近2万件次,面向群众开展法律咨询和法治宣传70多万人次。推进律师调解试点工作，共设立律师调解工作室8600多个，列入调解名册的律所9500多家，律师调解员4.9万多人。深化刑事案件律师辩护全覆盖试点，全国共有2368个县（市、区）开展试点工作，各地因开展试点扩大通知辩护法律援助案件达59.1万件。组织实施"援藏律师服务团"活动，从全国选派74名优秀律师到西藏无律师县开展法律援助和公益法律服务。截至2020年年底，全国律师事务所达到3.4万多家，同比增长5.7%，律师总数50.4万人，同比增长10.7%。

——公证、法律援助和仲裁工作。深化公证体制改革，激发公证行业活力。截至2020年年底，全国共有公证员1.3万余名，全年共办理公证事务1100余万件。完善法律援助制度，联合有关部门印发《关于进一步加强劳动人事争议调解仲裁法律援助工作的意见》，制定发布《法律援助值班律师工作办法》，出台刑事和民事行政法律援助案件质量同行评估规则。2020年，全国共组织办理法律援助案件140万件，提供法律咨询1500万人次，服务各类受援人216万人次。推进仲裁法修改，完善仲裁法律制度。推进国际商事仲裁中心建设。推进仲裁机构内部治理结构改革。推进中国仲裁协会筹建，完善行政指导与行业自律相结合的监管体制。2020年，全国263家仲裁机构，共处理民商事案件40余万件，案件标的额 7000 多亿元。

——人民调解和司法所工作。部署开展涉疫情矛盾纠纷排查化解工作。发布《全国人民调解工作规范》。推动粤港澳大湾区调解平台和国际商事调解组织建设。截至 2020 年年底，全国共有人民调解委员会 70.8 万个，人民调解员 320.9 万名，全年排查矛盾纠纷 470.9 万次，调解矛盾纠纷 819.6 万件。统筹推进新时代司法所工作，切实完善工作网络，充实工作队伍，司法所工作能力和服务水平不断提升，职能作用充分发挥，在维护社会和谐稳定、推进基层社会治理等方面发挥了重要作用。目前，全国共有司法所 3.9 万个，工作人员达到 14 万余人。

——国家统一法律职业资格考试工作。继续改革完善法律职业资格考试内容和方式，促进提高考试选拔的科学性和有效性。认真做好疫情防控常态化下法律职业资格考试组织实施工作，制定出台《新冠肺炎疫情防控常态化下国家统一法律职业资格考试组织实施与防疫工作指导意见》，70.8 万余人报名参加考试。规范法律职业资格服务管理行为，制定出台《法律职业资格管理办法》。研究推动建立法律职业人员统一职前培训制度。

——司法鉴定工作。全力推进司法鉴定管理体制改革，印发提高司法鉴定质量和公信力改革意见，出台法医、物证、声像资料"三大类"司法鉴定执业分类规定,建立完善干涉司法鉴定活动记录和报告制度、鉴定人出庭作证管理制度等。截至2020年年底,全国司法行政机关登记管理的司法鉴定机构共3100多家,鉴定人3.8万余人。

五、关于人权法治保障

2020年，面对突如其来的新冠肺炎疫情，中国坚持人民至上、生命至上，采取最严格、最彻底的疫情防控举措，全力以赴救治患者，统筹推进疫情防控和经济社会发展工作，全面保障人民权益，推动国家人权事业发展。

（一）生存权保障

——减少贫困。消除贫困是中国人权保障的重中之重，中国始终高度重视减贫工作。2020年2月，中共中央、国务院印发《关于抓好"三农"领域重点工作确保如期实现全面小康的意见》，把全面建成小康社会、全面打赢脱贫攻坚战作为两大目标任务；国务院扶贫开发领导小组对2019年年底全国未摘帽的52个贫困县以及贫困人口超过1000人和贫困发生率超过10%的共1113个贫困村进行挂牌督战，及时解决制约完成脱贫攻坚任务的突出问题，确保剩余贫困人口全部脱贫、剩余贫困县全部摘帽。6月，人力资源和社会保障部办公厅印发《关于做好疫情防控常态化条件下技能扶贫工作的通知》，指导各地采取更加有力、更有针对性的政策措施，积极克服面临的困难和问题，切实做好技能扶贫工作。7月，最高人民法院、最高人民检察院、公安部联合印发《关于刑事案件涉扶贫领域财物依法快速返还的若干规定》，以规范扶贫领域涉案财物快速返还工作，提高扶贫资金使用效能，促进国家惠民利民政策落实。8月，中华全国总工会印发《关于2020年度中央财政专项帮扶资金分配使用有关事项的通知》，下拨专项帮扶资金5.54亿元用于支持在档深度困难职工解困脱困。

——完善社会救助制度。2月，民政部、国务院扶贫办印发《社会救助兜底脱贫行动方案》，要求切实做到兜底保障"不漏一户、不落一人"。自5月起，民政部会同中央政法委等10部门联合开展生活无着的流浪乞讨人员救助管理服务质量大提升专项行动，及时为符合条件的流浪乞讨人员办理落户安置手续，摆脱生存困境。8月，中共中央办公厅、国务院办公厅印发《关于改革完善社会救助制度的意见》，围绕兜住兜牢基本民生保障底线，实现社会救助事业高质量发展，对改革完善社会救助制度进行了顶层设计，统筹发展社会救助体系，推进构建社会救助新格局。

（二）生命健康权保障

——积极抗疫。面对百年一遇的新冠肺炎疫情，中国坚持人民至上、生命至上,及时成立中央应对疫情工作领导小组,派出中央指导组,建立国务院联防联控机制,全国迅速形成统一指挥、全面部署、立体防控的战略布局,采取最严格、最彻底的疫情防控举措,全力以赴救治患者,用1个多月的时间初步遏制疫情蔓延势头,用2个月左右的时间将本土每日新增病例控制在个位数以内,用3个月左右的时间取得武汉保卫战、湖北保卫战的决定性成果,进而又接连打了几场局部地区聚集性疫情歼灭战,最大限度保护了人民生命安全和身体健康。

——完善食品药品制度建设。1月,国家市场监管总局、教育部、国家卫健委、公安部等4部门联合印发《关于落实主体责任强化校园食品安全管理的指导意见》,护航校园食品安全。3月,中共中央、国务院发布关于深化医疗保障制度改革的意见,就解决医疗保障发展不平衡不充分的问题提出意见。7月,国务院办公厅印发《深化医药卫生体制改革2020年下半年重点工作任务》,要求强化大卫生大健康理念,切实加强深化医改系统谋划和组织领导,统筹做好常态化疫情防控和深化医改各项工作。12月,十三届全国人大常委会第二十四次会议通过《中华人民共和国刑法修正案(十一)》,完善了关于药品犯罪的相关规定,药品使用单位的人员明知是假药、劣药而提供给他人使用的,以及违反药品管理法规而生产、销售国务院药品监督管理部门禁止使用的药品的，未取得药品相关批准证明文件生产、进口药品或者明知是上述药品而销售的，药品申请注册中提供虚假的证明、数据、资料、样品或者采取其他欺骗手段的，编造生产、检验记录的，依法承担刑事责任。

（三）劳动就业权益保障

——农民工劳动权益保障。2020年，检察机关将打击"恶意欠薪"等拒不支付劳动报酬犯罪作为服务保障"三大攻坚战"的重要举措之一。8月，人力资源社会保障部、国家发展改革委等15部门印发《关于做好当前农民工就业创业工作的意见》，提出拓宽外出就业渠道、促进就地就近就业、强化平等就业服务和权益保障、优先保障贫困劳动力稳岗就业等做好农民工就业创业工作的措施。

——多渠道支持就业，促进实现工作权。7月，按照国务院常务会议关于促进高校毕业生就业的部署要求，中央财政下达94.5亿元，支持农村教师特岗计划。7月，教育部办公厅等3部门联合印发《关于做好52个未摘帽贫困县建档立卡贫困家庭高校毕业生就业精准帮扶工作的通知》，进一步明确工作重点，全面提升贫困家庭毕业生就业帮扶精准性和实效性。7月，国务院办公厅印发《关于支持多渠道灵活就业的意见》，从就业发展渠道、创业环境、就业保障等三个方面提出具体政策措施。

(四)受教育权保障

6月,教育部印发《关于加强残疾儿童少年义务教育阶段随班就读工作的指导意见》,对新时代进一步加强残疾儿童少年义务教育阶段随班就读工作、完善随班就读工作机制提出意见,推动实现特殊教育公平而有质量发展。6月,教育部等10部门联合印发《关于进一步加强控辍保学工作 健全义务教育有保障长效机制的若干意见》,要求各地加强组织保障,更好地保障适龄儿童少年接受义务教育的权利。7月,财政部安排2020年义务教育薄弱环节改善与能力提升补助资金293.5亿元,继续支持地方基本消除城镇"大班额",基本补齐乡村小规模学校和乡镇寄宿制学校短板,实现农村义务教育学校网络教学环境全覆盖。8月,教育部等5部门印发《关于进一步加强和规范教育收费管理的意见》,要求进一步完善教育收费政策体系、制度体系、监管体系,持续巩固教育乱收费治理成果,促进教育公平而有质量的发展。12月,教育部公布《中小学教育惩戒规则(试行)》,第一次以部门规章的形式对教育惩戒作出规定,旨在把教育惩戒纳入法治轨道,更好地推动学校全面贯彻落实党的教育方针和立德树人根本任务。

（五）退役军人权益保障

1月，国务院退役军人事务部等20部门联合印发《关于加强军人军属、退役军人和其他优抚对象优待工作的意见》，要求规范优待内容，健全管理机制，建立优待证制度，明确优待目录，完善奖惩措施，努力让优抚对象受到全社会尊重，让军人成为全社会尊崇的职业。10月，教育部办公厅印发《关于进一步做好高职学校退役军人学生招收、培养与管理工作的通知》，要求提升退役军人技术技能水平和就业创业能力，促进其充分稳定就业。11月，十三届全国人大常委会第二十三次会议通过《中华人民共和国退役军人保障法》，系统规定退役军人移交接收、退役安置、教育培训、就业创业、优待抚恤、褒扬激励等方面内容，加强退役军人保障工作，维护退役军人合法权益。

（六）特定群体权益保障

——妇女儿童权益保障。1月，最高人民检察院、全国妇联联合下发《关于建立共同推动保护妇女儿童权益工作合作机制的通知》，要求加强侵害妇女儿童权益犯罪的惩治打击，推动未成年人司法保护社会支持体系建设，促进妇女儿童保护法律体系健全完善。3月，国务院联防联控机制印发《因新冠肺炎疫情影响造成监护缺失儿童救助保护工作方案》，就进一步做好因新冠肺炎疫情影响造成监护缺失儿童救助保护工作作出部署安排；民政部办公厅、教育部办公厅印发《关于统筹推进儿童福利领域疫情防控与复工复产复学相关工作的通知》，要求各地及时发现、报告和分类处置因新冠肺炎疫情影响造成监护缺失儿童，确保这类儿童群体的基本生活和照料照护得到基本保障。5月，最高人民检察院印发《最高人民检察院关于加强新时代未成年人检察工作的意见》，对加强新时代未成年人检察工作提出指导意见。5月，最高人民检察院等9部门联合印发《关于建立侵害未成年人案件强制报告制度的意见（试行）》，切实加强对未成年人的全面综合司法保护，及时有效惩治侵害未成年人违法犯罪。5月，十三届全国人大三次会议表决通过的民法典，注重维护妇女和未成年人权益，明确婚前告知重大疾病义务、设立离婚冷静期以及完善收养相关法律制度等，加大对妇女和未成年人保护力度。6月，最高人民检察院发布《未成年人检察工作白皮书（2014—2019）》，全面梳理总结了2014年至2019年全国检察机关未成年人司法保护工作，展示了未成年人检察工作的具体做法和明显成效。10月，十三届全国人大常委会第二十二次会议修订通过《未成年人保护法》，完善了家庭保护、学校保护、社会保护、网络保护、政府保护、司法保护等六大保护内容，提升了未成年人保护的法治化水平。12月，十三届全国人大常委会第二十四次会议修订通过《预防未成年人犯罪法》，明确了预防未成年人违法犯罪的原则和机制。12月，十三届全国人大常委会第二十四次会议通过了《中华人民共和国刑法修正案（十一）》，明确"奸淫不满十四周岁的幼女的，以强奸论，从重处罚"；增加了负有特殊职责人员性侵犯罪，规定"对已满十四周岁不满十六周岁的未成年女性负有监护、收养、看护、教育、医疗等特殊职责的人员，与该未成年女性发生性关系的"，应予以刑事处罚；细化了猥亵儿童罪适用更重刑罚的情节规定。

——老年人权益保障。5月，十三届全国人大三次会议表决通过的民法典，诸多条款涉及老年人的权益保护，主要体现：一是增设居住权规定，为"以房养老"提供法律支撑；二是确立成年人意定监护制度，最大限度尊重老年人意志；三是扩大了遗赠扶养人的范围。11月，国务院办公厅印发《关于切实解决老年人运用智能技术困难的实施方案》，就进一步推动解决老年人在运用智能技术方面遇到的困难，坚持传统服务方式与智能化服务创新并行，为老年人提供更周全、更贴心、更直接的便利化服务作出部署。12月，民政部等9部门发布《关于加快实施老年人居家适老化改造工程的指导意见》，旨在推动各地改善老年人居家生活照护条件，增强居家生活设施安全性、便利性和舒适性，提升居家养老服务质量。

——残疾人权益保障。

在坚决打赢脱贫攻坚战中,我国始终将贫困残疾人脱贫攻坚纳入其中,不断强化顶层设计,完善特别扶助措施。截至2020年年底,我国已稳定实现贫困残疾人及其家庭"不愁吃、不愁穿、义务教育、基本医疗、住房安全有保障"的目标。5年来,有700多万建档立卡贫困残疾人如期脱贫,平均每年减少100万人以上,创造了人类减贫史上残疾人这个特殊困难群体消除贫困的奇迹。

5月,十三届全国人大三次会议表决通过的民法典直接涉及残疾人权益保障的条款有30多条,通过给予残疾人民事权益平等保护、民事行为能力补正和支助、民事权利倾斜保护和导入社会责任等方式,构建了中国残疾人民事权利保护的制度体系,以实现残疾人平等享有和行使民事权利。9月,中国残联发起,联合国亚太经社会、联合国妇女署、联合国人口基金和康复国际共同支持的《行动呼吁:赋能残疾妇女和女童,共创我们想要的未来》发布,旨在进一步推动各国政府和国际社会将保障残疾妇女和女童平等权利、促进融合发展进一步纳入《消除对妇女一切形式歧视公约》《残疾人权利公约》和联合国2030年可持续发展议程等所有相关国际文书的落实中,并从残疾妇女和女童的生命安全、社会保障、医疗健康、教育就业、家居家庭、参与公共事务和国际合作等方面提出了具体的落实建议。9月，工业和信息化部、中国残联下发《关于推进信息无障碍的指导意见》，对完善信息无障碍环境建设顶层设计、进一步做好信息无障碍工作进行部署。10月，十三届全国人大常委会第二十二次会议修订通过《中华人民共和国未成年人保护法》，对包括残疾未成年人在内的需要特别照顾的未成年人权益和残疾未成年人受教育权的保护作出规定。9月，《重大传染病疫情残疾人防护指南（试行）》发布；11月，《重大传染病疫情残疾人防护社会支持服务指南（试行）》发布，填补了国家层面重大传染病疫情残疾人防护指南的空白。11月，《〈中华人民共和国国歌〉国家通用手语方案》（GF0024-2020）发布，这是首次以听力残疾人手语使用者为主体研制的国家通用手语规范化最新成果，切实解决了多年来听力残疾人手语使用者在奏唱国歌的场合，规范、统一、严肃地使用手语表达国歌的愿望。

（七）人权司法保障

1月，最高人民法院发布《关于在执行工作中进一步强化善意文明执行理念的意见》，要求人民法院在执行过程中要强化善意文明执行理念，严格规范公正保障各方当事人合法权益，在依法保障胜诉当事人合法权益的同时，最大限度减少对被执行人权益的影响。5月，司法部部署在全国开展"法援惠民生　扶贫奔小康"活动,从助力复工复产、助推脱贫攻坚、增强群众获得感3大方面提出了10项法律援助便民惠民措施。6月,最高人民法院发布《关于行政机关负责人出庭应诉若干问题的规定》,进一步规范行政机关负责人出庭应诉活动,切实保障人民群众合法权益。

六、关于知识产权保护

2020年,中国扎实推进知识产权保护各项工作,取得积极进展。

(一) 制度建设

审议通过《中华人民共和国专利法》《中华人民共和国著作权法》《中华人民共和国刑法修正案(十一)》。《行政执法机关移送涉嫌犯罪案件的规定》公布实施。推进《中华人民共和国专利法实施细则》《中华人民共和国植物新品种保护条例》修改工作。中共中央办公厅、国务院办公厅印发《2020—2021年贯彻落实〈关于强化知识产权保护的意见〉推进计划》。国务院知识产权战略实施工作部际联席会议办公室印发《2020年深入实施国家知识产权战略加快建设知识产权强国推进计划》。全国打击侵犯知识产权和制售假冒伪劣商品工作领导小组办公室、中央宣传部、最高人民法院、最高人民检察院、公安部、生态环境部、文化和旅游部、海关总署、国家市场监督管理总局联合印发《关于加强侵权假冒商品销毁工作的意见》。

(二) 审核登记

——专利方面。2020年，我国发明专利授权53.0万件，同比增长17.1%。实用新型专利授权237.7万件，同比增长50.2%。外观设计专利授权73.2万件，同比增长31.5%。截至2020年年底，我国发明专利有效量为305.8万件，同比增长14.5%。其中，国内（不含港澳台）发明专利有效量221.3万件，每万人口发明专利拥有量达到15.8件。实用新型专利有效量为694.8万件，同比增长32.0%。外观设计专利有效量为218.7万件，同比增长22.2%。专利审查周期保持稳定，高价值专利审查周期压缩至14个月。2020年，共受理依据《专利合作条约》提出的国际专利申请7.2万件，同比增长18.6%；其中，6.7万件来自国内，同比增长17.9%。

——商标方面。2020年，我国商标注册量为576.1万件，同比下降10.1%。截至2020年年底，商标累计注册量达3447.5万件，商标注册平均审查周期压缩至4个月。2020年，国内申请人提交马德里商标国际注册申请7553件，同比增长16.4%，在马德里联盟中排名第三。截至2020年年底，累计有效注册量达44,223件。2020年，外国申请人指定中国的马德里领土延伸申请24,524件（按一件商标多个类别折算），完成马德里领土延伸申请实质审查62,651类，审查周期缩短至4个月。

——著作权方面。2020年，著作权登记总量为503.9万件，同比增长20.37%。其中，作品登记量为331.6万件，同比增长22.75%；计算机软件著作权登记量为172.3万件，同比增长16.06%。全年共办理著作权质权登记量为384件，涉及主债务金额40.6亿元。

——地理标志、特殊标志和官方标志方面。截至2020年年底，累计批准地理标志产品2391个，核准及备案专用标志使用企业9479家，累计将地理标志作为集体商标、证明商标注册6085件。2020年，受理地理标志产品保护申请10件，批准保护地理标志产品6个，地理标志作为集体商标、证明商标注册765件，核准使用地理标志专用标志企业1052家。完成国家国际发展合作署、国家医疗保障局等有关官方标志备案工作；核准2022年第19届亚运会、第4届亚残会等37件特殊标志。对2022年冬奥会和冬残奥会吉祥物、志愿者标志等7件奥林匹克标志公告保护。

——集成电路布图设计方面。2020年，共受理集成电路布图设计登记申请14,375件，同比增长72.8%；予以登记公告并发出证书11,727件，同比增长77.3%。截至2020年年底，累计受理集成电路布图设计登记申请4.6万件，予以登记公告并发出证书共计3.9万件。

(三) 司法保护

2020 年,全国法院审结一审知识产权案件 46.6 万件,出台知识产权民事诉讼证据等 10 个司法解释和规范性文件。最高人民检察院组建知识产权检察办公室,整合刑事、民事、行政检察职能,统筹加强检察机关知识产权保护制度设计和研究指导。

——加强知识产权审判工作。2020 年,最高人民法院新收知识产权民事案件 3470 件,审结 3260 件;全国地方人民法院共新收知识产权民事一审案件 443,326 件,审结 442,722 件;全国地方人民法院共新收知识产权民事二审案件 42,975 件,审结 43,511 件。2020 年,最高人民法院新收知识产权行政案件 1909 件,审结 1735 件;全国地方人民法院共新收知识产权行政一审案件 18,464 件,审结 17,942 件;全国地方人民法院新收知识产权行政二审案件 6092 件,审结 6183 件。2020 年,全国地方人民法院共新收涉及知识产权的刑事一审案件 5544 件,审结 5520 件;全国地方人民法院新收涉及知识产权的刑事二审案件 869 件,审结 854 件。

——加大知识产权刑事犯罪打击力度。开展"昆仑 2020"专项行动,将打击侵犯知识产权犯罪作为重要内容。2020 年,侦破侵犯知识产权和制售伪劣商品犯罪案件 2.1 万余起,抓获犯罪嫌疑人 3.2 万余名,涉案总价值180余亿元。针对实体市场开展执法行动4.1万余次，组织开展销毁侵权假冒商品活动260余次。

——依法从严批捕知识产权犯罪案件。2020年，全国检察机关共批捕涉知识产权犯罪3930件7174人，起诉5848件12,152人。其中，批捕假冒注册商标罪1509件2879人，起诉2290件4891人；批捕销售假冒注册商标的商品罪1745件2970人，起诉2496件4947人；批捕非法制造、销售非法制造的注册商标标识罪270件498人，起诉403件972人；批捕侵犯著作权罪203件366人，起诉274件653人；批捕销售侵权复制品罪12件19人，起诉16件26人；批捕侵犯商业秘密罪30件52人，起诉30件50人；批捕数罪或他罪中含侵犯知识产权行为161件390人，起诉338件612人。

——加强刑事诉讼监督工作。检察机关及时纠正侵犯知识产权犯罪领域有案不移、有案不立、立案不当、以罚代刑、裁判不公等问题。2020年，经检察机关建议，行政执法机关移送侵犯知识产权涉嫌犯罪案件228件262人；经检察机关监督，公安机关立案181件230人，监督撤案243件304人。依法开展审判监督，纠正确有错误的刑事判决，提出二审抗诉、审判监督抗诉共计57件，法院改判15件18人。

（四）行政执法

——强化专利行政保护。组织开展执法保护专项行动，严厉查处专利侵权假冒违法行为。2020年，全国市场监管部门查处假冒专利案件0.71万件。全国知识产权管理部门办理专利侵权纠纷行政裁决案件4.2万余件，同比增长9.9%。

——强化商标行政执法保护。2020年，全国市场监管部门查处商标违法案件3.13万件，案值7.9亿元，罚没金额7亿元。其中，查处商标侵权假冒案件2.96万件，案值7.65亿元，罚没金额6.78万元。2020年，共依法向司法机关移送涉嫌商标侵权犯罪案件811件。

——强化版权行政执法保护。开展"剑网2020"专项行动，严厉打击视听作品、电商平台、社交平台、在线教育等领域侵权盗版行为，着力规范网络平台版权传播秩序，持续巩固专项治理成果。全国共删除侵权盗版链接323.94万条，关闭侵权盗版网站（APP）2884个，查办网络侵权盗版案件724件，其中刑事案件177件，涉案金额3.01亿元，调解网络版权纠纷案件925件。

——强化反不正当竞争行政执法保护。聚焦民生领域，坚持问题导向，组织开展重点领域反不正当竞争执法专项行动。加大对互联网等重点领域仿冒混淆、虚假宣传、侵犯商业秘密等不正当竞争行为的监管执法力度，依法维护公平竞争的市场秩序，保护经营者和消费者合法权益。2020年，专项行动期间共查办各类不正当竞争案件7371件，案值27.6亿元，罚没金额4.16亿元。

——强化植物新品种行政执法保护。开展打击侵犯植物新品种权行动，重点监督各类种苗、花卉博览会、交易会等，依法打击未经品种权人许可生产或者销售林业授权品种的繁殖材料、假冒林业授权品种的行为，以及销售林业授权品种时未使用其注册登记名称的行为。开展春夏秋冬种子市场专项抽检工作，净化种业市场环境。

——强化海关执法保护。2020年，共采取知识产权保护措施6.53万次，查扣进出口侵权嫌疑货物6.19万批次，同比增长20.11%，涉案货物数量5618.19万件，同比增长20.07%，保护了45个国家和地区近千家知识产权权利人的合法权益。

——强化网络市场行政执法保护。组建网络表演市场线上巡查工作组，开展在线执法检查，梳理排查网络表演APP 1623款次。开展集中执法检查和专项检查，依法查处42家违规网络表演平台、7家网络音乐网站，发现并清理下架违规歌曲940首，协调有关单位关闭7家非法网络动漫网站。

(五) 国际合作

——积极参与多双边磋商，主动参与国际规则制定。深度参与世界知识产权组织（WIPO）框架下全球知识产权治理工作。推动中华人民共和国成立以来第一个在我国缔结、以我国城市命名的国际知识产权条约《视听表演北京条约》生效（2020年4月28日）。完成《区域全面经济伙伴关系协定》（RCEP）知识产权章节谈判，推动协定正式签署。习近平主席与欧方领导人宣布正式签署《中华人民共和国政府与欧洲联盟地理标志保护与合作协定》。启动批准《关于为盲人、视力障碍者或其他印刷品阅读障碍者获得已出版作品提供便利的马拉喀什条约》国内程序。积极推进加入《工业品外观设计国际注册海牙协定》。推进世界知识产权组织《保护广播组织条约》《保护传统文化表现形式条约》谈判进程。

——积极参与国际会议论坛，贡献更多中国方案。积极参与世界贸易组织（WTO）与贸易有关的知识产权（TRIPS）理事会及相关会议，向各成员介绍中国应对新冠肺炎疫情的知识产权有关举措。在国际保护工业产权协会（AIPPI）世界知识产权大会特别会议、20国集团（G20）世界知识产权挑战论坛等重要会议上，与各方就新冠肺炎疫情应对政策和救济措施等进行探讨，并倡导运用知识产权独特优势促进全球创新和经济复苏。首次以视频形式主办第十三次中美欧日韩知识产权五局合作局长会，通过《2020年中美欧日韩知识产权五局合作局长联合声明》。参加中美欧日韩商标五局（TM5）和外观设计五局（ID5）年度会议。主办或联合主办第12届金砖国家知识产权局局长会议、第11届中国-东盟局长会议、第20次中日韩知识产权局局长会议、第8届中蒙俄知识产权研讨会等活动。

——加强司法交流合作及执法联合行动。世界知识产权组织（WIPO）仲裁与调解中心在上海自由贸易试验区临港新片区提供涉外知识产权争议案件的仲裁与调解服务。积极派员参加WIPO"全球知识产权法官论坛"、2020年国际知识产权法院会议等，宣传我国知识产权司法保护成就，提升国际影响力。2020年11月第三届中国国际进口博览会期间，与世界知识产权组织联合举办打击侵权假冒国际合作论坛。举办中欧植物新品种保护执法线上研讨会。围绕46起重点跨国境案件与相关国家执法部门开展线索核查、证据交换、联合行动、司法协助等多层面执法合作。应国际刑警组织邀请，继续深入参与打击互联网知识产权犯罪"网鹰"行动，取得积极成效，赢得国际社会理解与支持。

七、关于生态文明法治建设

2020年,中国立法、执法、司法等各方面积极服务生态文明建设,取得新成效。

(一) 生态文明立法

——出台一批指导性文件。3月,中共中央办公厅、国务院办公厅印发《关于构建现代环境治理体系的指导意见》,明确构建党委领导、政府主导、企业主体、社会组织和公众共同参与的系统化现代环境治理体系。4月,中央全面深化改革委员会第十三次会议审议通过《全国重要生态系统保护和修复重大工程总体规划(2021—2035年)》等6个文件,推进生态保护和修复工作。4月,中共中央办公厅、国务院办公厅印发《省(自治区、直辖市)污染防治攻坚战成效考核措施》,明确对各省(自治区、直辖市)党委、人大、政府污染防治攻坚战成效的考核内容。10月,中国共产党第十九届中央委员会第五次全体会议审议通过《中共中央关于制定国民经济和社会发展第十四个五年规划和二〇三五年远景目标的建议》(以下简称《建议》),指出"十四五"时期要将"生态文明建设实现新进步"作为经济社会发展必须遵循的原则，着力构建生态文明体系，完善生态文明领域统筹协调机制，建立健全生态文明领域各类制度和法律法规。11月，中央全面深化改革委员会第十六次会议审议通过《关于全面推行林长制的意见》，进一步压实地方各级党委和政府保护发展森林草原资源的主体责任。

——制定、修改、废止一批与环境资源保护相关的法律法规和规章。

在法律层面，2月，全国人大常委会审议通过《关于全面禁止非法野生动物交易、革除滥食野生动物陋习、切实保障人民群众生命健康安全的决定》，为全面禁食野生动物，严厉打击非法野生动物交易，从源头上防范和控制公共卫生安全风险提供了有力立法保障。4月，十三届全国人大常委会第十七次会议修订通过《中华人民共和国固体废物污染环境防治法》，明确国家推行生活垃圾分类制度，确立生活垃圾分类的原则；加强了工业固体废物和危险废物环境监管，完善了建筑垃圾、农业固体废物等污染环境防治制度；强化了违法行为的法律责任。5月，十三届全国人大三次会议通过《中华人民共和国民法典》，明确"民事主体从事民事活动，应当有利于节约资源、保护生态环境"的绿色原则，同时还规定民事主体从事民事活动应承担的环境保护义务和相关法律责任，全面开启环境资源保护的民法通道。10月，十三届全国人大常委会第二十二次会议通过《中华人民共和国生物安全法》，这是生物安全领域的基础性、综合性、系统性、统领性法律，系统梳理、全面规范各类生物安全风险，明确生物安全风险防控体制机制和基本制度，填补了生物安全领域基础性法律的空白。12月，十三届全国人大常委会第二十四次会议通过《中华人民共和国刑法修正案（十一）》，增加了污染环境罪的刑档并提高法定刑，将环评、环境监测"造假"、破坏自然保护地、非法引进、释放、丢弃外来入侵物种等行为入罪，增加了非法猎捕、收购、运输、出售陆生野生动物罪，打击滥食野生动物行为；通过《中华人民共和国长江保护法》，这是我国首部保护长江全流域生态系统、推进长江经济带绿色高质量发展的专门法律，以解决区域协调的重大问题为导向，就规划与管控、资源保护、水污染防治、生态环境修复、绿色发展、保障与监督等问题作出全面规定。

在行政法规和部门规章层面，3月，国务院第86次常务会议通过《农作物病虫害防治条例》，为病虫害防治工作提供了法律依据。12月，国务院第117次常务会议通过《排污许可管理条例》，规范排污许可证申请审批程序，要求排污单位建立台账制度，加强事中事后监管，为固定污染源按证排污、依证监管提供法治保障。

4月,生态环境部公布《新化学物质环境管理登记办法》,规范新化学物质环境管理登记行为及科学、有效评估和管控新化学物质环境风险,聚焦对环境和健康可能造成较大风险的新化学物质;原环境保护部发布的《新化学物质环境管理办法》废止。5月,交通运输部公布《高速铁路安全防护管理办法》,突出强化生态环境主管部门对高速铁路附近从事排放粉尘、烟尘及腐蚀性气体的生产活动的检查监督责任。7月,农业农村部公布《农用薄膜管理办法》,建立健全农用薄膜管理制度,构建全链条监管体系。8月,农业农村部、生态环境部公布《农药包装废弃物回收处理管理办法》,旨在防治农药包装废弃物污染,保障公众健康,保护生态环境。11月,生态环境部公布《生态环境部建设项目环境影响报告书(表)审批程序规定》,规范生态环境部建设项目环境影响报告书、环境影响报告表审批程序,提高审批效率和服务水平。12月,生态环境部公布《生态环境标准管理办法》,明确生态环境标准的制定、实施、备案和评估;同月,生态环境部公布《碳排放权交易管理办法(试行)》,对全国碳排放权交易及相关活动予以规范。

2020年,全国各地在环境资源立法方面也取得了积极成效。江苏省十三届人大常委会第十三次会议通过《江苏省生态环境监测条例》,这是全国首部生态环境监测地方性法规。重庆市五届人大常委会第二十次会议通过《重庆市水污染防治条例》。深圳市六届人大常委会第四十四次会议通过《深圳经济特区生态环境公益诉讼规定》。

——制定和修订一批环境资源相关的技术规范。2020年，我国共发布184份环保相关文件，122项国家环境标准。3月，国家林业和草原局发布《国家公园总体规划技术规范》等52项林业行业标准；其中，《国家公园总体规划技术规范》《国家公园资源调查与评价规范》《国家公园勘界立标规范》等3项国家公园行业标准和《林业和草原行政许可实施规范》《林业和草原行政许可评价规范》等2项行政许可行业标准，均属于首次发布。8月，自然资源部办公厅、财政部办公厅、生态环境部办公厅联合印发《山水林田湖草生态保护修复工程指南（试行）》。9月至12月，国家市场监督管理总局、国家标准化管理委员会先后批准发布《国家公园设立规范》《国家公园总体规划技术规范》《国家公园考核评价规范》《国家公园监测规范》《自然保护地勘界立标规范》等5项国家标准。11月，生态环境部、国家发展改革委、公安部、交通运输部、国家卫生健康委公布《国家危险废物名录（2021年版）》，生态环境部公布《建设项目环境影响评价分类管理名录（2021年版）》。

（二）生态文明执法

——持续推进生态文明监管领域改革。制定《生态环境损害赔偿资金管理办法（试行）》《关于推进生态环境损害赔偿制度改革若干具体问题的意见》，推进生态环境损害赔偿制度改革，全国31个省（区、市）和新疆生产建设兵团都印发省级改革实施方案。印发《关于实施生态环境违法行为举报奖励制度的指导意见》，指导各地建立实施生态环境违法行为举报奖励制度，推进生态环境监管制度改革。推进林长制改革、林权收储担保改革以及国有林场整合和集体林权流转改革。

——着力加强重点领域执法。全面推行"双随机、一公开"，开展执法检查58.74万家次。全国下达环境行政处罚决定书12.61万份，罚没款数额总计82.36亿元。成立生态环境部信访投诉举报工作领导小组及其办公室，推进信访投诉工作机制改革，整合投诉举报管理机构，着力解决突出问题，2020年共为各类专项行动转交提供线索近20万条。2020年，生态环境部调度处置各类环境应急事故157起，督办并处置34起重大及敏感突发环境事件。全国累计接收处理群众反映问题44.1万件，按期办结率100%。

——大力推进中央和省级生态环境保护督察。8月，开展第二轮第二批中央生态环境保护督察，对北京、天津、浙江3省（市），以及中国铝业集团、中国建材集团2家央企开展督察，并对国家能源局、国家林业和草原局2个部门开展督察试点，这是首次将国务院相关部门列为督察对象，共受理转办群众举报1.05万余件。全国31个省份和新疆生产建设兵团均设立了省级督察机构。制作完成2020年长江经济带生态环境警示片，梳理169个问题清单；完成整改226个2018年和2019年警示片披露的315个问题。

——扎实开展生态保护和建设。印发《山水林田湖草生态保护修复工程指南（试行）》，指导和规范各地山水林田湖草生态保护修复工程实施，推动山水林田湖草一体化保护和修复。出台《红树林保护修复专项行动计划（2020—2025年)》和《海岸带保护修复工程工作方案（2019—2022年)》，支持地方开展红树林生态修复。编制全国草原保护修复和草业发展规划，印发《全国草原监测评价工作指南》。出台《草原征占用审核审批管理规范》，明确征占用生态保护红线内草原的限制条件，严格限制建设项目征占用基本草原。扎实推进红树林保护修复专项行动，开展国际重要湿地生态状况监测，印发《中国国际重要湿地生态状况》白皮书。发布《2020年国家重要湿地名录》，新增国家重要湿地29处。全力推进国家公园体制试点工作，编制《国家公园空间布局方案》，制定《国家公园设立规范》等5项国家标准，印发《国家公园监测指标和监测技术体系（试行）》和东北虎豹、大熊猫、祁连山、海南热带雨林等4个国家公园总体规划（试行）。联合开展"绿盾2020""碧海2020"、长江非法码头整治、长江非法捕捞整治等专项行动，打击破坏自然保护地行为。

（三）生态文明司法

——出台一批环境资源司法文件。3月，最高人民法院出台《公益诉讼文书样式（试行）》，规范和统一公益诉讼裁判文书制作。6月，最高人民法院发布《关于为黄河流域生态保护和高质量发展提供司法服务与保障的意见》和黄河流域生态环境司法保护典型案例。9月，最高人民法院、最高人民检察院、生态环境部等10部门联合出台《关于推进生态环境损害赔偿制度改革若干具体问题的意见》，明确赔偿磋商、修复责任、资金管理等程序规则，强化生态环境损害赔偿执法司法衔接。12月，最高人民法院、最高人民检察院联合修订《关于检察公益诉讼案件适用法律若干问题的解释》，最高人民法院修订《关于审理环境民事公益诉讼案件适用法律若干问题的解释》，使相关规定与民法典一致。

——依法审理环境资源案件。2020年，全国各级人民法院受理环境资源刑事、民事、行政一审案件27.29万件，审结25.33万件。发挥环境公益诉讼、生态环境损害赔偿诉讼作用，促进环境保护。全国各级人民法院受理环境公益诉讼案件4679件，审结3557件；受理生态环境损害赔偿案件91件（包括生态环境损害赔偿司法确认案件和诉讼案件），审结62件。云南昆明中院审结"绿孔雀"案、四川甘孜州中院一审审结"五小叶槭"案两起预防性民事公益诉讼案，加强珍贵、濒危野生动植物生态环境保护。甘肃兰州中院、宁夏银川中院审理"弃风弃光"环境民事公益诉讼案，加强气候变化的司法应对。重庆、湖北、江苏等长江流域法院依法严厉打击长江流域非法捕捞行为及收购、加工、销售等产业链，保障长江十年禁渔部署顺利开局。

——发挥环境资源司法政策指引作用。1月，最高人民法院召开长江经济带生态环境司法保护工作情况暨典型案例发布会，通报司法服务保障长江经济带发展情况，发布《长江流域生态环境司法保护状况》（白皮书）。5月，最高人民法院发布《中国环境资源审判（2019）》（白皮书）、《中国环境司法发展报告（2019）》（绿皮书）、2019年度人民法院环境资源典型案例。2020年，最高人民法院发布环境资源保护类典型案例4批80例，最高人民检察院发布环境资源保护类典型案例3批34例。

——优化创新环境资源审判机制。持续推进专门机构建设，各级法院探索设立环境资源审判庭、环境资源法庭、巡回法庭等形式多样的环境资源专门审判机构。截至2020年年底，全国法院已设立1993个环境资源专门审判机构。推进集中管辖区、司法协作区建设。注重环境资源集中管辖法院和非集中管辖法院间协同，推动省级行政区划内集中管辖体系化。强化跨省域生态环境协同治理。黄河流域9省区高级人民法院签署环境资源审判协作框架协议，构建流域司法机制，推动黄河流域生态环境协同保护、系统治理。健全协调联动机制。与生态环境部、国家林业和草原局等加强合作交流，完善工作机制，共同维护环境资源安全。

——推进环境司法国际交流合作。邀请美国、英国、澳大利亚、新加坡等国家环境法学专家、资深法官，就土壤污染、气候变化应对、生物多样性保护等主题，以视频方式在全国法院环境资源审判工作培训班授课。派员参加由联合国环境规划署与亚洲开发银行共同举办的"亚太气候变化司法大会·新冠疫情时代的司法"国际研讨会，以及"中欧应对气候变化立法研讨会"等。

八、关于法治宣传、法学教育和法学研究

2020年，中国法治宣传、法学教育和法学研究工作紧紧围绕法治中国建设中的重大理论和实践问题展开，成效卓著。

（一）法治宣传

——深入学习宣传贯彻习近平法治思想。11月，中央全面依法治国工作会议召开，确立了习近平法治思想在全面依法治国中的指导地位，这是我国社会主义法治建设进程中具有重大现实意义和深远历史意义的大事。2020年，"宪法宣传周"以"深入学习宣传贯彻习近平法治思想　大力弘扬宪法精神"为主题开展活动，将学习宣传习近平法治思想同宪法宣传教育有力结合起来。全国人大常委会办公厅会同中央宣传部、司法部举行"深入学习宣传习近平法治思想　完善以宪法为核心的中国特色社会主义法律体系"座谈会，进一步将学习宣传贯彻习近平法治思想引向深入。组织中央有关国家机关干部学习习近平法治思想，发挥中央国家机关"头

雁"作用，推动全社会切实增强学习宣传贯彻习近平法治思想的思想自觉、政治自觉、行动自觉。以学习宣传习近平法治思想为重点内容，开展了进企业、进农村、进机关、进校园、进社区、进军营、进网络主题宣传，让基层群众感受到习近平法治思想的真理伟力，引导全社会坚定不移走中国特色社会主义法治道路。

——做好民法典普法工作。中央宣传部等8部门联合印发通知，部署开展民法典学习宣传工作。推出了12讲《民法典开讲》系列公益讲座，收看量突破千万人次。全国人大常委会法工委等单位的负责同志录制《民法典学习公开课》全网推送。以案例和漫画形式，制作了《生活中的民法典：看图学法》挂图，拍摄了《民法典：新时代的人民法典》专题片，广受欢迎。各地区各部门各行业结合实际，广泛开展了针对性强、社会覆盖面广、群众参与度高、形式生动直观的学习宣传活动，形成了全媒体立体传播的良好态势。

——开展疫情防控专项法治宣传行动。中央依法治国办、中央政法委等6单位以"防控疫情、法治保障"为主题，举行新闻发布会，公开发布贯彻习近平总书记重要讲话和中央全面依法治国委员会意见精神，制定实施《最高人民法院、最高人民检察院、公安部、司法部关于依法惩治妨害新型冠状病毒感染肺炎疫情防控违法犯罪的意见》有关情况。国务院新闻办就制定实施《关于政法机关依法保障疫情防控期间复工复产的意见》有关情况举行了新闻发布会。编写有关疫情防控的《法律知识问答》和《法律法规汇编》，发布"防控疫情 法治同行"专题宣传挂图，以"问题+案例+图片+法律点评+知识链接"的形式释法说理。重点向全国5亿多手机用户发送依法防控疫情的公益宣传短信。"中国普法"微信公众号发布疫情防控相关文章，总阅读量1.2亿人次。针对哄抬物价、破坏防疫秩序、危害公共安全、妨碍公务等行为，连续发布29组300多篇典型案例。各地各部门把疫情防控普法宣传与基层依法治理相结合，积极发挥基层社区、农村普法阵地的作用，引导全社会依法行动、依法行事。

——加强法治文化阵地建设。目前，全国共设立法治文化主题公园3500多个、广场1.2万多个、长廊3.4万多个，全国青少年法治教育基地3万多个。命名了第三批47个全国法治宣传教育基地，免费向社会开放。加强红色法治文化的宣传保护，传承红色法治文化基因。组织开展第八批"全国民主法治示范村（社区）"命名工作，总结、推广了一批先进典型。积极运用新媒体新技术普法，"中国普法"微信公众号粉丝数突破1600万，政法新媒体成为普法宣传重要阵地。

——组织评选2020年全国十大法治人物。制作播出《宪法的精神 法治的力量——2020年度法治人物特别节目》，在中央电视台 1 套和 12 套黄金时段播出，反映 2020 年依法抗疫、民法典编纂、扫黑除恶、法治扶贫、"七五"普法等各项工作取得的不凡成绩，进一步彰显广大干部群众特别是一线干警对宪法的信仰、对法治的坚守。

——开展"七五"普法总结验收。全国普法办制定印发了《"七五"普法总结验收工作方案》，明确总结验收的主要内容、验收标准、方法和步骤，坚持发现问题、帮助解决问题，避免形式主义、走过场。各省（区、市）和新疆生产建设兵团、中央和国家机关有关部门等，结合《全国"七五"普法规划总结验收考核评估指标体系》，进行自查和评估。司法部、全国普法办组织开展抽查调研，实地查看了基层乡村、社区、学校、企业等单位的普法情况，并结合开展个别谈话、随机线上法律知识测试和网上调查等方式，准确评估普法工作成效，推动各地查漏补缺，有力促进了"七五"普法各项措施落实落地。

——组织开展全国学生"学宪法 讲宪法"系列活动。举办第五届全国学生"学宪法 讲宪法"活动，推动各地各校将宪法学习宣传作为一项重要政治任务，引导教育系统干部师生广泛参与宪法法治学习教育。截至 2020 年 12 月 30 日，通过教育部全国青少年普法网参与学习的人次超过 71 亿，通过在线学习测评产生了 8900

多万名"宪法小卫士"。在国家宪法日举办第七届教育系统"宪法晨读"活动，36万多所学校的7200多万名师生同步参与了宪法诵读。

——继续开展"青年普法志愿者法治文化基层行"活动。2020年，"青年普法志愿者法治文化基层行"活动共组织现场普法活动51万多场次，线上普法活动71万多场次，参与法治宣传志愿者达93万多人次，受教育群众达1.25亿多人次。

（二）法学教育

——广泛开展线上线下相结合的专业教学，统筹推进疫情防控和法学教育。2020年，为统筹推进疫情防控和法学教育，各法科院校积极探索通过网络开展远程课程教学，确保课业平稳有序推进。2月，中国政法大学联合西南政法大学、华东政法大学共同推出《同心战"疫"三校说"法"》专题，集合3所学校的法学人才优势，对战"疫"期间发生的真实案例进行法理分析，普及法律知识，营造清新、健康、向上的社会环境，履行高校的社会服务职能。3月，为满足疫情防控期间法科生对学习专业知识的强烈需求，帮助各市场主体正确应对疫情带来的法律风险、疫情下的突发法律问题，来自北京大学、清华大学、中国人民大学、西南政法大学、华东政法大学、中南财经政法大学的13位法学名家携手推出"法学大家公益系列讲座",通过教授加平台面向全国免费直播。

——深化国际交流与合作。10月,第三届"21世纪世界百所著名大学法学院院长论坛"举行,来自牛津大学、耶鲁大学等国外大学法学院和国内法学院校的院(校)长与专家学者围绕文明转型时期的法学教育等进行交流。10月,以"'一带一路'背景下中非法律教育交流与合作"为主题的第四届中非法学院院长论坛以网络形式举行,与会嘉宾围绕"一带一路"背景下中非法律教育交流与合作的主题,聚焦疫情新形势下中非法学教育合作的热点问题进行交流。

——创建法学教育新平台。6月,天津大学举行首届中国高校法学教育创新研讨会暨天津大学法学院复建五周年座谈会,发布《法学教育创新联盟成立倡议书》,法学教育创新联盟正式成立。该联盟由全国若干知名法学院校发起,面向所有有志推动中国法学高等教育改革创新的高校开放,旨在建设成为全国高校探讨法学教育机遇挑战、共享法学教育改革创新经验的平台。

——组织评选第九届"全国杰出青年法学家"。第九届"全国杰出青年法学家"评选活动由中国法学会组织,自2019年5月启动,受到全国法学法律界和其他社会各界的高度重视和广泛关注,2020年11月完成,共评选出10名"全国杰出青年法学家"称号获得者和20

名提名奖获得者。12月，第九届"全国杰出青年法学家"座谈会在北京召开，10名"全国杰出青年法学家"称号获得者和20名提名奖获得者受到表彰。这10名"全国杰出青年法学家"称号获得者均是近年来活跃在我国法学界的"生力军"，在中国特色社会主义法治理论研究中作出了突出贡献。

——继续举办中国政法实务大讲堂。2020年，中国政法实务大讲堂走进清华大学、北京大学、中国人民大学、中国政法大学和西南政法大学等7所高校。7名政法系统副部级及以上领导围绕学习贯彻习近平法治思想、党的十九届五中全会精神等主题分别开展专题讲座，助力推动法学院校学生当好"接班人"，培养新时代法治人才。

（三）法学研究

——习近平法治思想的研究阐释进一步深化。11月，中央全面依法治国工作会议确立习近平法治思想为全面依法治国的指导思想。法学界深入学习研究宣传贯彻习近平法治思想，中国法学会设立"习近平法治思想研究"重大专项课题。中国人民大学、华东政法大学等高校陆续成立习近平法治思想研究中心（院）。国内重要法学学术期刊发表了对习近平法治思想的学术解读，有力推动了习近平法治思想的理论阐释。

——以制定和实施民法典为契机展开的民法学研究成果丰硕。2020年，民法学研究既达到一个新高度，又是多年民法学研究的集大成，这源于民法典的制定和通过。在"民法理论研究也达到较高水平"基础上，2020年刊发的许多重大理论创新成果，为民法典的制定和实施奠定了坚实的理论基础。代表文章有《以"生态恢复论"重构环境侵权救济体系》《行政许可的民法意义》等。在问题域拓展上，生态保护、营商环境优化、居住权、疫情防控等问题催生了大量创新性成果。从研究的理论目标看，以促进民法典实施为导向，从立法论转向司法适用层面，尤其是适用中与宪法、行政法、刑法、经济法等其他法律部门的关系衔接问题，产生大批研究成果。

——部门法学研究取得新发展。宪法学研究重点关注合宪性审查、宪法原则、宪法基本范畴、香港基本法30年、民法典与宪法、疫情与宪法、科技与宪法等议题。法理学围绕"全面依法治国与国家治理现代化"展开专题讨论。行政法学研究重点关注行政处罚法修订、行政法的法典化、法治政府建设、行政协议、公共卫生与应急法治体系更新、以行政复议为化解行政争议主渠道的复议制度改革、完善公益诉讼相关制度等议题。经济法学重点关注《中华人民共和国反垄断法》修订、系统性金融风险防控、数字经济的法律规制、外资利用、经济法的基础理论等问题。刑法学重点关注《中华人民共和国刑法修正案（十一）》、刑事合规和单位犯罪、疫情防控的刑法应对、现代科技风险的刑法应对、个人信息犯罪、黑社会性质组织犯罪等问题。刑事诉讼法学重点关注认罪认罚从宽制度、以企业合规加强民营经济的司法保护等议题。民事诉讼法学围绕民法典、新民事证据规定开展研究。行政诉讼法学聚焦行政公益诉讼、行政协议等展开研讨。国际法学就国内法的域外适用、国际知识产权保护、国际投资、全球抗疫等议题进行研究。法律史学重点研究了民法典编纂中传统法资源的整合、中国传统治理、传统法的体系化等议题。

九、关于国际交流与国际合作

2020年,中国大力推动抗击新冠肺炎疫情国际法治交流和合作,积极开展疫情形势下的司法协助和反腐败工作,深度参与有关国际立法活动,"一带一路"建设法律交流持续深入,国际法治对话不断推进,创新对外法学交流形式,取得了积极成果。

(一) 司法协助和国际反腐败合作

——司法协助缔约工作。2020年,我国批准了与土耳其、比利时、塞浦路斯的引渡条约,与巴基斯坦的移管被判刑人条约。

——司法协助办案。2020年,全国共审查办理民商事司法文书送达3817件,民商事调查取证及法律查明、民商事判决承认与执行案件67件。

——追逃专项工作。3月,"天网2020"行动启动。截至2020年年底,共追回外逃人员1421名,其中监察对象314人、"红通人员"28人,追赃金额约29.5亿元人民币。

——多边领域。10月,中方代表团视频参加二十国集团（G20）首次反腐败部长级会议并发言，与会各方就发挥G20引领作用、推动反腐败国际合作交换意见。会议通过《二十国集团反腐败部长级会议公报》，呼吁G20各方深化反腐败国际追逃追赃协作，加强应对疫情反腐败工作，共同打造廉洁的营商环境。10月，中方代表在第75届联大法律委员会"国内和国际法治"议题一般性辩论中发言，重点介绍中国全面推进依法治国和开展反腐败工作的情况。11月，习近平主席分别视频出席上海合作组织成员国元首理事会第二十次会议、金砖国家领导人第十二次会晤、二十国集团领导人第十五次峰会并发表重要讲话，与会领导人就加强反腐败国际合作达成重要共识并分别写入《上海合作组织成员国元首理事会莫斯科宣言》《金砖国家领导人第十二次会晤莫斯科宣言》《二十国集团领导人利雅得峰会宣言》。

——研讨工作。11月，"法治模式下的反腐败追逃追赃国际合作论坛"在北京召开。与会的国内外专家学者就"刑事缺席审判与正当程序""违法所得的没收与处置""引渡合作及其替代措施""企业的反腐败合规建设"等问题进行了研讨。

(二) 参与国际立法活动

——国际环境保护和气候变化方面。6月，《联合国气候变化框架公约》秘书处举行"六月造势"系列视频会议，会议由附属履行机构（SBI）和附属科技咨询机构（SBSTA）主席联合发起，内容涵盖疫后复苏、国家自主贡献（NDCs）、适应、资金、损失与损害、透明度等多个议题，此次会议是公约主渠道下首次集中举办线上交流活动，为2021年年底将在英国格拉斯哥召开的第26届联合国气候变化大会预做铺垫。9月，习近平主席在联合国生物多样性峰会上通过视频发表重要讲话，倡议各国坚持生态文明、坚持多边主义、保持绿色发展、增强责任心，强调中国努力建设人与自然和谐共生的现代化，并邀约各方参加2021年在昆明举办的《生物多样性公约》第十五次缔约方大会。9月，生态环境部和外交部共同举办了"2020年后生物多样性展望：共建地球生命共同体"部长级在线圆桌会，会议聚焦生物多样性与可持续发展、2020年后生物多样性全球治理等内容，来自巴西、哥斯达黎加、埃及等17个国家的部长级代表，以及联合国环境规划署等国际组织和非政府组织代表视频参会。11月下旬，习近平主席视频出席了二十国集团利雅得峰会，阐述了对恢复经济、可持续发展等问题的看法。峰会通过了《二十国集团领导人利雅得峰会宣言》。习近平主席在利雅得峰会"守护地球"主题边会上致辞，提出应加大应对气候变化力度、深入推进清洁能源转型、构筑尊重自然的生态系统。12月，习近平主席视频参加由联合国及有关国家倡议举办的纪念《巴黎协定》达成五周年的气候雄心峰会,并发表题为"继往开来,开启全球应对气候变化新征程"的重要讲话,宣布中国国家自主贡献一系列新举措。

——国际海洋法方面。2月,国际海底管理局第26届理事会第一期会议在牙买加举行,大会审议了国际海底区域内矿产资源开发规章草案,中国代表团就区域环境管理计划、国际海底资源、开发规章制定等问题进行了发言。12月,中国代表在第75届联大"海洋和海洋法"议题下呼吁各方携手构建海洋命运共同体,表示中方将积极支持根据《联合国海洋法公约》设立的国际海洋法法庭、国际海底管理局和大陆架界限委员会在全球海洋治理中的工作。

——网络方面。7月,联合国网络犯罪政府专家组召开第六次会议,会议重点讨论了打击网络犯罪国际合作和预防问题,围绕"国际合作"和"预防"形成了70多项具体建议。中国代表团线上参会并在专题讨论环节发言,介绍开展打击网络犯罪国际合作、企业助力预防网络犯罪的经验。

——国际刑事司法合作方面。9月,中国代表团视频参加金砖国家反恐工作组第五次会议,与会各方主要就国际地区反恐形势、各国反恐举措和金砖国家反恐合作交换意见。会前,由中方牵头的金砖国家反恐工作组去极端化分工作组首次会议以视频方式举行,中方代表主持会议并发言,全面阐述中方反恐和去极端化政策主张。10月,中国代表团参加《联合国打击跨国有组织犯罪公约》第十届缔约方大会,并强调跨国有组织犯罪形势依然严峻复杂,中国将始终做多边主义的践行者,坚定维护以联合国为核心的国际体系,与各国共同预防和打击跨国犯罪,推动构建普遍安全的人类命运共同体。12月,中国代表团视频参加联合国预防犯罪和刑事司法委员会第29届会议及续会并在3个议程项目下发言,积极宣介法治建设成就,并表示将认真参与第14届联合国预防犯罪和刑事司法大会筹备工作,积极参与联合国预防犯罪和刑事司法领域相关活动。

——外空法方面。10月,中国代表团参加第75届联合国大会裁军与国际安全委员会会议,会议表决通过"不首先在外空部署武器"决议,重申应研究和采取切实措施,达成防止外空军备竞赛条约,人类命运共同体理念再一次写入联合国外空决议中。

——人权方面。10月,中国代表团参加联合国人权理事会下设的"跨国公司及其他工商企业与人权问题"法律文书政府间工作组第六次会议,会议逐条讨论了"跨国公司及其他工商企业与人权问题"法律文书第二版修订案文。

——其他方面。2月和11月,海牙国际私法会议在荷兰海牙举行管辖权项目专家组第三次和第四次会议,探讨国际民商事领域直接管辖权规则相关议题，中国代表团通过视频参会。8月，《联合国海洋法公约》第30次缔约国会议在纽约联合国总部举行，与会缔约国投票选出了6名国际海洋法法庭法官，中国籍候选人成功当选。11月，国际法院法官选举在纽约联合国总部举行，选举5名国际法院法官，中国籍候选人、现任国际法院副院长薛捍勤法官成功连任。

（三）政府间法治对话

——联合国框架下的对话。9月，习近平主席出席联合国成立75周年纪念峰会并发表重要讲话，强调后疫情时代联合国应主持公道、厉行法治、促进合作、聚焦行动，重申中国将始终做多边主义的践行者，积极参与全球治理体系改革和建设，推动构建人类命运共同体。9月，习近平主席在第75届联合国大会一般性辩论上发表重要讲话，强调全球治理体系亟待改革和完善，要坚持走多边主义道路，维护以联合国为核心的国际体系，通过对话协商妥善化解国家间分歧，守住道德底线和国际规范。11月，中方代表在第75届联大全会"国际法院的报告"议题一般性辩论中发言，积极评价国际法院为维护多边主义、捍卫国际公平正义发挥的重要作用，重申中国积极倡导和平解决国际争端，将继续坚定支持国际法院工作。

——上海合作组织框架下的对话与合作。9月,国务委员兼公安部部长赵克志视频参加上海合作组织成员国安全会议秘书第十五次会议并发言,就加强上海合作组织安全合作提出五点建议,与会各方主要就当前国际和地区安全形势、上海合作组织成员国合作打击"三股势力"、贩毒、有组织犯罪以及维护信息安全等问题交换意见。10月,最高人民法院院长周强视频参加由哈萨克斯坦共和国最高法院主办的第十五次上海合作组织成员国最高法院院长会议,致开、闭幕式辞并作专题发言,提出广泛凝聚司法合作共识、不断健全司法合作机制、持续提升司法合作水平,与各方共同商讨新冠肺炎疫情形势下的司法交流合作;会议通过了《第十五次上海合作组织成员国最高法院院长会议联合声明》。10月,最高人民检察院检察长张军率团视频参加第十八次上海合作组织成员国总检察长会议并围绕"打击腐败的当前实践和有效机制"发言,介绍中国在治理腐败方面的主要措施和重大成效,围绕各国加强协作、共同打击腐败犯罪提出建议。

——东盟框架下的对话与合作。1月,最高人民法院院长周强接待泰国最高行政法院院长毕亚一行来华考察"法院信息化"工作。11月,最高人民法院院长周强以视频方式与新加坡最高法院首席大法官梅达顺举行工作会谈,并参加第四届中新法律和司法圆桌会议,致开、闭幕式辞并作专题发言,中新双方代表联合宣布《中国—新加坡"一带一路"国际商事审判案例选》正式出版发行。会议围绕"法院应对新冠疫情的最佳实践/新冠疫情给法院和法律界带来的挑战""如何通过案例指导和类案检索制度以及判例制度统一法律适用""一般法律原则在国际商事争议中的适用与限制""法院诉讼规则中与'一带一路'倡议相关的规定"等四个议题开展了交流研讨。

——金砖国家框架下的对话与合作。9月,中共中央政治局委员、中央外事工作委员会办公室主任杨洁篪出席第十次金砖国家安全事务高级代表视频会议,各方就国际和地区热点问题、生物安全、反恐和网络安全等交换意见,一致同意加强沟通协调合作,共同维护国际法、国际规则和多边主义。9月,最高人民法院院长周强出席金砖国家首席大法官论坛,致开、闭幕式辞,并在参加"通过行政诉讼保护经济参与者利益和营商环境"专题研讨时发言,介绍中国法院加强产权司法保护、服务优化营商环境的经验和做法,会议通过了《金砖国家首席大法官论坛联合声明》。10月,全国人大常委会委员长栗战书视频出席第六届金砖国家议会论坛并发表讲话,强调加强金砖国家立法机构合作;各方围绕"维护全球稳定、保障共同安全、促进创新增长的金砖国家伙伴关系:议会合作"的主题进行交流,金砖国家立法机构负责人视频参会，会议通过了《第六届金砖国家议会论坛宣言》。11月，习近平主席视频出席由俄罗斯主办的金砖国家领导人第十二次会晤，发表题为《守望相助共克疫情 携手同心推进合作》的重要讲话，强调坚持多边主义，合力克服疫情挑战，维护以世界贸易组织为核心的多边贸易体制，落实应对气候变化《巴黎协定》和联合国2030年可持续发展议程。各国领导人围绕"深化金砖伙伴关系，促进全球稳定、共同安全和创新增长"主题交换意见，会晤通过了《金砖国家领导人第十二次会晤莫斯科宣言》。12月，最高人民检察院检察长张军视频参加第四次金砖国家总检察长会议并致辞，围绕打击网络领域犯罪和经济领域犯罪提出建议。

——其他方面。4月，司法部部长傅政华在北京参加俄罗斯司法部主办的"新冠疫情，法制体系"国际视频连线论坛开幕式并发言，介绍中国为统筹疫情防控和经济社会发展提供优质高效的法律服务和法治保障的情况，并倡议加强法律司法界国际合作，携手共建人类命运共同体。

（四）对外法学交流

——东盟框架下的法学交流。10月，第17届中国—东盟商事法律合作研讨会在广西举办，与会代表围绕"中国—东盟自贸区多元化纠纷解决机制研究与实务"

主题，全方位就中国和东盟商事法律领域合作进行深入探讨，来自柬埔寨、马来西亚、缅甸、新加坡、越南等东盟国家的学者参与研讨。

——与非洲国家的法学交流。8月，中国法学会主办的"中非法律人才交流项目第七期研修班"在北京线上举办，围绕民法典、"一带一路"建设、外商投资保护、中国国际仲裁等专题展开研讨，来自非洲14个国家的70多名法律工作者参加了培训。

——与欧亚地区的法学交流。9月，由中国法学会主办的"'一带一路'欧亚地区法治研修班"在北京线上举办，围绕中国刑事司法、中国商事仲裁、中国公司法律制度、中国国际商事法庭、中国外商投资法律制度、"一带一路"等专题展开研讨，来自欧亚地区10个国家287名法律工作者参加了培训。9月至10月，中国法学会代表在北京分别同德国、俄罗斯、乌兹别克斯坦、哈萨克斯坦立法机构领导人举行视频会晤，并表示中国将与各方坚持互利共赢、开放合作，为促进中国与各国各领域关系发展提供良好法律保障。

——9月，由中国法学会主办的"国际投资经贸法律风险及对策"专题座谈会在北京线上召开。座谈会以"'一带一路'与中非联合仲裁机制"为主题，下设"中非联合仲裁中心规则""'一带一路'商事争议解决机制"等4个议题。来自中国和非洲法学界的代表参加了本次会议。

——9月，由外交部和中国南海研究院共同举办的"合作视角下的南海"视频国际研讨会在北京举行。会议围绕"南海问题的由来与现状""和平解决争议与《联合国海洋法公约》""落实《南海各方行为宣言》和区域海洋合作"等议题展开讨论。

——11月，由中国法学会主办的中国法治国际论坛（2020）在北京举行。国家主席习近平向论坛致信。习近平指出，共建"一带一路"需要良好法治营商环境。中国坚持开放包容、互利互赢，愿同各方一道，积极开展国际法治合作，为建设开放型经济、促进世界经济复苏提供法治支持。习近平表示，中方欢迎各国法学法律界朋友出席中国法治国际论坛（2020），希望大家围绕"新冠疫情背景下的国际法治合作"深入交流、凝聚共识，为运用法治手段推动共建"一带一路"、更加有力地应对全球性挑战贡献智慧和力量。论坛以"新冠疫情背景下的国际法治合作"为主题，发布了《中国法治国际论坛北京宣言》。来自中国、俄罗斯、巴西等18个国家和相关国际组织代表通过视频方式参加论坛。

——12月，由中国国际问题研究院主办的"共同应对新形势下的恐怖主义"国际研讨会在北京举行。与会各方围绕"疫情下国际地区反恐安全新形势及新挑战""各国反恐关切和经验做法""深化反恐国际合作的正确路径"进行了深入讨论。俄罗斯、法国、埃及、巴基斯坦等 12 国政府官员、反恐研究机构负责人和学者视频参会。

结束语

2021年是中国共产党成立100周年,是"十四五"开局之年,也是开启全面建设社会主义现代化国家新征程的第一年。党的十九届五中全会擘画了新时期党和国家事业发展宏伟蓝图,法治中国建设迈向新阶段。

中共中央印发《法治中国建设规划(2020—2025年)》(以下简称《规划》)。《规划》指出,建设法治中国应当实现法律规范科学完备统一,执法司法公正高效权威,权力运行受到有效制约监督,人民合法权益得到充分尊重保障,法治信仰普遍确立,法治国家、法治政府、法治社会全面建成。《规划》共分九个部分:一是坚定不移走中国特色社会主义法治道路,奋力建设良法善治的法治中国。二是全面贯彻实施宪法,坚定维护宪法尊严和权威。三是建设完备的法律规范体系,以良法促进发展、保障善治。四是建设高效的法治实施体系,深入推进严格执法、公正司法、全民守法。五是建设严密的法治监督体系,切实加强对立法、执法、司法工作的监督。六是建设有力的法治保障体系,筑牢法治中国建设的坚实后盾。七是建设完善的党内法规体系,坚定不移推进依规治党。八是紧紧围绕新时代党和国家工作大局，依法维护国家主权、安全、发展利益。九是加强党对法治中国建设的集中统一领导，充分发挥党总揽全局、协调各方的领导核心作用。《规划》作为新中国成立以来第一个关于法治中国建设的专门规划，是新时代推进全面依法治国的纲领性文件，为"十四五"时期统筹推进法治中国建设指明了方向、提供了遵循。

站在"两个一百年"的历史交汇点，中国人民在中国共产党的坚强领导下，坚持以习近平新时代中国特色社会主义思想为指导，深入贯彻落实习近平法治思想，坚定不移走中国特色社会主义法治道路，必将推进全面依法治国各项工作取得更大进展，为"十四五"开好局起好步提供有力的法治保障，以优异成绩庆祝中国共产党成立100周年。

附　录

一、2020 年全国人大及其常委会制定和修改的法律、法律解释及决定目录（33 件）

1. 中华人民共和国固体废物污染环境防治法
2. 中华人民共和国民法典
3. 中华人民共和国公职人员政务处分法
4. 中华人民共和国档案法
5. 中华人民共和国人民武装警察法
6. 中华人民共和国香港特别行政区维护国家安全法
7. 中华人民共和国城市维护建设税法
8. 中华人民共和国契税法
9. 全国人民代表大会常务委员会关于修改《中华人民共和国专利法》的决定
10. 中华人民共和国生物安全法
11. 中华人民共和国未成年人保护法
12. 中华人民共和国出口管制法
13. 全国人民代表大会常务委员会关于修改《中华人民共和国国旗法》的决定
14. 全国人民代表大会常务委员会关于修改《中华

人民共和国国徽法》的决定

16. 全国人民代表大会常务委员会关于修改《中华人民共和国全国人民代表大会和地方各级人民代表大会选举法》的决定

16. 全国人民代表大会常务委员会关于修改《中华人民共和国著作权法》的决定

17. 中华人民共和国退役军人保障法

18. 中华人民共和国预防未成年人犯罪法

19. 中华人民共和国长江保护法

20. 中华人民共和国刑法修正案（十一）

21. 中华人民共和国国防法

22. 全国人民代表大会常务委员会关于全面禁止非法野生动物交易、革除滥食野生动物陋习、切实保障人民群众生命健康安全的决定

23. 全国人民代表大会常务委员会关于推迟召开第十三届全国人民代表大会第三次会议的决定

24. 全国人民代表大会常务委员会关于授权国务院在中国（海南）自由贸易试验区暂时调整适用有关法律规定的决定

25. 全国人民代表大会常务委员会关于第十三届全国人民代表大会第三次会议召开时间的决定

26. 全国人民代表大会关于建立健全香港特别行政区维护国家安全的法律制度和执行机制的决定

27. 全国人民代表大会常务委员会关于增加《中华人民共和国香港特别行政区基本法》附件三所列全国性法律的决定

28. 全国人民代表大会常务委员会关于授予在抗击新冠肺炎疫情斗争中作出杰出贡献的人士国家勋章和国家荣誉称号的决定

29. 全国人民代表大会常务委员会关于香港特别行政区第六届立法会继续履行职责的决定

30. 全国人民代表大会常务委员会关于授权国务院在粤港澳大湾区内地九市开展香港法律执业者和澳门执业律师取得内地执业资质和从事律师职业试点工作的决定

31. 全国人民代表大会常务委员会关于香港特别行政区立法会议员资格问题的决定

32. 全国人民代表大会常务委员会关于加强国有资产管理情况监督的决定

33. 全国人民代表大会常务委员会关于设立海南自由贸易港知识产权法院的决定

二、2020年国务院制定和修改的行政法规目录（10件）

1. 农作物病虫害防治条例

2. 国务院关于修改和废止部分行政法规的决定（国务院号令第726号）

3. 化妆品监督管理条例

4. 保障中小企业款项支付条例

5. 中华人民共和国预算法实施条例

6. 国务院关于修改《行政执法机关移送涉嫌犯罪案件的规定》的决定

7. 国家科学技术奖励条例

8. 国务院关于修改和废止部分行政法规的决定（国务院号令第732号）

9. 政府督查工作条例

10. 企业名称登记管理规定

三、2020年最高人民法院、最高人民检察院发布的司法解释（32件）

1. 最高人民法院关于修改《关于内地与澳门特别行政区法院就民商事案件相互委托送达司法文书和调取证据的安排》的决定

2. 最高人民法院、最高人民检察院关于缓刑犯在考验期满后五年内再犯应当判处有期徒刑以上刑罚之罪应否认定为累犯问题的批复

3. 最高人民法院、最高人民检察院关于适用《中华人民共和国刑法》第三百四十四条有关问题的批复

4. 最高人民法院关于行政机关负责人出庭应诉若干问题的规定

5. 最高人民法院关于人民法院司法警察依法履行职权的规定

6. 最高人民法院关于证券纠纷代表人诉讼若干问题的规定

7. 最高人民法院关于修改《关于审理民间借贷案件适用法律若干问题的规定》的决定

8. 最高人民法院关于审理侵犯商业秘密民事案件适用法律若干问题的规定

9. 最高人民法院关于审理专利授权确权行政案件适用法律若干问题的规定（一）

10. 最高人民法院关于涉网络知识产权侵权纠纷几个法律适用问题的批复

11. 最高人民法院、最高人民检察院关于办理侵犯知识产权刑事案件具体应用法律若干问题的解释（三）

12. 最高人民法院关于审理涉船员纠纷案件若干问题的规定

13. 最高人民法院关于知识产权民事诉讼证据的若干规定

14. 最高人民法院关于内地与香港特别行政区相互执行仲裁裁决的补充安排

15. 最高人民法院关于审理食品安全民事纠纷案件适用法律若干问题的解释（一）

16. 最高人民法院关于适用《中华人民共和国民法

典》时间效力的若干规定

17. 最高人民法院关于废止部分司法解释及相关规范性文件的决定

18. 最高人民法院关于修改《最高人民法院关于在民事审判工作中适用〈中华人民共和国工会法〉若干问题的解释》等二十七件民事类司法解释的决定

19. 最高人民法院关于修改《最高人民法院关于破产企业国有划拨土地使用权应否列入破产财产等问题的批复》等二十九件商事类司法解释的决定

20. 最高人民法院关于修改《最高人民法院关于审理侵犯专利权纠纷案件应用法律若干问题的解释（二）》等十八件知识产权类司法解释的决定

21. 最高人民法院关于修改《最高人民法院关于人民法院民事调解工作若干问题的规定》等十九件民事诉讼类司法解释的决定

22. 最高人民法院关于修改《最高人民法院关于人民法院扣押铁路运输货物若干问题的规定》等十八件执行类司法解释的决定

23. 最高人民法院关于适用《中华人民共和国民法典》婚姻家庭编的解释（一）

24. 最高人民法院关于适用《中华人民共和国民法典》继承编的解释（一）

25. 最高人民法院关于适用《中华人民共和国民法

典》物权编的解释（一）

26. 最高人民法院关于审理建设工程施工合同纠纷案件适用法律问题的解释（一）

27. 最高人民法院关于审理劳动争议案件适用法律问题的解释（一）

28. 最高人民法院关于新民间借贷司法解释适用范围问题的批复

29. 最高人民法院关于适用《中华人民共和国民法典》有关担保制度的解释

30. 最高人民检察院关于废止《最高人民检察院关于办理非法经营食盐刑事案件具体应用法律若干问题的解释》的决定

31. 人民检察院检察委员会工作规则

32. 最高人民检察院关于废止部分司法解释和司法解释性质文件的决定

Preface

The year 2020 was an extremely extraordinary year in the history of the People's Republic of China. In the face of the complicated international situation, the arduous domestic reform, development and stability tasks, especially the serious impact of the Covid-19 epidemic, under the strong leadership of the Central Committee of the Communist Party of China (CPC) with Xi Jinping at the core, all the Chinese people have struggled tenaciously to achieve significant strategic results in the prevention and control of the epidemic. China was the only major economy in the world to achieve positive economic growth. Complete victory was achieved in the battle against poverty, and the decisive achievement was made in completing a moderately prosperous society in all respects. China achieved impressive results that satisfy the people and will go down into annals The year 2020 also marked an important milestone for China's rule of law development. In the year, the Central Working Conference on Comprehensive Law-Based Governance was held, clarifying the guiding position of Xi Jinping's thinking on the rule of law in comprehensive law-based governance. In the year, the Third Session of the 13th National People's Congress (NPC) voted to adopt the Civil Code of the People's Republic of China. In the year, the CPC Central Committee issued the Plan for Building the Rule of Law in China (2020-2025) and the Program for Developing a Law-Based Society (2020-2025), which clearly defined the roadmap and plan for developing the rule of law in China and a law-based society. In the year, judicial and law enforcement organs nationwide gave full play to their functions and worked to do a good job of epidemic prevention and control and contribute to the fight against poverty, helping to continue to write a new chapter about the two miracles: rapid economic development and long-term social stability. In the year, fresh progress was made in developing the law-based government, new breakthroughs were made in comprehensively deepening judicial and law enforcement reform, and the struggle to combat organized crime and root out local criminal gangs was completed. Our ability to administer justice for the people and ensure impartial administration of justice significantly improved. Fresh progress was made in building a safe China and the rule of law in China. New achievements were made in legal publicity, legal education and legal research. The significant progress China made in the development of the rule of law in 2020 will surely inspire the people of China to advance in the great journey of the rule of law more proudly and actively.

Unswervingly Follow the Socialist Legal Path with Chinese Characteristics to Provide a Strong Legal Guarantee for Building a Modern Socialist Country in All Respects[1]

Xi Jinping

The main task of this Central Working Conference on Comprehensive Law-Based Governance is to review experience, analyze the situation, define tasks, make plans for the current and future periods of comprehensive law-based governance, and mobilize the whole Party, the entire country and the whole of society to work together to further promote comprehensive law-based governance, accelerate the development of a socialist legal system with Chinese characteristics, and build a socialist law-based country.

---

[1] Excerpts from General Secretary Xi Jinping's speech at the Central Working Conference on Comprehensive Law-Based Governance on November 16, 2020. Source: *Qiushi*, No. 5, 2021.

Our Party has always attached importance to the development of the rule of law. During the new-democratic revolution, the Party formulated the Constitution of the Chinese Soviet Republic and a large number of laws and decrees, and created the Ma Xiwu trial method. After the founding of the People's Republic of China, during the period of socialist revolution and socialist construction, the Party led the people in enacting the May Fourth Constitution and a series of important laws and regulations, such as the Organic Law of State Institutions, the Election Law and the Marriage Law, establishing a socialist legal framework and system and a socialist judicial system. In a new period of reform and opening up, the Party put forward the policy of seeing that laws are in place wherever necessary and that laws are observed and strictly enforced and lawbreakers are prosecuted. It emphasized that promoting law-based governance is the basic strategy of the Party in leading the people in governing the country, that law-based government administration is the basic way of the Party in governing the country, and that continuous efforts must be made to promote socialist rule of law.

Since the 18th National Party Congress, the Party Central Committee has clearly put forward comprehensive law-based governance and promoted it as part of the four-pronged comprehensive strategy.[1] The Fourth Plenary Session of the 18th CPC Central Committee was devoted to research in law-based governance and made a decision on major issues regarding the comprehensive promotion of law-based governance. After the 19th Party Congress, the Party Central Committee set up the Central Commission for Law-Based Governance, and made a series of major decisions and plans for comprehensive law-based governance from a global and strategic perspective, promoting the historic changes and achievements in the development of socialist rule of law in China. We wrote "the leadership of the Communist Party of China is the most essential feature of socialism with Chinese characteristics" into the Constitution, and improved the Party's system of leading legislation, ensuring law enforcement, supporting justice and taking the lead in abiding by the law, so that the Party's leadership of comprehensive law-based governance is stronger. We improved the top-level design and coordinated the legal norms, the implementation of laws, legal supervision, and the development intra-Party rules

---

[1] The four-pronged comprehensive strategy is to make comprehensive moves to finish building a moderately prosperous society in all respects, deepen reform, advance law-based governance, and strengthen Party self-governance.

and regulations, and the overall pattern of comprehensive law-based governance has been basically formed. We promoted important areas of legislation, deepened the reform of the rule of law, promote the development of the law-based government, established state supervisory agencies, reformed and improved the judicial system, increased public awareness of the law, deepened law-based military governance, strengthened the ranks of legal professionals, resolutely safeguarded social justice, corrected a number of wrongful cases in accordance with the law, and made significant progress in comprehensive law-based governance.

At present and in the coming period, to promote comprehensive law-based governance, we must fully implement the guiding principles from the 19th CPC National Congress and the second through fifth plenary sessions of the 19th CPC Central Committee. To achieve the overall goal of building a socialist legal system with Chinese characteristics and a socialist law-based country, we must ensure the unity of Party leadership, the running of the country by the people, and law-based governance. With a focus on solving the outstanding problems in the field of the rule of law, we must unswervingly keep to the socialist legal path with Chinese characteristics, modernize the system and capacity for national governance under the framework of law, and provide a strong legal guarantee for building a modern socialist country in all respects and realizing the Chinese Dream of National Rejuvenation. Our priorities are as follows:

First, we must adhere to the Party's leadership of comprehensive law-based governance. The leadership of the Party is the fundamental guarantee for promoting comprehensive law-based governance. Our Party is the world's largest ruling party of the world's most populous country. How to effectively wield power, provide good governance, and better organize and mobilize the 1.4 billion people to build a socialist modern country in all respects is a major issue always demanding our great attention. History is the best textbook and it is the best way to help us stay sober. Our Party has led the development of socialist rule of law, with both successful experiences and lessons from mistakes. Especially during the ten years of civil unrest, the legal system was seriously damaged, and the Party and the people paid a heavy price. After the end of the Cultural Revolution, Deng Xiaoping brought this issue to the height of the future fate of the Party and the country, emphasizing that, "We must strengthen our legal system. Democracy has to be institutionalized and written into law." Both positive and negative experiences tell us that the more complex the international and domestic environment, the more complicated the task of reform and opening up and socialist modernization, the more we must use the rule of law thinking and means to consolidate our ruling position, improve the way of governance, and become better able to govern, in order to ensure the long-term stability of the Party and the state.

All Party members must be soberly aware that comprehensive law-based governance is never to weaken the leadership of the Party, but to strengthen and improve it. We must improve the system and working mechanism of the Party's leadership of comprehensive law-based governance, institutionalize the Party's leadership, write it into law, and ensure the effective implementation of the Party's line and policy through the legal system. We must promote both the law-based governance of the country and the law-based based governance of the Party and ensure that the Party both governs the country in accordance with the Constitution and law and exercises strict self-governance in accordance with the intra-Party rules and regulations.

In 2015, when I listened to the work reports of the leading Party members' groups of the Supreme People's Court and the Supreme People's Procuratorate at a meeting of the

Standing Committee of the CPC Central Committee's Political Bureau, at a seminar for principal provincial and ministerial level leaders on the guiding principles from the Fourth Plenary Session of the 18th CPC Central Committee and on comprehensively advancing the law-based governance of China, and on other occasions, I categorically pointed out that placing rule of law in competition with Party leadership is a political trap and a pseudo-proposition. We must not speak in ambiguous or vague terms on this issue; our answer must be unequivocal. The leadership of the Party and law-based governance are not opposites, but unified. Our laws fully reflect the will of the Party and the people, and our Party acts in accordance with the law; this relationship is a mutually unified relationship. Party members must bear in mind that the leadership of the Party is the soul of our socialist rule of law and is the biggest difference between the rule of law in China and the rule of law in Western capitalist countries. Without the leadership of the Party, comprehensive law-based governance will be difficult to be effectively promoted and the law-based socialist country will not be built.

Of course, when we say it is wrong to placing rule of law in competition with Party leadership, we put the Party as a ruling whole, and we are talking about the Party's ruling position and leadership, and when it comes to each Party and government organization and each official, they must obey and comply with the Constitution and laws. Some things should be submitted to Party committees to decide, but such decisions are not for private ends; they are not covert interventions, but are political, procedural, duty-bond decisions. This line must be clearly delineated.

Second, we must keep the people at the center. The people are the broadest and deepest basis of comprehensive law-based governance. We must uphold the principle of doing everything for the people and rely on the people. We must reflect the interests of the people, reflect the aspirations of the people, safeguard the rights and interests of the people, and promote the wellbeing of the people in the whole process and all aspects of comprehensive law-based governance. We must ensure that the people, under the leadership of the Party, manage state affairs, economic and cultural undertakings, and social affairs through various ways and forms. We must ensure that the people enjoy a wide range of rights and freedoms and assume their obligations in accordance with the law.

The fundamental purpose of promoting comprehensive law-based governance is to protect the rights and interests of the people in accordance with the law. With China's sustained economic and social development and the people's living standards continuing to improve, the people's demand for democracy, rule of law, fairness, justice, security, and the environment keep growing. We must actively respond to the people's new requirements and new expectations, and stay problem-oriented and goal-oriented. We must establish dialectical thinking and keep the picture in mind. We must carry out systematic research and planning and solve the outstanding legal problems of major concern to the public, continue to enhance people's sense of gain, happiness and security, and use the rule of law to ensure that people live and work in peace and happiness.

Third, we must keep to the socialist legal path with Chinese characteristics. As I said, our socialist legal path with Chinese characteristics is a specific embodiment of upholding the rule of law; our theory of Chinese socialist rule of law is a theoretical achievement in developing the rule of law; our Chinese socialist rule of law system is a legal manifestation of building the socialist system with Chinese characteristics. We should not only be based on the present and use the rule of law thinking and the rule of law to solve the deep-rooted problems facing economic and social development, but also focus on the long term in building the foundation of the rule of law, the force of the rule of law, and the momentum of the rule of law, in order to make various systems more mature and well-defined and provide long-term institutional safeguards for the development of the Party and the state.

Since ancient times, China has formed a unique Chinese law in world law history and accumulated a profound legal culture. Chinese law was formed in the Qin Dynasty, and gradually matured in the Sui and Tang dynasties, with the *Tang Code* being the representative code. Chinese law gradually faded away after the late Qing Dynasty. Unlike civil law, common law, and Islamic law, Chinese law was formed under specific historical conditions in China, demonstrating the great creativity of the Chinese nation and the profound foundation of Chinese legal culture. Chinese law has brought together the spirit and wisdom of the Chinese nation, and it has many excellent ideas and concepts worthy of our inheritance. These include the national governance strategy of making ritual and rite violations criminal offenses and valuing rites and laws; the concept that the people are the foundation of a nation, and a nation can enjoy peace only when its foundation is strong; the value that the country should be free from litigation and harmony is precious; the idea of "prudent punishment," the idea of prioritizing virtues over sanctions; the equality concept of making sanctions appropriate to the crime in accordance with the law' and the principle of protecting those who have no kin and cannot support themselves as well as the elderly, minors, women, and those with disabilities. All this shows the wisdom of the excellent Chinese traditional legal culture. After the modern times, many people have tried to copy the Western model of rule of law in China, but all of them failed in the end. History and reality tell us that only by inheriting the excellent Chinese traditional legal culture, exploring the appropriate rule of law from the practice of China's revolution, construction and reform, and at the same time drawing on the beneficial achievements of foreign rule of law, can we consolidate the legal foundation for building a socialist modern country in all respects and realizing the rejuvenation of the Chinese nation.

One thing should be clear: we promote comprehensive law-based governance, but under no circumstance should we imitate the models and practices of other countries indiscriminately or adopt the Western models of "constitutionalism," "separation of powers," and "judicial independence." Practice has proved that our political system and legal system are suitable for our national conditions and realities and have significant advantages. On this issue, we must be confident and determined. Facts have educated our people, who are becoming more and more confident.

In the face of the sudden Covid-19 outbreak, we have always adhered to the general requirement to stay confident, stand united, and adopt both a science-based approach and targeted measures. On February 5, I chaired the Third Meeting of the Central Commission for Law-Based Governance to plan law-based work for the prevention and control of the epidemic in accordance with the law at a critical moment. I particularly stressed that the more challenging the work for epidemic prevention and control became, the more we must adhere to prevention and control in accordance with the law and coordinate all prevention and control work within the framework of the law. All regions and departments have made comprehensive efforts in legislation, law enforcement, justice, law promotion and law compliance, implemented measures such as regional blockade, patient isolation, traffic control and disposal of human remains in strict accordance with legal authority and procedures, cracked down on illegal and criminal acts that hinder epidemic prevention and control, and resolved epidemic-related conflicts and disputes in accordance with the law, providing a strong legal guarantee for major strategic achievements in epidemic prevention and control.

Fourth, we must govern the country and exercise state power within the framework of the Constitution. The Constitution is the fundamental law of the country and has the highest legal effect. The Party led the people in formulating and implementing the Constitution and laws, and the Party itself must operate within the scope of the Constitution and laws. All the Chinese people, all state organs and armed forces, all political parties and social organizations, all enterprises and institutions must take the Constitution as the fundamental guideline for their activities, and all have the responsibility to safeguard the dignity of the Constitution and ensure its implementation. No organization or individual may have privileges beyond the Constitution and laws, and all violations of the Constitution and laws must be investigated.

The Fourth Plenary Session of the 18th CPC Central Committee clearly stated that to uphold the law-based governance of the country, we must first uphold governance based on the Constitution; to uphold the law-based exercise of state power, we must first uphold the exercise of power based on the Constitution. We stress governing the country and exercise state power within the framework of the Constitution, but that is essentially different from the so-called constitutionalism in the West and the two cannot be confused with each other. To govern the country and exercise state power within the framework of the Constitution, we must unswervingly adhere to the leadership of the CPC, the state system of the people's democratic dictatorship and the system of people's congresses that are enshrined in the Constitution.

Maintaining the legal unity in the country is a serious political issue. China is a unitary state, so it is vital to maintain its legal unity. The Legislation Law revised in 2015 gives the cities divided into districts local legislative power, local legislation has made positive progress, and the overall situation is good. However, some localities run counter to superior legislation and fail to treat legislation seriously with very bad impact. We must will strengthen oversight to ensure compliance with the Constitution, advance constitutionality review, and safeguard the authority of the Constitution. In addition, local legislation must have local characteristics and must be as concise as are needed: if three or five articles will do, then it is unnecessary to make the legislation too long. The key is to fully understand the guiding principles from the Party Central Committee and proceed from local conditions to solve prominent problems.

Fifth, we must modernize the system and capacity for national governance within the legal framework. The rule of law is an important foundation for the system and capacity for national governance. Only comprehensive law-based governance can effectively ensure the national governance system is systemic, standard and coordinated and maximize social consensus.

Over the past 70 years since the founding of the People's Republic of China, China has created two miracles: rapid economic development and long-term social stability, which are very closely related to our continuous promotion of socialist rule of law. In response to the Covid-19 epidemic, we have used the rule of law to coordinate the prevention and control of the epidemic and economic and social development, maintained social stability in accordance with the law, promoted reopening in an orderly manner, and achieved significant strategic results in the prevention and control of the epidemic in China. China will become the only major economy in the world to resume positive economic growth this year. As we integrate the great struggle, the great project, the great cause and the great dream in practice and embark on the new journey of building a socialist modern country in all respects, we must pay more attention to the rule of law, implement the rule of law, and give a better play to the role of the rule of law in strengthening the fundamentals, keeping expectations stable, and yielding long-term benefits. We must use the law to deal with major challenges, resist major risks, overcome major resistance, and resolve major conflicts.

Sixth, we must continue to build the socialist legal system with Chinese characteristics. The socialist legal system with Chinese characteristics is integral for promoting the rule of law across the board. We need to move faster to form a complete system of legal norms, an efficient system of law compliance, a tight system of legal supervision, a strong system of legal protection, and a sound system of intra-Party regulations. We must integrate the rule of law and the rule by virtue and ensure that the rule of law and the rule by virtue complement each other.

"Governance without law leads to chaos; keeping laws unnecessarily unchanged leads to decline." We must accelerate the improvement of the socialist legal system with Chinese characteristics, so that it becomes more scientific, complete, unified and authoritative. Since the 18th National Party Congress, the NPC and its Standing Committee have adopted amendments to the Constitution, enacted 48 laws, revised laws 203 times, made 9 legal interpretations, and adopted 79 decisions on legal issues and major problems. Up to now, there are 282 laws, 608 government regulations and more than 12,000 local regulations in force. The Civil Code provides a good example for the codification of legislation in other areas. We should review the experience of codification of the Civil Code, and in due course promote the codification of legislative in areas where conditions are ripe. We must study the rich form of legislation. We may develop some big laws, but also may develop some smaller ones and enhance the relevance, applicability and operability of legislation.

We must actively promote legislation in national security, science and technology innovation, public health, biosecurity, ecological civilization, risk prevention, foreign-related rule of law and other important areas of legislation. We should improve the legal systems that are urgently needed for national governance and are essential for meeting the growing needs of the people for a better life, fill the gaps and shore up areas of weakness. The digital economy, internet finance, artificial intelligence, big data, cloud computing and other new technologies and new applications are developing rapidly, giving rise to a series of new industries and new models, but some laws are still not readily available or are not there at all. Cybercrime has become one of the important risks that endanger our national political security, network security, social security, economic security.

Seventh, we must push forward coordinated progress in law-based governance, exercise of state power, and government administration, and promote the integrated development of the law-based country, government, and society. Comprehensive law-based of law is a systemic project; we need to plan it in an integrated way, with greater emphasis on a systemic, holistic and coordinated approach. Law-based governance, exercise of state power, and government administration are an organic whole, and the key lies in the Party implementing law-based governance and the governments at all levels adhering to law-based government administration. The law-based country, government, and society complement each other, the law-based country is the goal of the development of the rule of law, the law-based government is the focus of building the law-based country, and the law-based society is the basis for the development of the law-based country.

I have repeatedly stressed that in the promotion of comprehensive law-based governance, developing a law-based government is the key task and the main project and plays a demonstrative and driving role in developing a law-based country and society, and breakthroughs must be made in this area first. Now, there are still some difficult problems to be solved in developing the law-based government. Problems such as the infirm concept law-based government administration and the meaningless formalities in legality reviews of administrative decision-making have not been fundamentally resolved. We should use the rule of law to set the rules and delineate the boundaries for the exercise of administrative power, standardize administrative decision-making procedures, and improve the mechanisms whereby government keeps its word and raise the level of law-based government administration. In accordance with the characteristics of the new development stage, and with a focus on the promotion of high-quality development and the building of a new development pattern, we should accelerate the transformation of government functions, move faster to create a market-oriented, law-based, and international business environment, break the industry monopoly and local protectionism, remove the obstacles to economic circulation, and promote the formation of a national unified, standard and orderly market system for fair competition.

Administrative law enforcement work is extensive, relates the government to the people, and has a direct bearing on the people's trust in the Party and the government and their confidence in the rule of law. To promote strict, fair and appropriate law enforcement, we must improve judicial credibility. In recent years, we have rectified irregularities and malfeasance in law enforcement with great results. At the same time, problems such as some places carry out law enforcement like a movement and apply a one-size-fits-all approach still occur from time to time, and malfeasance in law enforcement remains a prominent problem. Emphasis on strict law enforcement to ensure that violators respect the law and hold it in awe does absolutely not advocate violent law enforcement and excessive law enforcement. We must enforce the law both with tensity and with warmth. We need to strengthen the establishment of a system of coordination and supervision of administrative law enforcement that covers all provinces, cities, counties and townships, strengthen all-around and process-wide supervision, and improve the quality of law enforcement.

All people abiding by the law is the foundation for law-based society. Popularization of the law should keep up with the times. Greater efforts should be made to improve relevance and effectiveness, carry out a responsibility program in which those who enforce the law are responsible for strengthening public legal awareness. In particular, we should strengthen youth education on the rule of law, and constantly improve all citizens' awareness of the rule of law, so at to make the rule of law become a social consensus and basic norm. We should strengthen governance in accordance with the law and cultivate the legal environment in which all of our people work in accordance with the law, look to the law when running into problems, and rely on the law to resolve problems and conflicts.

An ancient Chinese said, "It is essential to eliminate the scourge before it arises, cure the disease before it becomes severe, and provide preventive care before a disease develops." By the same token, to develop the rule of law, we should not only address crime but more importantly, prevent crime. China's national conditions determine that we cannot afford to have too many litigation cases. China has a population of 1.4 billion and if we resort to the court of law to resolve all large and small things, the country is bound to be overwhelmed. We should ensure promote more legal professionals work more on guidance and counseling, improve the preventive legal system, adhere to and develop the Fengqiao model[1] in the new era, improve the comprehensive mechanism for the prevention, mediation and resolution of social conflicts and disputes, pay more attention to the basic work at the grassroots level, give full play to the role of the policy of establishing a social governance model based on collaboration, participation, and common interests at the grassroots level, and promote social harmony and stability.

Eighth, we must comprehensively promote scientific legislation, strict law enforcement, impartial justice, and universal compliance with the law. We should continue to promote reform in the field of the rule of law, and solve the outstanding contradictions and problems in the field of legislation, law enforcement, justice, and law-abiding.

Fairness and justice is the soul and life of justice. We should deepen the comprehensive reform of the judicial responsibility system, strengthen judicial constraints and supervision, refine personnel management by type, improve judicial career security, regulate the operation of judicial power, and improve the quality and efficiency of judicial cases. We need to improve the system of legal protection of

---

1 In the early 1960s, the officials and citizenry of Fengqiao Town in Zhejiang Province created the Fengqiao practice, which emphasized solving problems *in situ* rather than passing them up to higher authorities.

social fairness and justice, and strive to ensure that the people can see in every judicial case that justice is served. We should continue to improve the public interest litigation system, and effectively safeguard public interest. Since the 18th National Party Congress, the Party Central Committee has some major reforms to improve the institutions and mechanisms whereby inspection and supervision organs, public security organs, procuratorial organs, judicial organs, judicial administrative organs fulfill their respective duties and investigative powers, procuratorial powers, judicial powers, executive powers are wielded in support of each other. These reforms must be carried out through to the end with real results.

In recent years, many judicial corruption cases have revealed the problem of inadequate constraints and supervision of power. Some people have bought their way to become above the law with the support of dozens judicial and law enforcement officers, rendering supervision null and void. We must speed up the establishment of a standard and efficient system of constraints and supervision to resolutely break the "social connection network" and cut off the "chain of interests," leaving no room for underhanded activity.

Since January 2018, a three-year special struggle to combat organized crime and root out local criminal gangs has been rolled out nationwide. The special struggle has integrated efforts to combat organized crime and root out local criminal gangs with efforts to take out the umbrella protecting criminal gangs and destroy their social connection networks, removing a number of rotten apples. In the past three years, the number of mafia-like organizations taken out is equivalent to the sum of the previous 10 years, forming a strong deterrent to criminal gangs. We must continue to crack down on illegal and criminal acts that disrupt public order. In particular, we must regularize the struggle to combat organized crime and root out local criminal gangs, and persistently and unswervingly crack down on criminal gangs and their protective umbrellas, so that both the cities and the countryside will be more peaceful and the public more comfortable.

Ninth, we must coordinate efforts to promote of the rule of law at home and foreign-related rule of law. The rule of law is an important element of the country's core competitiveness. At present, profound changes of a kind unseen in a century facing the world are accelerating, peace and development are still the themes of the times, but the international environment is becoming significantly more instable and uncertain, and the impact of the Covid-19 pandemic is widespread and far-reaching. China continues to develop and grow, and is increasingly approaching the center of the world stage. We must accelerate the strategic layout of foreign-related rule of law work, coordinate domestic and international governance, and better safeguard national sovereignty, security and development interests. We should accelerate the formation of a systematic and complete system of foreign-related laws and regulations, and improve the judicial effectiveness of foreign-related law enforcement. We must guide enterprises and citizens in more consciously complying with local laws and regulations and customs in the process of going global and using the rule of law and rules to protect their legitimate rights and interests. We should focus on cultivating a number of international first-class arbitration institutions and law firms to make the work of foreign-related rule of law protection and services more effective.

We must firmly uphold the international system with the United Nations at its core, firmly uphold the international order based on international law, and firmly uphold the basic principles of international law and the basic norms of international relations based on the purposes and principles of the UN Charter. We should put forward reform proposals for international rules and international mechanisms that are unjust and unreasonable and do not conform to the general trend of the evolution of the international landscape, promote changes in global governance, and build a human community with a shared future.

Tenth, we must build a high-quality rule of law workforce with both moral integrity and professional competence. To comprehensively promote law-based governance, we must, first and foremost, build a good team of professionals. We should strengthen education on ideals and convictions, carry out in-depth education on the core socialist values and the socialist concept of the rule of law, and ensure that the rule of law workforce is revolutionary, regularized, specialized and professional and is loyal to the Party, the country, the people and the law.

The management of the rule of law professionals must adhere to stricter standards and higher requirements. Some law enforcement and judicial personnel with great power lack in self-respect. They are guilty of corruption, favoritism and abuse of the law and handle cases manipulated by money, power, and personal favor, seriously undermining the authority of the rule of law. We must develop and improve the iron rules, regulations, disciplinary provisions, and use institutions to manage key personnel, key positions, and key tasks. We must resolutely investigate and prosecute those who are corrupt, disloyal and dishonest to the Party and thoroughly investigate corruption in law-enforcement and judicial activities. Recently, judicial and law enforcement departments have carried out team education and pilot rectification work, investigating and prosecuting a number of rotten apples and winning public praise. We should consolidate and expand the results of the pilot work, have zero tolerance for corruption, be strict with ourselves, and remove all irregularities despite pains.

Legal service personnel are an important force in comprehensive law-based governance. Overall, they are good, but there are also many problems. Some are keen to "seek fame and profit," have misconduct, lack in integrity, and have a poor image. Very few individual legal practitioners have little political awareness, and even maliciously attack China's political system and legal system. Supporting the leadership of the CPC and China's socialist rule of law must be made the basic requirements for legal services personnel. We should strengthen education, management, and guidance, guide legal service workers in adhering to the correct political direction, practicing in accordance with the law, regulations, and integrity, conscientiously fulfilling their social responsibilities, and enthusiastically building a socialist law-based country. We should promote the reform and development of law schools to improve the quality of personnel training. We should strengthen foreign-related legal education, focusing on the training of foreign-related law enforcement, judicial and legal services personnel and the training of legal professionals for international organizations, and better serve the overall situation of foreign work.

Eleventh, we must focus on a small number of key officials. Officials specifically exercise the Party's ruling power and national legislative, executive, supervisory and judicial power, and are the key to comprehensive law-based governance. Officials at all levels should resolutely implement the major decisions and plans of the Party Central Committee on comprehensive law-based governance, take the lead in respecting the rule of law, holding the law in awe, understanding the law, and mastering the law, and constantly become better able to use the rule of law thinking and the rule of law to deepen reform, promote development, resolve conflicts, maintain stability and deal with risks, and serve as the models for respecting, learning, abiding by and using the law. The rule of law literacy and the performance of duties in accordance with the law should be included in the assessment and evaluation of officials, so that respecting, learning and abiding by the law becomes the conscious behavior and the necessary quality of officials.

To deeply promote comprehensive law-based governance, we must adhere to the centralized and unified leadership of the Party. Party committees and governments at all levels must strengthen the organization and leadership of the rule of law, grasp major plans, important tasks, key work, and ensure their implementation. They must thoroughly implement the guiding principles from of the Fifth Plenary Session of the 19th CPC Central Committee, and simultaneously plan, deploy, and advance economic and social development and rule of law development during the 14th Five-Year Plan period. The Party Central Committee will soon issue a plan for building the rule of law in China and a program for building a law-based society. The new program for building a law-based government will also soon be introduced. Party committees and governments at all levels must implement them properly. All fronts and all departments must strengthen the concept of the rule of law, act strictly in accordance with the law, and constantly improve the level of the rule of law in the work of all areas. Legal departments must fully perform their duties and responsibilities. The Central Office for Law-Based Governance must coordinate efforts, carry out supervision and inspection, and promote implementation, identify problems in a timely manner, and work to solve them. It must quit meaningless formalities and bureaucracy to ensure that the tasks of comprehensive law-based governance are completed.

Promoting comprehensive law-based governance is a profound change in national governance. We must be guided by scientific theory, strengthen theoretical thinking, and theoretically answer the question of why comprehensive law-based governance must be carried out as a major task of the times and how it can be carried out. We must constantly achieve new results in integrating theory and practice, summarize and apply the Party's ideological and theoretical achievements in strengthening the rule of law in the new era, and better guide the work of comprehensive law-based governance.

I. The Legislative and Supervisory Work of the National People's Congress and Its Standing Committee

In 2020, China's NPC and its Standing Committee enacted 9 laws, revised 12 laws, and adopted 12 decisions on legal issues and major issues. As of the end of December 2020, there were 283 laws in force in China. On May 28, 2020, the Third Session of the 13th NPC adopted the Civil Code of the People's Republic of China. The law came into effect on January 1, 2021. The Marriage Law of the People's Republic of China, the Inheritance Law of the People's Republic of China, the General Principles of the Civil Law of the People's Republic of China, the Adoption Law of the People's Republic of China, the Security Law of the People's Republic of China, the Contract Law of the People's Republic of China, the Property Rights Law of the People's Republic of China, the Tort Liability Law of the People's Republic of China, and the General Principles of the Civil Law of the

People's Republic of China were simultaneously repealed. This left 274 effective laws currently in force in China on January 1, 2021.

1. Implementing important constitutional institutions through legislation

- Convening meetings of the NPC is a constitutional mandate of the NPC Standing Committee

In light of the developments in the Covid-19 epidemic and the needs of prevention and control, in February, the NPC Standing Committee made the Decision on Postponing the Third Session of the 13th NPC, which was the first time in more than 40 years of reform and opening up that an NPC session was postponed. This decision was in line with the principles and spirit of the Constitution and the relevant laws, and was conducive to implementing the major decisions and plans of the Party Central Committee for promoting the prevention and control of the epidemics and economic and social development, to safeguarding people's life safety and health, and to ensuring that the NPC session focuses on the theme and successfully completes its tasks. In April, a timely decision was made on the timing of the Third Session of the 13th NPC, which was held in Beijing on May 22, 2020.

- The awarding of state decorations and honors is an important institution provided for in the Constitution

On the occasion of the significant strategic achievements in the fight against the Covid-19 epidemic, in accordance with the Constitution and the Law on State Decorations and Honors, in August the NPC Standing Committee made a decision on awarding state decorations and honors to those who made outstanding contributions in the fight against the Covid-19 epidemic, and the Chinese President signed a presidential decree to award Zhong Nanshan the Order of the Republic and Zhang Boli, Zhang Dingyu and Chen Wei the title of the People's Hero, to honor exemplary figures who made outstanding contributions in the fight against the epidemic, and to promote their loyalty, commitment and dedication.

- Efforts were made to resolutely maintain the constitutional order of the Hong Kong Special Administrative Region as determined by the Constitution and the Hong Kong Basic Law, and strengthen the legislation on safeguarding national security legislation in the Hong Kong Special Administrative Region

In accordance with the Constitution and the Basic Law of the Hong Kong Special Administrative Region, the Third Session of the 13th NPC made the Decision on the Establishment of a Sound Legal System and Implementation Mechanism for Safeguarding National Security in the Hong Kong Special Administrative Region. In June, the NPC Standing Committee enacted the Law of the People's Republic of China on Safeguarding National Security in the Hong Kong Special Administrative Region and decided to include it in Annex III of the Basic Law of the Hong Kong Special Administrative Region, to be promulgated and implemented locally by the authorities of the Hong Kong Special Administrative Region. In November, the NPC Standing Committee adopted the Decision on the Qualifications of Members of the Legislative Council of the Hong Kong Special Administrative Region, which clearly defines the statutory requirements and qualifications for members of the Legislative Council of the Hong Kong Special Administrative Region and ensures that Hong Kong is governed mainly by those who love China. This series of legislative initiatives provided a constitutional basis and a legal guarantee for upholding and improving the "one country, two systems" system, safeguarding national sovereignty, security and development interests, and ensuring the long-term stability, prosperity and stability of Hong Kong.

- The Election Law is an important law that guarantees the exercise of citizens' right to vote and stand for election and the election of deputies to people's congresses at all levels in accordance with the law

In response to the actual situation that the grassroots administrative divisions around the country have abolished townships and towns have been merged to be converted into subdistricts, cutting the number of deputies to grassroots people's congresses year by year, in October, the NPC Standing Committee revised the Election Law. The revised law appropriately increased the base number of deputies to county and township people's congresses, increasing the base number of deputies to the people's congresses of cities not divided into districts, districts of cities, counties, and autonomous counties from 120 to 140, and the base number of deputies to people's congresses of townships, ethnic townships, and towns from 40 to 45. In addition, the revised law made it clear that the new number of deputies shall be reported for the record. This was conducive to better protecting the people's right to run the country and to further consolidating the foundation of the system of people's congresses.

- The system of laws regarding national symbols and emblems was improved to maintain the authority and dignity of the state

In October, the NPC Standing Committee revised the National Flag Law and the National Emblem Law to further regulate the flying and use of the national flag, the national emblem and their designs This was conducive to strengthening citizens' concept of the state, promoting the spirit of patriotism, cultivating and practicing the core socialist values, and gathering cultural strength for realizing the rejuvenation of the Chinese nation.

- The reform of the national supervision system was deepened to strengthen the supervision and management of all public employees

In June, the NPC Standing Committee passed the Law on Administrative Action for Public Employees. The law concretizes the principled provisions of the Supervision Law, incorporates the statutory objects into the scope of administrative action, matches administrative action with Party disciplinary action and integrates it with criminal penalties. The law defines the targets, grounds, authority and procedures for imposing administrative action, and the ways of relief for the disciplined personnel to safeguard their legitimate rights and interests. This is conducive to strengthening the concept of rule of law and procedural awareness of the decision-making bodies and units for administrative action, promoting the standardization of disciplinary actions, and making administrative action more law-based and standard, and ensuring that public employees perform their duties in accordance with the law, exercise their powers impartially, and maintain integrity in their official duties and business.

2. Strengthening legislation in key areas

- Completing the codification of the Civil Code

As the first law named after a code in the People's Republic of China, the Civil Code has confirmed, consolidated and developed the achievements of civil rule of law since the reform and opening up in a codified manner and created a precedent for codification legislation in China, which is a milestone. In March 2017, the Fifth Session of the 12th NPC adopted the General Part of the Civil Code. In December 2018 and April, June, August and October 2019, the Standing Committee of the 13th NPC reviewed each of the draft books of the Civil Code, reviewed six draft books for the second time, and reviewed the three draft books on personality rights, marriage and family, and tort liability, which are of greater concern to various parties, for the third time. On this basis, the General Provisions of the Civil Code were merged with the draft books that had been reviewed and revised to form the draft Civil Code. In December 2019, the NPC Standing Committee reviewed the draft Civil Code and made a decision to submit the draft Civil Code to the Third Session of the 13th NPC for deliberation. On May 28, 2020, the Third Session of the 13th NPC adopted the Civil Code of the People's Republic of China. The Civil Code consists of seven books and 1,260 articles. The books are: General Part, Real Rights, Contracts, Personality Rights, Marriage and Family, Inheritance, Tort Liability, and Supplementary Provisions. The NPC session further improved the basic legal system and rules of conduct in the civil and commercial fields in China, providing basic guidelines for all kinds of civil and commercial activities. This was of great importance to uphold and improve the basic socialist economy, promote high-quality development, enhance people's welfare and safeguard the fundamental interests of the people.

- Reinforcing legislation on public health rule of law

In order to impose a complete ban and punish illegal wildlife trade and eliminate the unhealthy habit of indiscriminate wild animal meat consumption, in February, the NPC Standing Committee enacted the Decision on a Complete Ban of Illegal

Wildlife Trade and the Elimination of the Unhealthy Habit of Indiscriminate Wild Animal Meat Consumption for the Protection of Human Life and Health. With a focus on the outstanding problem of indiscriminate of wild animal meat consumption, the decision imposes a complete ban on wild animal meat consumption, strengthens the management of non-food use of wild animals, and strictly prohibits the trade of illegal wild animals. This provides strong legislative protection to safeguard public safety and ecological security and protect the lives and health of the people.

In response to the shortcomings of the rule of law and prevention of public health risks revealed in Covid-19 response, in April, the NPC Standing Committee heard and reviewed the report on legislation and law amendments and the work plan designed to strengthen legal protection of public health. This is the first time the NPC Standing Committee has developed a special legislative work plan and heard a report on the legislative work in a special area. The special work plan for legislation and law amendments proposed the laws to be enacted and revised, including 17 laws to be enacted and revised in 2020 and 2021, 13 laws to be enacted and revised in a comprehensive and timely manner, and other relevant laws to be enacted and revised, to provide legal support for the prevention and control of the Covid-19 epidemic, and to improve and strengthen the public health legal law protection system.

- Improving national security legislation

The Biosecurity Law was developed. The Biosecurity Law is the basic law in the field of biosecurity. In October, the NPC Standing Committee passed the Biosecurity Law. The law implements the holistic approach to national security, integrates development and security, establishes a sound national biosecurity leadership mechanism, builds a scientific and complete biosecurity risk prevention and control system, and makes specific arrangements for biosecurity risk monitoring, assessment, early warning, and response. The law devotes a special chapter to the prevention and control measures for major new outbreaks of infectious diseases and animal and plant epidemics. It focuses on improving China's biosecurity governance capacity. All this is conducive to protecting people's lives and health, maintaining biosecurity and ecological security, and promoting the orderly and healthy development of the biological industry.

The Export Control Law was developed. In October, the NPC Standing Committee passed the Export Control Law. The law is aimed at better implementing China's international obligations such as non-proliferation, and provides for the basic systems of export control lists, export licenses, end-user and end-use management on the basis of practical experience and internationally accepted systems, providing a strong legal guarantee for effective export control in the new era.

- Improving legislation on the market economy

The Law on Urban Maintenance and Development Tax and the Deed Transfer Tax Law were developed. In August, the NPC Standing Committee adopted the formulated the Law on Urban Maintenance and Development Tax and the Deed Transfer Tax Law. The principle of statutory taxation was implemented, the existing tax framework and tax burden level were left generally unchanged in accordance with the idea of tax shift, and the relevant temporary regulations became laws. So far, 11 of the 18 existing taxes have been made statutory.

The Patent Law and Copyright Law were revised. Efforts were made to strengthen the protection of intellectual property rights and promote the development of scientific and technological innovation and cultural development in China. In October, the NPC Standing Committee revised the Patent Law, adding the principle of honesty and credit, establishing a new system of compensation for the duration of patent rights and an early settlement mechanism for pharmaceutical patent disputes, extending the protection period for design patent rights, strengthening the protection of the legitimate rights and interests of patentees, and increasing the punishment for patent infringement; making it clear units have the right to dispose of service inventions and creations, strengthening patent services, setting up a new open patent licensing system, and promoting the implementation and application of patents; establishing a new domestic priority system for application of design patents, making it clear that patent rights for certain designs shall be granted, improving the patent authorization system, and encouraging scientific and technological innovation. In November, the NPC Standing Committee revised the Copyright Law. In adapting to the development of network and digital technology applications, the NPC Standing Committee improved the definition and type of works and protected the copyright of audiovisual works by category. It made provisions regarding the pledge of copyright, performance on duty and pre-litigation preservation measures, introduced a punitive compensation system, significantly increased the upper limit of statutory compensation, and strengthened legal convergence, providing a powerful legal weapon for the protection of the legitimate rights and interests of copyright owners.

- Improving legislation on society and livelihood

The Law on Support for Veterans was developed. The Law on Support for Veterans is a basic, systematic and comprehensive law on the support for of veterans. In November, the NPC Standing Committee adopted the Law on Support for Veterans. The law highlights the positioning of the support law, coordinates the relevant national and military policies and institutional reforms, stresses the need to strengthen the development of the system of support for veterans, provides detailed principles for resettling and paying veterans, clarifies the content of support services for veterans and the responsibilities of the competent departments for veterans' work, enhances the relevance of education and training measures for veterans, and provides legal protection for strengthening the support for veterans and safeguarding the legitimate rights and interests of veterans.

The Law on the Protection of Minors was amended. In October, the NPC Standing Committee revised the Law on the Protection of Minors. The revised law strengthens the protection measures by family, school, society, government and judiciary, improves the coordination mechanism for the protection of minors, highlights the responsibility of judicial organs for protecting minors, establishes a mandatory reporting system for cases against minors, improves the protection measures on the Internet, adds provisions on the right to education and discipline, ascertains legal responsibilities, protects the legitimate rights and interests of minors, and promotes the well-rounded development of minors.

The Law on the Prevention of Juvenile Delinquency was amended. In December, the NPC Standing Committee revised the Law on the Prevention of Juvenile Delinquency. The amendment clearly implements graded prevention, provides detailed education and correctional measures, strengthens family guardianship responsibilities, enriches school discipline responsibilities, consolidates the protection responsibilities of state organs, gives full play to the advantages of groups and organizations, and promotes extensive social participation, providing a strong legal guarantee for the prevention of juvenile delinquency.

- Improving eco-environmental legislation

The Yangtze River Protection Law was developed. In December, the NPC Standing Committee adopted the Yangtze River Protection Law, which is the first law to protect the Yangtze River basin-wide ecosystem and promote the green and high-quality development of the Yangtze River Economic Belt. The law is guided by Xi Jinping's thinking on ecological civilization, prioritizes ecological conservation and boosts green development, and makes the concept of promoting well-coordinated environmental conservation and avoiding excessive development a legal principle. The law establishes sound institutions and measures for the protection of the Yangtze River, strengthens eco-environmental protection and restoration in the Yangtze River basin, promotes efficient and rational use of resources, ensures ecological security, and uses the law to protect the mother river of Yangtze and achieve harmony between man and nature.

- Improving military legislation

The National Defense Law was amended. In December, the NPC Standing Committee amended the National Defense Law. As the basic national defense law, the law implements Xi Jinping's idea of strengthening the military, consolidates the achievements of national defense and military reform, and provides for a series of major issues such as the national defense leadership system, the tasks of the armed forces, security and defense policies, national defense research and production, and the national defense mobilization system. All this is of great significance for improving the system of military laws and regulations with Chinese characteristics and laying the cornerstone of the legal system for strengthening the military and defending the country.

The Law on the People's Armed Police was amended. In June, the NPC Standing Committee revised the Law on the People's Armed Police. The law implements Xi Jinping's idea of strengthening the military. With a focus on the need of the reform to adjust the armed police force leadership and command system and expand the armed policy forces' missions and tasks, the law comprehensively reflects the results of the reform, regulates and protects the armed police force to perform its duties and missions. The law is in line with the new system, new functions, and new requirements of the armed police force and maintain national security and social stability.

- Adopting the Amendments to the Criminal Law (XI)

In December, the NPC Standing Committee adopted the Amendments to the Criminal Law (XI). The amendments to 47 articles strengthen the prevention and punishment of workplace safety crimes. They improve the provisions on the punishment of food and drug crimes, on the crimes of disrupting the financial order and the order of social management, and juvenile crimes. They strengthen the protection of enterprise property rights, intellectual property rights, and public health under criminal law. They also respond directly

Taipei such issues of public concern as taking impersonation, seizing the steering wheel of a bus, and throwing objects from a high altitude as crimes, increasing the punishment for illegal fund-raising, and lowering the minimum age of legal criminal responsibility.

In 2020, the NPC Standing Committee also amended the Law on Prevention and Control of Solid Waste Pollution and the Archives Law, and reviewed the Law on the Promotion of Rural Revitalization, the Law on Data Security, the Law on the Protection of Personal Information, the Law on Maritime Police, the Law on the Hainan Free Trade Port, the Law on Anti-Food Waste, the Law on Anti-Organized Crime, the Supervisors Law, the draft Law on the Protection of the Status and Rights and Interests of Military Personnel as well as the draft amendments to the Law on Animal Epidemic Prevention, the Law on Administrative Punishment, the Law on Wildlife Protection, the Law on Maritime Traffic Safety, the Military Service Law, and the Law on the Protection of Military Facilities. The draft amendments to the Organic Law of the NPC and the Rules of Procedure of the NPC were reviewed by two meetings of the NPC Standing Committee before being submitted to the Fourth Session of the 13th NPC for adoption.

3. Providing the legal basis and guarantee for deepening reform and expanding opening up in related areas

In implementing the strategy of the Party Central Committee for supporting Hainan in deepening reform and opening up, the NPC Standing Committee made a decision to authorize the State Council to temporarily adjust the application of relevant legal provisions in the China (Hainan) Pilot Free Trade Zone, using legal means to support Hainan in building a pilot free trade zone and a free trade port with Chinese characteristics. In order to promote the building of free trade ports with Chinese characteristics, increase the protection of intellectual property rights and create a good business environment, in December, the NPC Standing Committee made a decision to establish the Hainan Free Trade Port Intellectual Property Court.

The NPC Standing Committee made a decision to strengthen supervision of state-owned assets administration. In performing the NPC's function of supervising state-owned assets, the NPC Standing Committee implemented the state-owned assets administration reporting system, improved working mechanisms concerning report, review, and correction and accountability mechanism, and making results public in order to better play the important role of the NPC in supervising state-owned assets administration and governing state-owned assets.

The NPC Standing Committee made a decision to authorize the State Council to carry out pilot work in nine cities in the Guangdong-Hong Kong-Macao Greater Bay Area for Hong Kong legal practitioners and Macao practicing lawyers to obtain a license to practice in the mainland and to engage in the profession of lawyer, which is conducive to giving full play to the professional advantages of legal talents in Hong Kong and Macao, promoting the development of the Guangdong-Hong Kong-Macao Greater Bay Area, and promoting better integration of Hong Kong and Macao into the overall development of China.

4. Continuing to promote scientific, democratic and law-based legislation

The NPC Standing Committee further implemented and improved the institutions and mechanisms for scientific, democratic and law-based legislation, and constantly improved the quality and efficiency of legislation, and made solid efforts to deliver good performance in legislation and related work. First, the NPC Standing Committee strengthened the organization and coordination of legislative work and gave full play to the leading role of the NPC in the legislative work. Second, it remained committed to make draft laws public for comments. Throughout the year, a total of 42 draft laws were made public on the NPC's website for comments, and a total of 306,090 people put forward 1,351,869 comments. Third, the NPC Standing Committee deepened NPC deputies' participation in the legislative work and paid more attention to giving play to the role of deputies specializing in legal work, as well as deputies who have put forward relevant bills and proposals in recent years, in the legislative work. Fourth, the NPC Standing Committee strengthened the development of grassroots legislative contact points. Six additional grassroots legislative contact points were established, the rules of work of grassroots legislative contact points were revised and improved, and the contact points were guided to improve institutions and mechanisms. Throughout the year, a total of 18 draft laws, such as the Civil Code, Amendments to the Criminal Law (XI), and the Anti-Food Waste Law were made available to 10 contact points for comments, and more than 1,300 suggestions have been reported back, making the legislative work in line with local conditions and public sentiment. Fifth, the NPC Standing Committee strengthened the contact guidance of local legislative work. It convened 26 national forums on local legislation and held the First NPC Meeting on Record and Review Work Experience and the Record Review Training Course.

5. The NPC Standing Committee's supervision work

In 2020, with a focus on the overall work of the Party and the country, the NPC Standing Committee exercised constitutional and legal supervision as a means of support. It carried out orderly work supervision and legal supervision, improved the supervision work institutions and mechanisms, created new supervision methods, and enhanced the effectiveness of supervision to ensure that the Party Central Committee's decisions and plans are implemented, the law is effectively implemented, and power is exercised correctly.

- Checking legal compliance

In 2020, the NPC Standing Committee checked compliance with the Decision on a Complete Ban of Illegal Wildlife Trade and the Elimination of the Unhealthy Habit of Indiscriminate Wild Animal Meat Consumption for the Protection of Human Life and Health, the Wildlife Protection Law, the Law on the Promotion of Agricultural Mechanization, the Law on the Prevention and Control of Soil Pollution, the Charity Law, the Anti-Unfair Competition Law, and the Law on Public Cultural Services. In addition, special inquiries were conducted in conjunction with the deliberation of the inspection report on the enforcement of the Law on the Prevention and Control of Soil Pollution.

As for the Decision on a Complete Ban of Illegal Wildlife Trade and the Elimination of the Unhealthy Habit of Indiscriminate Wild Animal Meat Consumption for the Protection of Human Life and Health, the Wildlife Protection Law, the focus of the check was on combatting indiscriminate consumption and illegal hunting and trading, strengthening the protection of wildlife and their habitats, improving the supporting laws, regulations and relevant lists, law enforcement supervision and implementation of legal responsibilities, the disposal of artificially bred wildlife, and the shift of wildlife breeders to other industries to promote the formation of a scientific and healthy lifestyle. As for the Law on the Promotion of Agricultural Mechanization, the focus of the check was on the standardized implementation of the scientific research and development system, the implementation of legal responsibilities for quality assurance, the promotion of advanced and applicable agricultural machinery, the standardized management of commercial service organizations, the implementation of supportive policies, and the formulation of supporting laws and regulations, so as to promote the improvement of agricultural productivity. As for the Law on the Prevention and Control of Soil Pollution, the focus of the check was on soil pollution survey, investigation, monitoring, prevention, the development of regulations and standards, the safe use of farmland and land for construction purposes, soil pollution risk control and soil repair, as well as special funds and the implementation of other supporting and supervision systems. This was the third consecutive year the NPC Standing Committee has carried out law enforcement inspection in the field of eco-environmental protection and used the rule of law to help prevent and control pollution and the battle and promote ecological civilization. As for the Charity law, the focus was on the inspection of whether charitable organizations carried out activities in accordance with the law, standardized fund-raising, property trust and management, donor rights protection and donors' fulfillment of obligations, the development of charitable services, information disclosure, and the promotion of charitable innovation, to promote the healthy and orderly development of charity. As for the Anti-Unfair Competition Law, the focus was on increasing public law awareness, the development of laws and regulations, the establishment and implementation of work coordination mechanisms, and the investigation and punishment of various types of unfair competition. A special check was conducted of online unfair competition and other outstanding issues. As for the Law On The Protection Of Public Cultural Services, the focus was on the inspection of the establishment and implementation of relevant standards and institutions, infrastructure construction and utilization, digitalization and network development, the implementation of government responsibilities for the organization, management, provision and protection of of public cultural services to promote the development of public culture and meet the growing needs of the people for a better life.

In the process law enforcement inspections and special inquiries, the NPC Standing Committee members put forward comments and suggestions on improving the legal system, promoting the implementation of the law, and strengthening and improving the relevant work and. The State Council and relevant departments attached great importance to these comments and suggestions, and proposed and took a series of measures to improve and implement the work.

- Hearing and reviewing special work reports, and conducting inquiries and research on special topics

In 2020, the NPC Standing Committee strengthened its

supervision of the State Council, the National Supervisory Commission, the Supreme People's Court and the Supreme People's Procuratorate by hearing and reviewing 18 special work reports and conducting two special inquiries and six special studies.

The NPC Standing Committee helped fight the three major battles. It heard and deliberated the State Council's report on the annual report on environmental status and the completion of environmental protection goals, the report on the study of the law enforcement inspection on the implementation of the Water Pollution Prevention and Control Law and the report on result of its deliberations. The NPC Standing Committee conducted special research and hearing and deliberating the research report on the implementation of the resolution of the NPC Standing Committee on comprehensively strengthening eco-environmental protection and promoting pollution prevention and control in accordance with the law. This promoted the continuous improvement of environmental quality and helped with pollution prevention and control. The NPC Standing Committee of the People's Republic of China heard and deliberated the report of the State Council on the work of poverty eradication and the report on the allocation and use of financial agricultural and rural funds, prioritizing agricultural and rural development and supporting the fight against poverty.

The NPC Standing Committee promoted high-quality economic development. It heard and reviewed the report on the implementation of China's plan for economic and social development, ensured that the State Council and relevant parties to uphold the policy of making progress while maintaining stable performance, better coordinate the work of epidemic prevention and control and economic and social development, do a solid job in ensuring stability on six fronts, fully carry out the task of maintaining security in six areas[1] and strive to complete the annual economic and social development objectives and tasks. The NPC Standing Committee carried out research on several important issues in the preparation of the 14th Five-Year Plan for National Economic and Social Development, writing 22 research reports, which provided important reference for the decision-making of the Party Central Committee and the formulating of the plan by the State Council, and also provided necessary

---

1 The six fronts refer to employment, the financial sector, foreign trade, foreign investment, domestic investment, and expectations. The six areas refer to job security, basic living needs, operations of market entities, food and energy security, stable industrial and supply chains, and the normal functioning of primary-level governments.

conditions for the review and approval of the 14th Five-Year Plan at the Fourth Session of the 13th NPC. The NPC Standing Committee heard and reviewed the report of the State Council on implementing the innovation-driven development strategy and promoting the implementation of the Law on Scientific and Technological Progress. It ensured that the State Council and relevant departments strengthen basic research and key core technology research, deepen the new round of science and technology reform, and promote the integration of industrial and innovation chains. The NPC Standing Committe heard and reviewed the report of the State Council on the reform of the rural collective property rights system, promoted the formation of new forms of operational mechanisms of the rural collective economy, safeguarded the legitimate rights and interests of farmers, and helped the comprehensive revitalization of the countryside. The NPC Standing Committe heard and reviewed the report of the State Council on the reform to introduce the registration system for stock issuance, helping the State Council actively and steadily promote this reform on the basis of fully estimating and effectively preventing risks, and improving the capacity of the financial sector to serve the real economy. The NPC Standing Committee conducted research on the management and reform of government investment funds to further clarify the functions and positioning of government investment funds and improved the system and mechanism in order to better serve national strategies.

The NPC Standing Committee promoted the development of social programs and undertakings for improving people's lives. It carried out research on saving food and opposing waste, which is an additional supervisory project for 2020. The NPC Standing Committee promoted the establishment of a sound long-term mechanism to ensure food security and stop food waste in the catering industry, enhance public awareness of the need to save food, and create an atmosphere of shame for wasting food and pride for saving it throughout the whole of society. The NPC Standing Committee carried out research on the reform of the social insurance system and the implementation of the Social Insurance Law, and promoted the improvement of the sustainable multitiered social security system that covers the entire population in both urban and rural areas, with clearly defined rights and responsibilities, and support that hits the right level. It carried out research on the work to ensure ethnic unity and progress to promote the firm sense of a Chinese national community.

The NPC Standing Committee strengthened the supervision of law enforcement, supervision and judicial work. It heard and reviewed the State Council's report on the standardization of law enforcement by public security organs, promoting strict, standardized, fair and appropriate law enforcement, and enhancing the level of rule of law and the credibility of law enforcement. It implemented the Supervision Law. It heard and reviewed for the first time the report of the National Supervisory Commission on international anti-corruption efforts to track down and recover stolen goods and money, and promoted the establishment of a sound leadership system, coordination mechanism and legal system for tracking down and recovering stolen goods and money. The NPC Standing Committe heard and reviewed the report of the Supreme People's Court on strengthening the work of civil trials, ensuring the judiciary strengthens the protection of civil rights and interests, and providing strong judicial services and protection for economic and social development. The NPC Standing Committe heard and reviewed the report of the Supreme People's Procuratorate on the application of the penal policy of severity tempered with mercy, promoting the enhancement of litigation efficiency, saving judicial resources, quickly resolving social conflicts, and realizing the organic unity of judicial justice and efficiency.

- The NPC Standing Committee strengthened the NPC's review and supervision of China's budgets and final accounts and supervision of state-owned assets administration

It heard and reviewed the report on the central final accounts, the audit report and the budget execution report, reviewed and approved the central final accounts for 2020. It heard and reviewed the report on the rectification and reform of the problems identified by the audit and conduct special inquiries. It promoted a more proactive fiscal policy, improved the efficiency of the use of funds, and ensured that policies for epidemic prevention and control and for benefiting enterprises and the people are put into practice. It continued to promote the reform to expand the focus of the NPC's budget review and supervision, formulated the decision on strengthening the review and supervision of the central budget, formulated the guidelines on strengthening the review and supervision of government debt by local people's congresses, and increased the full-caliber review and supervision of the entire process. It established a mechanism for hearing the performance evaluation of the government budget and briefing relevant departments on the performance of important policies and key funds, and made the review and supervision more targeted and effective.

While reviewing the State Council's comprehensive report

on strengthening state-owned assets administration, the NPC Standing Committee heard and reviewed the State Council's two special reports on the Ministry of Finance's administration of enterprises' state-owned assets by performing the responsibility as an investor and assets regulator, and on the administration of state-owned assets of enterprises under the State-owned assets administration information system in 2019, to deepen of the reform of state-owned assets and state-owned enterprises and ensure the preservation and appreciation of state-owned capital. The NPC Standing Committee reviewed practical experience, made a decision on strengthening supervision of state-owned assets administration, further improved the reporting mechanism and related work system, made supervision more mandatory, deepened and expanded the NPC's supervision of state-owned assets administration and improved quality and efficiency. The NPC Standing Committee promoted the online supervision of state-owned assets administration and basically ensured that a reporting system is established nationwide for all state-owned assets administration at the county level and above.

- The NPC Standing Committee did a good job in reviewing normative documents reported for the record

In accordance with the requirements that all documents should be reported for the record, all documents that have been reported for the record should be reviewed, and all mistakes the have been identified are corrected, the NPC Standing Committee stepped up efforts to review documents reported for the record and urged the correction of a number of normative documents that are inconsistent with the Constitution and laws, so as to effectively maintain the legal unity of the country. Throughout the year, the NPC Standing Committee accepted a total of 1,310 government regulations, local regulations, judicial interpretations, special administrative region laws submitted for the record, reviewed each of them, and dealt with them in accordance with different circumstances. In line with the epidemic prevention and control, the implementation of the Civil Code, and the improvement of the business environment, the NPC Standing Committee organized special reviews and centralized cleanup in five areas, found 3,372 normative documents that need to be revised or repealed, and urged the relevant parties to correct the mistakes in a timely manner. The NPC Standing Committee took solid steps to conduct examination on application and transfer, accepted 5,146 review proposals from citizens and organizations, studied each of the 3,378 cases belonging to the scope of the Standing Committee's review, made comments and gave feedback to the review proposers; those not belonging to the scope of the

Standing Committee's review were transferred to relevant authorities for handling in accordance with the regulations. The NPC Standing Committee researched and reviewed 58 local regulations transferred through the coordinated mechanism for reviewing documents submitted for the record and urged the revision or repealing of 27 them by authorities that had developed them. The NPC Standing Committee continued to improve institution and capacity building for reviewing documents submitted for the record and completed the national laws and regulations database (Phase I). It ensured that the standing committees of local people's congresses at all levels generally establish a system to report to the standing committees on the review of documents submitted for the record in order to put this system in all standing committees of local people's congresses.

II. Law-Based Government Administration

In 2020, the Chinese government performed all its functions in accordance with the law, and further promoted the development of law-based government. It provided strong and quality legal services to coordinate the prevention and control of the epidemic and economic and social development, and achieved new results and new developments in developing law-based government work to achieve new results.

1. Legislative work of the State Council

In 2020, the State Council submitted nine legislative proposals to the NPC Standing Committee for review, enacted four government regulations, revised 33 government regulations, and repealed 11 government regulations. Eighteen treaties were submitted by the State Council to the NPC Standing Committee for review and approval and were approved by the State Council.

- The State Council developed the Regulations on Crop Pest Control

In order to clarify the responsibility of crop pest control, standardize the control protocols and control methods, and encourage professional and green prevention and control, in March, the State Council promulgated the Regulations on Crop Pest Control, which became effective on May 1, 2020. The Regulations clearly stipulated the prevention and control responsibilities of the people's governments at all levels and their relevant departments as well as agricultural producers and operators, further improved the systems for monitoring and forecasting crop diseases and insect pests and for preventing and controlling crop diseases and insect pests, strengthened the emergency management of crop diseases and insect pests, and provided a strong legal guarantee for the prevention and control of crop diseases and insect pests.

- The State Council developed the Regulations on Safeguarding Payments to Small and Medium Enterprises (SMEs)

In order to establish a long-term mechanism for preventing and resolving payments owed to SMEs, and further implement the provisions of the Law on Promoting Small and Medium-Sized Enterprises that state organs, public institutions and large enterprises shall not default on payments for goods, work and services owed to SMEs, in July, the State Council promulgated the Regulations on Safeguarding Payments to SMEs, which came into effect on September 1, 2020. The Regulations have provisions concerning standardizing the payment terms of organs, public institutions and large enterprises, clarifying the inspection and acceptance requirements, prohibiting disguised arrears, regulating the collection and settlement of security deposits, publicizing information on arrears, establishing a sound complaint and monitoring and evaluation mechanism, and clarifying the responsibility for late payment in order to ensure that SME payments are paid in a timely manner, relieve the pressure on SMEs for funds, and effectively protect the legitimate rights and interests of SMEs.

• The State Council developed the Regulations on Government Supervision Work

In order to implement the requirements of the Party Central Committee on coordinating and standardizing supervision, inspection and assessment work, strengthen and standardize government supervision work, and better promote the implementation of the Party Central Committee and the State Council's decisions and plans, in December, the State Council promulgated the Regulations on Government Supervision Work, which came into effect on February 1, 2021. The Regulations institutionalize the mature experience and practices of government inspection work at all levels in recent years, clarify the positioning of government inspection, regulate government inspection procedures, and provide legal regulation and institutional guarantee for government inspection work.

• The State Council revised the Regulations on the Implementation of the Budget Law of the People's Republic of China

To reflect the achievements of deepening the reform of the fiscal and taxation systems and make the relevant provisions of the Budget Law more detailed, in August, the State Council revised the Regulations on the Implementation of the Budget Law of the People's Republic of China, which took effect as of October 1, 2020. The revised Regulations incorporate into the rule of law the State Council's regulations on deepening the reform of the budget management system and other relevant provisions enacted after the implementation of the Budget Law, specify the matters on which the State Council is authorized to make regulations, and make corresponding provisions on the scope of budgetary revenues and expenditures, transfer payments, and local government debts in light of the practice of recent years.

• The State Council revised the Regulations on the Administration of Enterprise Name Registration

In order to further release enterprise name resources and

highlight the service functions of enterprise registration authorities, in December, the State Council revised the Regulations on the Administration of Enterprise Name Registration, which became effective as of March 1, 2021. The revised Regulations fully respect the right of enterprises to choose their own business names, make it clear that enterprises are independent in declaring their business names, simplify the process of business name registration, reduce business startup costs, strengthen ongoing and ex-post supervision, and safeguard the legitimate rights and interests of enterprises and the good market order.

In 2020, the State Council also developed the Regulations on the Supervision and Administration of Cosmetics, revised the Regulations on the Transfer of Suspected Crime Cases by Administrative Law Enforcement Organs, the Regulations on National Science and Technology Awards, the Regulations on Urban Water Supply, the Regulations on Urban Real Estate Development and Operation, the Regulations on the Management of Artificially Influenced Weather, the Regulations on Radio and Television Administration, the Regulations on Nurses, the Measures for the Public Security Management of the Hotel Industry, and the Regulations on the Implementation of International Copyright Treaties, and other government regulations.

2. Law-based government administration

• Supervision work was carried out on building law-based governments

On the basis of the supervision work on building a law-based government in 2019, the supervision of the main Party and government leaders fulfilling the responsibility of those assuming the primary responsibility for advancing the rule of law and the building of a law-based government was continued in 2020. Led by the Central Office for Law-Based Governance, a supervision team was established by 24 central Party and government departments. Led by provincial and ministerial leaders, the team carried out on-the-spot supervision in Shanghai, Inner Mongolia, Heilongjiang, Jiangsu, Shandong, Guangxi, Hainan, and Qinghai. It held 589 talks with leaders and law enforcement officers and paid 1,073 visits to lawyers, private-sector entrepreneurs, and members of the public in 32 cities and prefectures and 68 counties and districts. The team discovered and promote the rectification of various problems, effectively transmitted the pressure and ensured responsibilities are fulfilled.

- Demonstration initiatives were concept for building law-based governments

The evaluation and naming of the first batch of national demonstration projects was conducted for building law-based governments. After the provincial preliminary review, third-Party assessment, people's satisfaction assessment, field verification, and public announcement, 40 comprehensive demonstration areas and 24 single demonstration projects were selected. The State Council organized demonstration areas and projects to promote exchange activities. The column "demonstration areas and projects for building law-based governments" was opened in *Legal Daily* to publish the achievements and experience of demonstration areas and projects. This effectively gave play to the exemplary and leading role of the progressives and promoted the overall improvement of efforts to build law-based governments.

- A special review of government regulations was carried out

With a focus on the implementation of high-level opening up, a package of 22 sets of government regulations were revised and one set of government regulations inconsistent with the Foreign Investment Law was repealed. With a focus on promoting the reform to delegate power, improve regulation, and upgrade services, a package of seven sets profit government regulations were revised and 10 sets of government regulations were repealed. With a view to implementing the Civil Code, government regulations, rules and normative government documents related to the content of the Civil Code were reviewed.

● A database of government regulations currently in force was established and made public

All government regulations enacted by the State Council since the founding of the People's Republic of China were reviewed. The catalogue and standard texts of government regulations currently in force were checked and made public, providing the public with public products that are "visible, accessible and usable."

● Efforts were stepped up to review regulations and rules submitted for the record

In 2020, all localities and departments submitted 2,071 sets of regulations and rules to the State Council for the record. The State Council reviewed them one by one in accordance with the law, registering 2,046 sets for the record and suspending 25 others. The problematic regulations and rules were handled in accordance with the legal authority and procedures. The General Office of the NPC Standing Committee and the Ministry of Justice jointly issued the Circular on the Standardized and Orderly Unified Reporting of Local Regulations for the Record, and completed the integration of the reporting platform. The Ministry of Justice set up an expert committee for the record and review of regulations and rules to make the report and review more standard, scientific and professional.

- Law-based government administration was promoted during the epidemic prevention and control

The Ministry of Justice issued Guidelines on Promoting Strict, Fair and Appropriate Law Enforcement to Provide Strong Legal Protection for Epidemic Prevention and Control. This encouraged administrative law enforcement organs at all levels to punish all kinds of resistance to epidemic prevention and control measures in accordance with the law, strengthened supervision of administrative law enforcement, and promptly dealt with problems of law enforcement officers' inaction, indiscriminate action and excessive law enforcement in epidemic prevention and control.

- Administrative law enforcement was made more standard

The special supervision of the implementation of the three systems for administrative law enforcement was carried out to ensure that these systems are implemented in all city and county law enforcement units. The national unified and standard administrative law enforcement certificates were introduced. Certificate management was strengthened. The administrative law enforcement certificates issuing authority, their job responsibilities, and numbering rules were clarified, thus solving the problems of diversified certificate standards, duplicate issuance of certificates, and certificates being issued by multiple authorities at the source. The special supervision of the implementation of the legality review mechanism of administrative regulatory documents was carried out to supervise and guide all regions and departments to improve their work. The mechanism for integrating administrative law enforcement and criminal justice was further improved and the Regulations on the Transfer of Suspected Criminal Cases by Administrative Law Enforcement Agencies. Efforts were made to accelerate the development and application of the National Comprehensive Administrative Law Enforcement Management and Supervision Information System, which has initially realized the data connection with all provinces, autonomous regions, and municipalities directly under the central government.

- The work of administrative adjudication was promoted Relevant departments of the State Council developed administrative adjudication demonstration stations, and established a demonstration development contact mechanism for departments in key areas of administrative adjudication. Continuous efforts were made to review administrative adjudication matters and the List of Administrative Adjudication in State Council Departments (Ⅱ) was issued.

- The system of informing commitment on certification matters was fully implemented

Since the pilot in 2019, 18 regions and departments have piloted the system of informing the commitment to certify matters related to a total of more than 2,000 items in over 60 areas including household registration management, market entities quasi-operating, qualification examinations, social insurance, and social assistance. This effectively gave the people great access to government services and improved the business environment. Based on the review of the experience from the pilot project, the General Office of the State Council issued the Guidelines on the Full Implementation of the Informing Commitment System concerning Certification Matters and Business-Related Business License Matters, and promoted the system nationwide.

- Administrative reconsideration and response to lawsuits were strengthened

In 2020, administrative reconsideration organs at all levels nationwide finalized 211,000 cases of administrative reconsideration. In response to the common illegal issues found in the cases, 4,726 administrative reconsideration comments were issued, and in 26,000 of the finalized cases, corrective awards such as revocation, change, confirmation of illegality and order to perform decisions were made, with a direct error correction rate of 14.6%. The court appearance rate of the leaders of administrative authorities nationwide was 41.8%, and the average rate of administrative authorities lost lawsuits was 17.8% nationwide. The State Council concluded 2,693 administrative reconsideration cases, the error correction rate of the State Council administrative reconsideration ruling cases was 11.8% and the error correction rate of the State Council administrative reconsideration supervision cases was 19.2%. Correcting errors in cases and issuing awards and proposals actively resolved administrative disputes, promoted law-based government administration, and promoted the building of law-based governments. The reform of the administrative reconsideration institutions and mechanisms was deepened. The Plan for Administrative Reconsideration Reform of the Central

Commission for Law-Based Governance was implemented. Efforts were made to promote the implementation of the reform plan through the establishment of ledgers, research and supervision, and the convening of special video promotion conferences. The revision of the Administrative Reconsideration Law was accelerated, and greater efforts were made to make administrative reconsideration work more standard, IT-based, and specialized.

III. Judicial and Law Enforcement Reform

In 2020, China's judicial and law enforcement reform focused on the outstanding issues of great concern to the public. New breakthroughs were made in all the work to accelerate the reform and development of law enforcement and judicial constraint and supervision system, and comprehensively enhance the credibility of law enforcement and justice.

1. Accelerating the establishment of the law enforcement and judicial constraint and supervision system

- Meeting were held to make a special plan

In January, the Central Political and Legal Work Conference was held in Beijing. The meeting planned to, led by the efforts to comprehensively deepen judicial and law enforcement reform, to address the new situation and new problems facing judicial and law enforcement work, and comprehensively improve the modernization of judicial and law enforcement work. The company's main goal was to improve the quality of its products and services, and to improve the quality of its products and services. The meeting called for efforts to remove the institutions, mechanisms, and policies to make way for reform. To address the problem of insufficient oversight and management after delegating power, the meeting stressed the need to further improve the policies and measures for judicial oversight in judicial and law enforcement departments, strengthen internal oversight and accountability of judicial and law enforcement units, and minimize the space for rent-seeking by power. In August, the Central Judicial and Law Enforcement Commission held a meeting to fully deepen judicial and law enforcement reform and gain a thorough understanding and implement the guiding principles from the major speeches of General Secretary Xi Jinping. The meeting defined the direction and priorities of the next step of reform: speeding up the development of a law enforcement and judicial constraint and supervision system that is coherent, standard and efficient, integrates internal and external factors, and is complete in system in order to ensure that law enforcement and judicial justice is fair and clean, efficient and authoritative. A plenary session of the Central Judicial and Law Enforcement Commission and a meeting of the Central Leading Group for Judicial Reform also put forward clear requirements for accelerating the development of a law enforcement and judicial constraint and supervision system. Central judicial and law enforcement units held a special meeting to plan to implement the guiding principles from the meeting to fully deepen judicial and law enforcement reform.

- The constraint and supervision system was strengthened

The Central Judicial and Law Enforcement Commission formulated the Guidelines on Strengthening the Law Enforcement and Judicial Constraint and Supervision System, which put forward a series of reform measures for improving the supervision system of the Party's absolute leadership of judicial and law enforcement work, the constraint and supervision system of judicial and law enforcement organs, the constraint and supervision mechanism of law enforcement and judicial power operation, the supervision system of judicial and law enforcement service management, the supervision system of the management of judicial and law enforcement officers, and the intelligent constraint and supervision system. Central judicial and law enforcement units formulated documents on improving the positioning of the four levels of court trial, strengthening the legal supervision of the procuratorial organs, promoting the reform of the law enforcement supervision and management mechanism of public security, strengthening the law enforcement constraint and supervision of state security organs, and deepening the reform of the notary systems and mechanisms in order to improve the internal constraint and supervision mechanism of judicial and law enforcement departments.

- The assessment and supervision of reform was carried out

The reform tasks assigned by the Party Central Committee since the Third Plenary Session of the 18th CPC Central Committee were comprehensively assessed, major theoretical achievements, institutional achievements, and practical achievements were systematically sorted out, reform experience was reviewed, areas of weakness were identified, and comments and suggestions were studied. All this contributed to the Report for Reviewing and Assessing the Efforts to Comprehensively Deepen Judicial and Law Enforcement Reform since the Third Plenary Session of the 18th CPC Central Committee. The Central Judicial and Law Enforcement Commission organized a special supervision of judicial and law enforcement reform, focusing on strengthening key elements such as law enforcement and judicial constraint and supervision, understanding in detail the implementation of reform initiatives, analyzing in depth the institutions and mechanisms affecting reform and innovation and implementation, and putting forward policy recommendations for improvement.

2. Further improving the functions of judicial and law enforcement agencies

- The functions of Party committee judicial and law enforcement commissions were straightened out

The Regulations of the Communist Party of China on Judicial and Law Enforcement Work. The Central Judicial and Law Enforcement Commission organized a supervision of the implementation of the Regulations and improved the institutions and mechanism for Party leadership of judicial and law enforcement work in the new era. Central judicial and law enforcement units and the provincial, autonomous regional and municipal authorities formulated detailed rules or measures for the implementation of the Regulations. The relationships between Party committee judicial and law enforcement commissions and Party committees and judicial and law enforcement units and between the Party committee judicial and law enforcement commissions at all levels were further straightened out. The institutions and mechanisms were further improved to ensure the Party's political, ideological, and organizational leadership of judicial and law enforcement work. The mechanism whereby Party committee judicial and law enforcement commissions comprehensively coordinates judicial and law enforcement work was improved, and the mechanism for coordinating efforts to build the Peaceful China was developed. the party's judicial and law enforcement committee comprehensive coordination of judicial and law enforcement work mechanism, the establishment of a coordination mechanism for the development of safe China. At present, all towns and townships in 18 provinces, autonomous regions and municipalities directly under the central government nationwide have judicial and law enforcement commissioners.

- The organizational system of courts and procuratorates was improved

The Beijing Financial Court and the Hainan Free Trade Port Intellectual Property Court were established to enhance the level of specialization in handling cases and the ability to serve overall economic and social development. The Supreme People's Court formulated the Reform Plan on Improving the Four-Level Trial Functions of Courts, and the allocation of functions and powers, case jurisdiction, and institutional settings were promoted in the four levels of courts. The reform of the trial mechanism of the circuit courts of the Supreme People's Court was deepened, and intellectual property courts and international commercial courts were strengthened. The functions of national procuratorial organs were systematically and holistically reorganized, and a new pattern of procuratorial work has been formed to include criminal prosecution, civil prosecution, administrative prosecution, and public interest litigation prosecution as well as general criminal prosecution, major criminal prosecution, office crime prosecution, economic crime prosecution, criminal enforcement prosecution, civil prosecution, administrative prosecution, public interest litigation, juvenile prosecution, and complaint and appeal prosecution.

- The system of institutions and functions of public security organs was improved

The administrative resettlement of 300,000 former public security officers was completed, and solid progress was made in adjusting the management system of industrial public security organs. The development of a one-stop case management model was promoted for law enforcement, supervision and management, and service guarantee. More than 2,100 law enforcement case management centers have been built nationwide, centralizing the handling of criminal cases and realizing supervision of the whole process and all elements.

- The reform of law societies was deepened

In May, the General Office of the CPC Central Committee

issued and implemented the Guidelines on Further Strengthening Law Societies, which provide rules for effectively maintaining and enhancing the political, advanced and popular nature of law societies and further strengthening their development. The China Law Society thoroughly implemented the Reform Plan of the China Law Society, guided 32 provincial law societies in formulating and issuing reform plans. Now almost all provinces, cities, and counties have their law societies.

3. Deepening the comprehensive reform of the judicial accountability system

- The establishment of a new mechanism for the operation of judicial power with consistent authority and responsibility was accelerated

In March, the General Office of the CPC Central Committee issued and implemented the Guidelines on Deepening the Comprehensive Reform of the Judicial Responsibility System, which systematically makes provisions for improving management by category, regulating the operation of powers, strengthening supervision and management, improving professional security, and enhancing the effectiveness of case handling, so as to promote the full implementation of the judicial responsibility system. The Supreme People's Court issued the Guidelines on

Deepening the Comprehensive Reform of the Judicial Responsibility System, supervised and guided people's courts at all levels to implement the Guidelines on Improving the List of Judicial Powers and Responsibilities of the People's Courts, and further improved the trial power operation mechanism. The Supreme People's Procuratorate formulated the Regulations on Judicial Accountability of People's Procuratorates to clarify the scope, procedures and forms of judicial accountability for public procurators and other personnel, and promote the formation of an effective closed system of internal oversight of judicial case handling. At present, the principal position of judges and public procurators in handling cases has been basically established, with more than 98% of the adjudication documents of cases in courts nationwide being issued directly by single judges and collegial courts, and more than 90% of cases in procuratorates nationwide being decided directly by the public procurators in charge.

- The improvement of the mechanism for the dynamic adjustment of judges and public procurators' posts, post withdrawal and disciplinary action was accelerated

The Supreme People's Court formulated the Measures for Judge' Post Withdrawal (for Trial Implementation) and the Guidelines on the Dynamic Adjustment to Judges' Posts in

People's Courts at or below the Provincial Level (for Trial Implementation) to promote the improvement of the mechanism for dynamic adjustment to judges' posts and the implementation of the post withdrawal mechanism. The Supreme People's Court formulated the Regulations on the Disciplinary Procedures for Judges (for Trial Implementation) and the Charter of the Judges' Disciplinary Action Committee of the Supreme People's Court, established the Judges' Disciplinary Action Committee of the Supreme People's Court, and promoted the establishment of provincial-level judges' disciplinary action committees nationwide. The judges' disciplinary action system gradually entered into substantive operation. The Supreme People's Procuratorate formulated the Charter of the Public Procurators' Disciplinary Action Committee and the Procedural Provisions for the Disciplinary Work of Public Procurators. All this made it possible for the courts and procuratorates to accelerate the improvement of the disciplinary action systems and the implementation of the trial accountability mechanisms.

- Sound performance appraisal systems were established for judges and public procurators

The Supreme People's Court formulated a guiding document on improving the working mechanism for judges assessment. The Supreme People's Procuratorate issued the

Main Evaluation Indicators of the Quality of Cases in the Procuratorial Organs, and made the actual case-to-handled case ratio as the core case quality evaluation index, thus further improving the performance assessment system. Only qualified officers handling cases has basically become a regular practice, and a number of officers who failed in their performance assessment and handled cases in violation of discipline and law were disqualified and held accountable.

- The funding reform for the local courts and procuratorates at or below the provincial level was carried out

The Supreme People's Court, in conjunction with the Ministry of Finance, issued five documents, including the Interim Measures for the Management of the Refund of Litigation Expenses of the People's Courts, to improve the supporting mechanism for the unified management of financial and material resources. The model of unified provincial management of finance and material resources of local courts and procuratorates at or below the provincial level was standardized. Localities were supervised to improve the relevant policies and programs, and the funding mechanism whereby courts and procuratorates exercise their powers independently and impartially in accordance with the law became increasingly sound.

4. Deepening litigation reform

- The governance of the source of litigation was deepened

The Central Judicial and Law Enforcement Commission formulated the Guidelines on Strengthening the Governance of the Source of Litigation and Promote the Resolution of Conflicts at the Source. The document stresses the need to uphold and develop the Fengqiao model for the new era, give top priority to the resolution of non-litigation disputes, encourage more legal forces to make greater efforts toward guidance and persuasion, strengthen the prevention of disputes at the source, resolve them at the front end, and control them at the key points, improve the preventive legal system, and curtail the increase in litigation at the source.

- Litigation reform was deepened

The trial-centered reform of the criminal procedure system continued. The Supreme People's Court, the Supreme People's Procuratorate, the Ministry of Public Security, the Ministry of State Security and the Ministry of Justice issued on the Guidelines on Issues concerning the Standardization of Sentencing Procedures (for Trial Implementation) and the Legal Aid Duty Lawyer Work Measures. The mechanism for judicial experts to testify in court was improved. Supplementary investigation work was strengthened and standardized. The legality of interrogation before the end of the investigation of major cases was verified. The implementation of the system of sentence bargaining was deepened, the penal policy of severity tempered with mercy, the principle of commensurate crime with punishment and the principle of evidential adjudication were always adhered to. Efforts were made to ensure that the handling of cases of sentence of bargaining achieves the unity of political, legal and social effects.

• Trials were carried out for the reform to separate simplified and complicated civil proceedings

According to the central leadership's plan and the authorization of the NPC Standing Committee, the Supreme People's Court issued the plan for the trials for the reform to separate simplified and complicated civil proceedings and the measures for implementing the plan. The trials were started in 305 courts in 15 provinces and 20 cities. The six mechanisms of organizational leadership of the trials, working liaison meetings, policy and document review, monthly reports on the trials, data aggregation and evaluation, and policy dissemination and interpretation were improved. Five supporting documents, including those on the caliber of questions and answers, the style of documents, and the data index system, were issued for the trials. The effect of the reform gradually emerged, the quality and efficiency of the judiciary were further improved, the allocation of judicial resources was more reasonable and was further improved, the people's sense of fairness and justice was constantly enhanced, and the trials achieved initial results.

- The system of enforcing penal decisions was improved

  General Secretary Xi Jinping's important instructions on the outstanding issues in the enforcement of penal decisions were thoroughly implemented. The areas of weakness, risks, and loopholes that may be caused by commutation, parole, and temporary execution outside prison to institutions and mechanisms were comprehensively analyzed. Suggestions were put forward on improving the systems and mechanisms of commutation, parole and temporary execution outside prison. The implementation of the Community Corrections Law was promoted. Continued efforts were made to integrate penalty execution, and the mechanism was constantly improved to attach equal importance to the management of criminals and education and rehabilitation a native of coordinate professionals and amateurs.

5. Improving the institutions and mechanisms of judicial and law enforcement public services

- More convenient litigation services were provided

The Supreme People's Court issued the general framework guidelines on developing one-stop services and 21 special standards. Nationwide 98% of the courts built litigation service halls; 98% of the courts opened litigation service networks; 95% of the courts opened 12368 litigation service hotlines; and 95% of the courts realized online filing. During the epidemic, the number of online court sessions increased by more than 450% year-on-year; that means online court hearings are always available in the fight against Covid-19. A total of 195 million judicial documents were published on https://wenshu.court.gov.cn/, and the total number of live broadcasts on http://tingshen.court.gov.cn/ exceeded 10 million, making them the world's largest websites for the disclosure of judicial documents and live video broadcasts of government affairs respectively.

- The scope of public interest litigation cases was actively and steadily expanded

The Supreme People's Court and the Supreme People's Procuratorate jointly revised the Interpretation of Issues on the Application of Law to Procuratorate Public Interest Litigation

Cases, and the Supreme People's Court revised the Interpretation of Issues on the Application of Law to the Trial of Environmental Civil Public Interest Litigation Cases to standardize the procedures and rules on the application of law to environmental public interest cases. The Supreme People's Procuratorate deployed to actively handle public interest damage cases in the areas of workplace safety, public health, biosecurity, protection of the rights and interests of women and children and persons with disabilities, network infringement, poverty alleviation, cultural relics and cultural heritage protection that had aroused strong public complaints. The Supreme People's Court issued the Guidelines on Actively and Steadily Expanding the Scope of Public Interest Litigation Cases, strictly grasping the conditions for filing cases in new areas and strengthening procedural safeguards. The Supreme People's Court released leading cases of public interest litigation in the areas of sales of counterfeit and shoddy masks, military and civilian collaboration, and cultural relics and cultural heritage protection.

- The public service system of judicial and law enforcement was improved

The judicial administrative organs sped up the development of public legal service system, improved and unified the judicial appraisal management system, and established and implemented a national unified legal qualification examination system. Public legal service networks began to provide services 24 hours a day and seven days a week on all businesses. The total number of public legal service institutions and personnel reached a historical high.

- The reform to delegate power, improve regulation, and upgrade services in public security and judicial administration was deepened

Fifteen measures to facilitate public security management during the prevention and control of the Covid-19 epidemic, and 10 measures to combat crimes in the field of food, drug, environment and intellectual property rights to ensure reopening during the prevention and control of the epidemic. Documents such as the Guidelines on Further Deepening the Reform to Delegate Power, Improve Regulation, and Upgrade Services to Promote the Convenience of Examination and Approval Services.

IV. Judicial, Procuratorial, Public Security and Judicial Administrative Work

1. Judicial work

In 2020, the Supreme People's Court accepted 39,347 cases and concluded 35,773 cases; local people's courts at all levels accepted 30,805,000 cases and concluded and executed 28,705,000 cases, with a total value of 7.1 trillion yuan.

- Criminal judicial work

In 2020, courts at all levels adjudicated 1.116 million criminal cases of first instance and sentenced 1.527 million criminals. They strictly punished various crimes of infiltration, subversion and sabotage, violent terrorism, ethnic separatism and religious extremism in accordance with the law, and firmly safeguarded the security of state power and the system. They concluded 47,000 cases of serious violent crimes in accordance with the law. The courts also promoted the fight against drugs and concluded 68,000 cases of drug crimes. To safeguard the order of epidemic prevention, the courts concluded 5,474 cases of epidemic-related crimes involving

6,443 persons in accordance with the law. The courts completed the trial and execution tasks of the campaign to combat organized crime and root out local criminal gangs. Since the campaign, 33,053 cases involving 226,495 persons involved in cases of organized crime and local criminal gangs have been tried and concluded in accordance with the law. The court strictly punished the crimes of corruption and bribery in accordance with the law, and adjudicated 22,000 cases of corruption and bribery and dereliction of duty involving 26,000 persons. The courts actively cooperated with the international anti-corruption efforts to track down and recover stolen goods and money, and tried 316 cases of tracking down and recovering stolen goods and money and confiscating illegal proceeds. They ruled to confiscate 1.15 billion yuan of illegal proceeds from 164 people, including Yao Jinqi, for whom a red notice had been issued. The courts severely punished cybercrime and concluded 33,000 cases of telecommunication network fraud, online marketing, online gambling, online hacking, online rumors, and online violence in accordance with the law. They concluded 15,000 cases of crowdsourced economic crimes, such as fund-raising fraud, involving 2.9 trillion yuan, in accordance with the law.

- Civil and commercial judicial work

In 2020, the courts at all levels adjudicated 13.306 million civil and commercial cases in the first instance, including 1.347 million cases involving education, employment, medical care, housing, social security and other livelihood issues. They concluded 1.649 million marriage and family cases and issued 2,169 writs of habeas corpus. In conjunction with the All-China Women's Federation and other units, they deepened the reform of family trials and improved the system of family mediation, family investigation and psychological counseling. They concluded 253,000 first instance environmental resource cases and 3,557 environmental public interest litigation cases. The courts concluded 10,132 bankruptcy cases in accordance with the law, involving 1.2 trillion yuan of claims. They adjudicated 18,163 first instance foreign-related civil and commercial cases in accordance with the law.

- Administrative trial and national compensation work

In 2020, the courts at all levels adjudicated 266,000 first-instance administrative cases to serve the reform to delegate power, improve regulation, and upgrade services and promote the development law-based governments and government integrity. The courts concluded 18,000 cases of state compensation.

- Filing cases, addressing public complaints and proposals, and supervising trials

In 2020, the courts at all levels re-tried and re-sentenced 1,818 criminal cases in accordance with trial supervision procedures. Adhering to the principles legality, the benefit of the doubt, and evidentiary adjudication, they acquitted 656 defendants in public prosecution cases and 384 defendants in private prosecution cases in accordance with the law. A one-stop multi-means mechanism for settling disputes was generally established. Making full use of their mediation platforms, the courts successfully mediated 4.24 million civil cases without litigation. The one-stop litigation service center was basically completed, and 6.933 million cases were speedily adjudicated and quickly tried in the litigation service center. The courts nationwide provided cross-domain filing services in all areas, providing cross-domain filing services for 82,000 cases in total.

2. Execution work

In 2020, the courts nationwide did not relax their efforts, continuously consolidating the achievements of "basically solving the difficulties in execution," further improving the long-term mechanism for solving the difficulties in execution.

They made all-out efforts to handle cases well and persistently grasped quality and efficiency, improving execution in all respects. The courts accepted 10,592,000 execution cases and executed 9,958,000 cases, involving 1.9 trillion yuan, an increase of 1.7%, 4.3% and 8.1% year-on-year respectively. The number of new cases accepted, cases concluded and the amount money involved increased, and the number of old and outstanding cases decreased, realizing a virtuous cycle of execution work and regularizing the high standard operation of the "3 + 1" core indicators. As a result, in spite of the Covid-19 epidemic and trade friction, the people earned more money through execution work.

• The work pattern of comprehensively addressing execution difficulties under the leadership of the Party further deepened

The No. 1 document issued by the Central Commission for Law-Based Governance in 2019 was implemented to ensure that all localities introduce specific measures for implementing the document and plans for attaining the tasks, in order to a solve the execution difficulties at the source. The assessment methods for building the Peaceful China were implemented and responsibilities were ascertained for relevant authorities to assist in execution. The relevant authorities were urged to become connected as soon as possible with the national "Internet + supervision" system and the national credit information sharing platform's joint disciplinary action system and share information. Tianjin established the Joint Judicial Execution Center. Under the leadership of the Tianjin Municipal Party Committee's Judicial and Law Enforcement Commission, the key members of the Joint Judicial Execution Center sent personnel to become stationed at the Tianjin Higher People's Court's Execution Bureau to directly participate in the work of the center and study and solve major problems. In collaboration with the public security organs, the Tianjin Higher People's Court launched the online case handling system for motor vehicles, shortening the time to seize and release local motor vehicles from a day to minutes. In Kashi, Xinjiang, a collaborative execution mechanism was established in villages and towns which, led by the judicial and law enforcement committees of county Party committees, issued briefings notices on a monthly basis. Towns and townships set up a special team for collaborative execution to bring cases to rural areas on a regular basis. This further improved the grassroots governance pattern and further enhanced the identification with socialist rule of law in ethnic border areas. The Jiangxi Provincial Party Committee's

Judicial and Law Enforcement Commissions led the convening of a work conference to comprehensively address execution difficulties, established a sound long-term working mechanism for joint execution and realized the regular and physical operation of joint execution under the leadership of Party committees' judicial and law enforcement commissions.

• Execution work played an increasingly prominent role in serving efforts to improve the business environment, develop the social integrity system and establish a new development pattern

An execution campaign was launched to do a solid job in ensuring stability on six fronts and maintaining security in six areas in order to provide strong judicial services and guarantees for routine epidemic control efforts and economic and social development work. Execution leggers were established for criminal cases involving property in criminal cases involving organized crimes and local criminal gangs and job-related criminal case, departmental coordination was strengthened, and a "green channel" was opened to actively promote the execution work involving property in criminal cases involving organized crimes and local criminal gangs and job-related criminal cases, cut the source of income of organized criminals and local criminal gangs. This demonstrated the Party Central Committee's strong determination to consolidate the overwhelming victory in the fight against organized crimes and local criminal gangs. The Beijing Higher People's Court and the Beijing Municipal Finance Bureau signed minutes of meeting to jointly regulate the surrender of criminal-related property to the government. Guangdong courts deployed to carry out the "thunderbolt action" for the execution of property in cases of organized crimes and local criminal gangs, ensuring that "not a single case" and "not a single piece of property is left out," forcefully cutting the source of income of organized criminals and local criminal gangs, and promoting the confiscation of all the property involved with obvious results. Full play was given to the function of execution, active response was made to the profound changes in the international and domestic situation, and the vitality of market entities was constantly stimulated to create a strong atmosphere to encourage entrepreneurs to work and start business. The Fujian Higher People's Court established a mechanism to remove the barriers to execution and bankruptcy procedures to promote market clearing and improve the business environment. Shandong courts carried out special cleanup of seized land and sea use rights, releasing 46,000 *mu* of land resources and 3,888 hectares of sea use rights through judicial auctions and execution settlements, releasing production factors in accordance with the law and improving the investment environment. In view of the special situation that the property of the executees in agricultural and pastoral areas are mostly cattle, sheep and livestock, seedlings and dried fruits, and the property is seasonal and cyclical, the Xinjiang courts integrated compulsory supervision and flexible management, and actively guided the parties to reach settlement agreements to achieve a "win-win" solution for creditors and debtors.

- Information technology and intelligence helped to improve the execution ability

Efforts were made to further integrate execution work and modern technology, and make the execution information system more intensive, refined and intelligent. With the help of blockchain technology, the intelligent inspection system for terminating this execution procedure, which was tried out in some courts. The coverage of network inspection and control was expanded, including the entry and exit records, tax registration information, insurance and financial products of the executes. Cross-domain services with China Post EMS were actively promoted, and electronic delivery of documents, remote printing and packaging, and local delivery were used to reduce costs, improve efficiency and promote energy conservation and emission reduction and the development of a Beautiful China. The Supreme People's Court issued a circular to further regulate the auxiliary work of judicial online auction. In collaboration with relevant industry associations, work specifications for commissioned appraisals were issued. The use of online inquiry and appraisal systems was promoted to make appraisals more scientific and precise. During the epidemic period, the results of making execution more IT-based and intelligent were fully tested, the network investigation and control system ran smoothly, the number of matters entrusted online increased by nearly 40%, and the mobile execution platform became prominent, keeping execution work going. The judicial online auction work continued to maintain good momentum, with more and more online auctions, larger and larger auction amounts, and better and better auction results with zero complaints. The physical operation of execution command centers was promoted. The execution command management platform was relied on. The visual regulation and automated warning of key areas of execution were improved. The downward supervision, hierarchical time-sharing supervision and other work mechanisms was refined. The whole-process and all-around management of cases, people and things was carried out. Active efforts were made to promote the extension of execution management from private networks to the internet. Full arrangements were made to apply mobile execution platforms. The development of the emergency response system was accelerated. Full play was given to the supervisory and service role of the Smart Execution APP and expanded it to deputies to people's congresses, members of CPPCC committees, parties and units to assist in execution, so that the deputies, members, and the general public can understand and participate in execution more comprehensively. Jiangsu courts actively developed the Internet of Things (IoT) property seizure supervision system, IoT electronic seal and IoT weighing system to realize the "wise" supervision, "live" seizure and "fast" disposal of the property under execution. This effectively improved the security of the seized property and reduced the circumstance of evasion of execution by the executees.

- The execution ecology which is law-based, standard, goodwilled and appropriate was further strengthened

A sound "one case, two investigators" working mechanism was established whereby execution departments and supervisory departments jointly investigate and deal with illegal and irregular execution as well as the failure to implement management responsibilities and other issues. With the help of the national system for handling execution appeals, public complaints and proposals, and supervision cases, the supervision and management of key cases such as public complaints and proposals and cases of concern to the deputies to people's congresses and members of the CPPCC members was strengthened. The development of the national court "one case, one account" case management mechanism was basically completed to further standardize case fund management and make payments more efficient. The Supreme People's Court, in conjunction with the Supreme People's Procuratorate, issued guidelines to establish a national platform for execution and legal supervision, and to strengthen and standardize the legal supervision of execution by people's procuratorates. Greater efforts were made to further eliminate the space for negative, selective and indiscriminate execution, resolutely stop cases from being influenced by social connections, personal favors, or money, and establish the authority and credibility of execution. Guangdong courts comprehensively implemented the three mechanisms of intensively handle affairs, separating simple and complicated cases, and encouraging, which have greatly improved the quality and efficiency of execution. The judicial interpretation of execution was strengthened, and the system of standardizing execution with operating procedures at the core was strengthened and improved. Accurate measures for punishing breach of trust and restricting consumption were adopted, and the focus of credit disciplinary action was shifted to combat the few illegal and untrustworthy behaviors such as circumvention and resistance to execution. Goodwilled and appropriate execution was promoted, a graded and classified management and credit repair mechanism was established for the list of defaulters, disciplinary action for breach of trust and consumption restrictions were made more targeted and predictable, and opportunities were given to honest but unfortunate operators and entrepreneurs to make a fortune again. The Jiangxi Higher People's Court and the Ningbo Intermediate People's Court established credit commitment and credit repair mechanisms for defaulted executees, which are highly targeted and operative, and have exemplary significance. The Guangzhou internet Court, together with the Guangzhou Municipal Committee of the Communist Youth League, launched the Guangzhou Legal Aid Project for Youth, adopting "online + offline," "repair + recognition" and "grading + classification" measures to provide diversified support and credit incentives to promote goodwilled execution against young executees.

Seizures in excess of standards and indiscriminate seizures were prohibited, and it was made clear that rigid seizures should never be used where flexible seizures are an option. Everything was done to ensure that enterprise properties are put to best use and operate normally. Full play was given to online judicial auctions to speed up property liquidation and appropriate flexible liquidation was used to prevent the seized property from being sold cheaply. During the Covid-19 epidemic, the Supreme People's Court issued a number of judicial documents, including a circular on matters related to doing good execution work, a circular on doing a good job in renewing real estate seizures and bank deposit freezing, and the guidelines on issues related to the execution of cases involving the Covid-19 epidemic in accordance with the law, to ensure smooth and orderly execution work and help small, medium and micro enterprises and other entities in difficulty by all means to alleviate and overcome their difficulties. Nearly 300 execution cases for serving the prevention and control of the Covid-19 epidemic and reopening were collected, and 13 leading cases were selected for publication to serve as guidance. Hunan court carried out execution of a number of engineering machinery cases to serve the healthy development of manufacturing industry.

- Outstanding issues of concern to the people were further resolved

Regularly carry out special enforcement actions for cases involving people's lives were regularly carried out. For cases concerning people's lives, high priority was given to filing and executing them and disbursing execution funds. Communication was strengthened government departments to seek policy support in including include eligible parties into social security and poverty alleviation so that they could accept judicial assistance or social assistance. Around New Year's Day and the Spring Festival, execution actions for large numbers of cases involving people's lives were carried out, and 25.4 billion yuan was released in cases involving people's lives, enhancing the people's sense of gain. Fully understanding the extreme importance of arable land protection, relevant authorities used judicial means to curb the indiscriminate occupation of arable land, supporting local governments and relevant departments in cracking down on all kinds of illegal occupation of arable land in accordance with the law, and ensuring the redline for arable land is not crossed and food security is secured. Efforts were continuously increased to execute cases of debts owed by Party and government organs and state-owned enterprises to private enterprises and small and medium-sized enterprises. Communication with local authorities responsible for debt clearance was strengthened and work measures were made more detailed to guarantee the timely realization of the rights and interests of private enterprises and small and medium-sized enterprises that had won the lawsuits and create a business environment based on the rule of law. Shandong courts increased efforts to ensure Party and government organs and large enterprises pay the debts they default on their debts to small and medium-sized enterprises. In particular in conjunction with the development and reform commission and other important Party and government departments, Party and government organs that default on business debts were incorporated into the pre-notification system for the list of defaulters, with obvious effect. The higher people's courts in Inner Mongolia, Zhejiang and Hubei issued a series of judicial policy documents to provide strong support and guarantee for the survival and development of small, medium-sized and micro businesses. The Jiangxi Higher People's Court organized a series of thematic activities to resolutely solve the difficulties of execution, and the Jilin Higher People's Court organized a series of activities on the theme of "execution work into ten thousand homes with the execution director broadcasting live," using vivid cases to increase public awareness of the law and integrity and create a more favorable public opinion environment and social atmosphere for comprehensively address execution difficulties. The Jiangsu Higher People's Court issued the guidelines on the substantive resolution of the cases involving public complaints and proposals, implemented the execution director's responsibility system, adhered to the principle of substantive handling, focused on solving practical problems, and effectively safeguarded the legitimate rights and interests of the people.

3. Procuratorial work

In 2020, procuratorial organs nationwide handled a total of 3.01 million cases of various types, down 19.4% year-on-year. The number of cases accepted for review and arrest, review and prosecution, and complaints fell by 30.6%, 12.4%, and 46.1%, respectively, year-on-year; the number of public interest litigation and litigation supervision cases performed proactively rose by 19.2% and 9.6%, respectively.

• Performing functions such as approving arrests and prosecutions in accordance with the law

In 2020, procuratorial organs nationwide approved the arrest of 770,561 suspects and the public prosecution of

157,2971 people. They resolutely safeguarded national security and social stability, and cracked down on the infiltration, subversion and sabotage activities of hostile forces inside and outside the country. They severely punished serious violent crimes such as murder and robbery, and prosecuted 57,000 people. High priority was given to addressing frequent property-related crimes such as theft, fraud, and robbery, prosecuting 350,000 people. The crimes of pornography, gambling and drugs were punished in accordance with the law, prosecuting 212,000 people. There was a timely introduction of a series of judicial policies to guide the prosecution of crimes that hindered the prevention and control of the Covid-19 epidemics in accordance with the law, arresting 7,227 people for epidemic-related crimes and prosecuting 11,000 others. Procuratorial organs contributed to the comprehensive victory in combatting organized crime and rooting out local criminal gangs. Since 2018, a total of 149,000 people have been arrested for related crimes, and 230,000 people have been prosecuted. Procuratorial organs actively participated in network governance, prosecuting 142,000 people for network crimes. They continued to promote the fight against corruption, accepting 19,760 people referred by the supervisory commissions at all levels for job-related crimes, prosecuting 15,346 of them, not prosecuting 662 of them, and instituting public prosecutions against 12 former provincial and ministerial officials, including Zhao Zhengyong. The penal policy of severity tempered with mercy was thoroughly implemented, with 88,000 people not being arrested and 202,000 people not being prosecuted for crimes that are minor and do not require a prison sentence; 25,000 people were released or had their compulsory measures changed as they pleaded guilty to punishment after arrest and could no longer be detained.

• Services to ensure high-quality economic and social development

Procuratorial organs helped to fight poverty, assisting 32,000 people with 420 million yuan. They helped to prevent and control pollution, prosecuting 51,000 people for crimes against ecological and environmental resources, and handling 84,000 cases of public interest litigation. They strictly prosecuted financial fraud and crimes against the order of financial management, prosecuting 41,000 people. They severely punished money laundering, prosecuting 707 people for money laundering crimes, 4.7 times more than in 2019. Working with the National Copyright Administration and other authorities, they supervised 49 major infringement and piracy cases, prosecuting 12,000 people for crimes against intellectual property rights. Special rules were formulated to serve the development of the free trade zones and support the development of the Hainan Free Trade Port. Twenty-one initiatives were issued to support the development of the Guangdong-Hong Kong-Macao Greater Bay Area. Procuratorial organs held video conferences with the prosecution authorities of the Shanghai Cooperation Organization (SCO) member states and BRICS countries to discuss the punishment and prevention of transnational crimes while adhering to routine Covid-19 control measures, and to improve the mechanism of cross-border judicial assistance.

- Strengthening legal supervision of litigation activities

In 2020, procuratorial organs urged the investigative authorities to file 22,000 cases in accordance with the law, and supervised the withdrawal of 24,000 cases. They made 20,000 additional arrests and 29,000 additional prosecutions in cases that arrests should have been made or that should have prosecuted but had not been transferred in accordance with the law; and did not approve 138,000 arrests and 41,000 prosecutions in cases that did not constitute crimes or for which there were insufficient evidence. The number of protests against criminal decisions that were considered to be wrong was 8,903; 4,994 civil protests were filed, and 9,900 proposals for retrial were made. Some 182 protests were filed against administrative decisions that were considered to be wrong, and 198 proposals for retrial were made, 2.4 times more than in 2019. Procuratorial organs nationwide supervised the correction of 51,000 cases of improper commutation of sentence, parole and provisional release from prison, and made 37,000 procuratorial recommendations for violations in civil enforcement activities and 25,000 for violations in administrative execution activities. Procuratorial organs continued to deepen special supervision, correcting 10,090 cases of false lawsuits and prosecuting 1,352 people for suspected crimes. They effectively resolved 6,304 administrative disputes in response to some administrative litigation procedures being left idle. They expanded public interest litigation prosecution in an orderly manner, filing 151,260 public interest litigation cases. To protect the legal practice of lawyers, they supervised the correction of 958 cases of law enforcement and judicial organs obstructing lawyers' exercise of litigation rights.

- Ensuring procuratorial services are for the people and promote their wellbeing

Procuratorial organs prosecuted 8,268 people for crimes

such as manufacturing and selling toxic and harmful food, fake drugs and substandard medicines, and handled 27,000 public interest litigation cases for food and drug safety. They handled 106 criminal cases involving manhole covers and 424 public interest litigation cases. They adhered to developed the Fengqiao model in the new era and handled 25,000 longstanding cases involving public complaints and proposals. In protecting the safe and healthy growth of minors, procuratorial organs prosecuted 57,000 people for sexual assault, abuse of minors and child trafficking. In resolutely safeguarding the interests of national defense and the legitimate rights and interests of military personnel and their families, they prosecuted 381 people for military-related crimes such as destruction of military facilities and military marriages. To resolutely and severely punish crimes against doctors, they prosecuted 496 people.

4. judicial interpretation and case guidance work

In 2020, the Supreme People's Court and the Supreme People's Procuratorate jointly issued two sets of judicial interpretations, and the Supreme People's Court alone issued 26 sets of judicial interpretations, consisting of two sets of criminal judicial interpretations, 20 sets of civil judicial interpretations, two sets of administrative judicial interpretations, and four sets of other judicial interpretations. The Supreme People's Procuratorate alone issued three sets of judicial interpretations. The Supreme People's Court issued 17 sets of leading cases, and the Supreme People's Procuratorate issued 34 leading cases. These judicial interpretations and leading cases played a positive role in the correct implementation of the law.

• Providing guidance on the correct handling of major and complex issues in criminal justice work

In March, the Supreme People's Court and the Supreme People's Procuratorate jointly issued the Reply on the Application of Article 344 of the Criminal Law of the People's Republic of China, guiding the judicial organs nationwide to apply the crime of illegal logging of plants of national importance in accordance with the law, so as to ensure the compatibility of crime with punishment. In September, the Supreme People's Court and the Supreme People's Procuratorate jointly issued the Interpretation of the Supreme People's Court and the Supreme People's Procuratorate on Issues concerning the Specific Application of Law in Handling Criminal Cases of Infringement of Intellectual Property Rights (Ⅲ) to punish crimes of infringement of intellectual property rights in accordance with the law and maintain the socialist market economic order.

• Giving guidance on how to properly handle new developments and problems in economic and social development and people's lives

In July, the Supreme People's Court issued the Regulations on Issues concerning Representative Proceedings in Securities Disputes to improve the securities class action system, effectively punish securities violations of laws and disciplines and protect the legitimate rights and interests of investors. In September, the Supreme People's Court issued the Reply on Issues concerning the Application of Law in Internet-Related Intellectual Property Infringement Disputes. In November, the Supreme People's Court issued the Regulations on Evidence in Civil Intellectual Property Litigation to protect and facilitate the exercise of litigation rights by parties in accordance with the law and to ensure that the people's courts hear civil intellectual property cases in a fair and timely manner. In December, the Supreme People's Court promulgated the Interpretation of the Supreme People's Court on Issues concerning the Application of Law to the Trial of Civil Dispute Cases on Food Safety (Ⅰ) to guide the people's courts in the proper trial of civil disputes on food safety and to protect people's health and life. In accordance with the Civil Code of the People's Republic of China and other legal provisions, and taking into account the actual trial practice, the 591 sets of judicial interpretations and 139 leading cases currently in effect were reviewed, and the formulation of new judicial interpretations was advanced in an orderly manner to ensure the uniform and correct implementation of the Civil Code.

- Giving guidance on how to properly handle new situations and new problems in administrative litigation

In June, the Supreme People's Court promulgated the Regulations on Issues concerning the Appearance of Leaders of Administrative Organs in Court to Respond to Lawsuits to further regulate the appearance of leaders of administrative organs to respond to lawsuits and promote the substantive resolution of administrative disputes. In September, the Supreme People's Court promulgated the Regulations of the Supreme People's Court on Issues concerning the Application of Law to the Trial of Administrative Cases of Patent Granting and Confirmation of Rights (Ⅰ) to guide the people's courts in properly trying administrative cases of patent granting and confirmation of rights.

- Providing guidance over how to properly handle foreign-related commercial maritime disputes

In June, the Supreme People's Court issued the Guidelines on Issues concerning the Proper Trial of Covid-19-Related Civil Cases in Accordance with the Law (Ⅲ) to properly hear Covid-19- and foreign-related cases involving commercial and maritime disputes, and to provide equal protection of the legitimate rights and interests of Chinese and foreign parties. In September, the Supreme People's Court issued the Guidelines on the People's Courts Serving and Safeguarding Further Expansion of Opening to the Outside World to provide judicial services and safeguards for a higher level of opening to the outside world. In December, the Supreme People's Court issued the Annual Report on Judicial Review of Commercial Arbitration (2019) to promote the development of a mechanism for resolving non-litigation disputes. In 2020, the Supreme People's Court selected and issued eight leading cases of safeguarding the legitimate rights and interests of crew members and 11 leading cases of national maritime maritime trials.

5. Public security work

In 2020, the CPC Central Committee established the

People's Police Day and held the flag-awarding ceremony of the Chinese People's Police. General Secretary Xi Jinping awarded the flag and delivered an important message, which greatly stimulated the motivation of the police to forge the police soul, stay true to the Party's founding aspiration and carry out the mission. This provided the fundamental guidelines and charted the course for promoting the development of public security under the rule of law in the new era.

- Fighting the Covid-19 epidemic in accordance with the law

After the outbreak of the epidemic, public security organs nationwide strictly implemented preventive and control measures, quickly organized the closure and control of the epidemic area, order maintenance and other work, strengthened the control of air, sea and land ports, adjusted entry and exit policies in a timely manner, and established a solid defense line for the prevention and control of the epidemic. The Ministry of Public Security, in conjunction with the Supreme People's Court, the Supreme People's Procuratorate and other departments, issued guidelines to provide timely and effective legal basis for punishing epidemic-related crimes. Public security organs at all levels standardized law enforcement and case handling during epidemic prevention and control, accurately grasped the tensity of law enforcement, and cracked down on epidemic-related crimes such as hurting doctors and disturbing the order, making and selling fake and shoddy epidemic prevention materials and fake vaccines, and destroying wild animal resources, thus effectively preventing law enforcement risks and epidemic prevention and control risks. To integrate epidemic prevention and control and economic and social development, public security organs launched a series of new initiatives to benefit the people and enterprises and to effectively serve efforts to ensure stability on six fronts and maintain security in six areas.

• Cracking down on prominent crimes in accordance with the law

The public security organs nationwide adhered to the strict policy of cracking down on crimes in accordance with the law and achieved decisive victory in the three-year campaign to combat organized crime and root out local criminal gangs, prosecuting a total of 3,392 mafia-like organizations n 11,000 criminal groups. Measures were strengthened to oppose and prevent terrorism, maintaining zero occurrence of violent terrorism cases nationwide. Public secretary organs launched a campaign to investigate longstanding murder cases, solving 6,270 cases, with a 99.8% detection rate of active murder cases nationwide. Public secretary organs carried out a new round of special operations to combat and rectify gun-and-explosive related crimes, and 153 cities across the country destroyed illegal guns and explosives at the same time. In response to the prominent problems that aroused the great resentment of the people, public secretary organs organized crackdowns and rectification, solved 322,000 criminal cases of telecommunication network fraud, 75,000 criminal cases in the field of food, medicine, environment and knowledge, and arrested 75,000 suspects of cross-border gambling and related crimes, and 596 suspects of economic crimes who had fled the country. They carried out in-depth operations to address crimes on the border. In addition, public secretary organs made greater efforts to address the problems of foreigners entering, residing or working in China illegally. In accordance with the law, they cracked down on all kinds of illegal and criminal activities that impaired border control, illegal fishing in the Yangtze River valley, infringement of citizens' personal information, illegal fund-raising, and new types of drugs. They fully implemented crime prevention and control measures to enhance the sense of security of the people. In 2020, the number of criminal cases dropped by 1.8% compared to 2019, of which, the eight major cases dropped by 8.7%; the number of security cases found and accepted fell by 10.4% year-on-year; and the numbers of larger road accidents and prison security accidents fell by 24% and 60% respectively.

- Continuously improving social management services

Adhering to and developing the Fengqiao model in the new era, public secretary organs carried out "millions of police into millions of homes" activities, to solve all kinds of conflicts and disputes and defuse security risks. They deepened the development of the crime prevention and control system, carry out special investigation and rectification of official use of guns, strengthen the IT-based supervision of civilian firearms and ammunition, strengthen the basic control of explosives, and carry out the campaign to create "model cities" and keep schools and hospitals safe to further improve the level of ability to maintain public security. Public secretary organs successfully completed the security tasks for a series of major events such as the sessions of the NPC and the CPPCC National Committee, the China International Fair for Trade in Services in Beijing, the China International Import Expo in Shanghai, the celebrations for the 40th anniversary of the establishment of the Shenzhen Special Economic Zone.

Focusing on solving the "urgent, difficult, worrying and pending" problems of the public, the Ministry of Public Security launched high-quality convenience service initiatives and put online the "internet plus government service" platform, unifying for the first time online national public security services and providing more than 900 types of public security services for the public. The practice of issuing resident identity cards of other localities was encouraged and made it possible to obtain household registration-related certificates five types of household registration transfer business on an inter-provincial basis. Off-site traffic violations by non-local penetrators were dealt with in all areas, and 5.22 million traffic violations were handled on an inter-provincial basis. The traffic control internet service platform and traffic control "12123" cell phone APP were used comprehensively, and internet users reached 360 million. Online services reached 2.4 billion times. The new policy was introduced for changing and renewing Hong Kong and Macao residents' entry and exit permits in the mainland and made it possible for Hong Kong and Macao residents and overseas Chinese to enjoy 35 types of services in nine areas such as transportation, education, medical care by producing entry and exit documents.

- Deepening the standardization of law enforcement

General Secretary Xi Jinping's important instructions on promoting strict, standardized, fair and appropriate law enforcement was fully implemented. Persistent efforts were made to deepen the standardization of law enforcement. In August, the NPC Standing Committee heard and reviewed the report on the standardization of law enforcement by public security organs, and fully affirmed the effectiveness of the standardization of law enforcement by public security organs. Great efforts were made to promote the revision of laws in the fields of punishment of crimes against public security, road traffic safety, anti-organized crime, cybercrime prevention and control, and immigration management. The development of law enforcement and case handling management centers was promoted, 2,167 such centers were established nationwide, and 28 provinces, autonomous regions and municipalities directly under the central government introduced development standards, work norms and management and operation systems. Supervision was organized for the prominent problems facing nationwide public secretary organs' online law enforcement inspection and the acceptance and filing of criminal cases, rectifying outstanding problems in law enforcement and case handling. Continuous efforts were made to strengthen and improve the management of law enforcement in detention centers, and lawyers' visits to clients were protected and served in accordance with the law. Extensive combat training was carried out to enhance the legal and law enforcement capabilities of the police. Efforts were made to continue to implement the law enforcement qualification examination system, a total of 1.805 million police officers in service nationwide obtained the basic level of law enforcement qualifications, and 60,000 police officers in service obtained senior law enforcement qualifications.

6. Judicial administration work

- Prison work

In 2020, the security and stability of prisons nationwide continued to improve, with no escape of criminals for the second consecutive year. The integration of cultural education and vocational skills training for criminals into local government plans was promoted. The system of commutation, parole, and temporary execution outside prison was further improved, and more than 600 prisons nationwide completed IT-based platforms for handling cases relating to commutation and parole. All prisons worked to make their affairs transparent, promoted law-based prison governance and constantly improved the credibility of prison law enforcement. Measures were strengthened for the prevention and control of the Covid-19 epidemic. Work was done to incorporate prisons into the local joint Covid-19 prevention and control mechanism, 99.3% of the country's prisons achieved zero infection, and all confirmed cases were cured.

- Community correction work

The Community Correction Law of the People's Republic of China was conscientiously studied and implemented. The Measures for the Implementation of the Community Correction Law of the People's Republic of China were developed. The institutions and mechanisms for community correction were improved in accordance with the law. Community correction institutions and teams were strengthened. Public participation was actively guided. The development of a unified and coordinated punishment execution system that coordinates custodial and non-custodial penalties was accelerated, efforts were made to constantly make community correction work more standard, detailed, and IT-based. As of the end of 2020, the country accepted 530,000 new offenders for community correction, completed community correction for 558,000 offenders, and there are now 645,000 offenders receiving community correction. China now has accepted a total of 5,371,000 offenders for community corrections and completed community correction for 4,726,000 offenders, and the recidivism rate during correction has been at a relatively low level of about 0.2%. Community correction agencies around the year completed a total of 2,753,000 cases of investigation and evaluation, to give 30,061 warnings to offenders receiving community correction for their violation of law, 1,820 punishments were meted out for crime, 3,272 people had their probation revoked, 61 people had their parole revoked, and 1,399 people were admitted to prison for offenders on provisional release.

- Judicial administrative drug rehabilitation work

All efforts were made to promote the establishment of a unified basic model of judicial administrative drug rehabilitation work. Rehabilitation training guidelines were introduced. The systems and standards for the operation of the unified model were improved, and assessment and acceptance work was arranged. The drug rehabilitation project based on one education and drug rehabilitation resource bank, 40 superior education and treatment programs, 100 education and treatment experts and 4,000 drug treatment cases was deepened. Superior education and drug rehabilitation projects were upgraded. Rehabilitation training was made more professional. The "year of consolidation of medical work in drug rehabilitation facilities" was conducted. There was active involvement in the development of regional medical associations, medical communities and specialist alliances. The capacity and level of medical work in drug rehabilitation facilities were improved comprehensively. Drug rehabilitation facilities were strengthened. Intelligent drug rehabilitation was improved. The theoretical research and external publicity of drug rehabilitation were deepened. Great efforts were made to improve the ability of drug rehabilitation officers to perform their duties. By the end of 2020, there were 381 drug rehabilitation facilities for interpretation administration nationwide, which had accepted and treated a total of nearly 1.57 million drug addicts. There were zero Covid-19 infections in drug rehabilitation facilities for judicial administration nationwide.

- Developing the public legal service system

The three platforms of physical, hotline and network public legal services platforms were integrated, and the public awareness rate, preferred rate and satisfaction rate were further enhanced. A sound mechanism for the government to purchase legal services was established and funding for public legal services was improved. By the end of 2020, 566,000 physical public legal service platforms had been built at the provincial, prefectural (city), county (district), township (town) and village levels.

- Work related to lawyers

The Guidelines on Public Interest Legal Services of Lawyers for Business Reopening. The initiative to provide legal services to private enterprises was carried out. Guiding cases were written about lawyers' public interest legal services for the Covid-19 epidemic prevention and control and business reopening to guide lawyers in actively serving the epidemic prevention and control and economic and social development. During the epidemic outbreak, more than 3,300 public interest legal service groups and professional service groups of lawyers were formed, and nearly 20,000 legality reviews and legal arguments were provided for the decisions of Party committee and government on epidemic prevention and control, and more than 700,000 legal consultations and rule of law publicity activities were carried out for the public. The pilot work of lawyer mediation was promoted, setting up more than 8,600 lawyer mediation centers and incorporating more than 9,500 law firms and more than 49,000 lawyer mediators into the list of mediators. The pilot project of full coverage of lawyer's defense in criminal cases was deepened. A total of 2,368 counties (cities and districts) nationwide carried out the pilot project, and courts made legal aid available in 591,000 cases due to the expanded pilot project. The "legal aid to Tibet" activities were organized, during which, 74 excellent lawyers were selected to provide legal aid and public welfare legal services in Tibet's counties without lawyers. By the end of 2020, the number of law firms nationwide had reached more than 34,000, up 5.7% year-on-year, and the total number of lawyers had been 504,000, up 10.7% year-on-year.

- Notary public, legal aid and arbitration

The reform of the notary system was deepened to stimulate the vitality of the notary industry. By the end of 2020, there had been more than 13,000 notaries nationwide, and they handled than 11 million notarial matters in the year. The legal aid system was improved. In collaboration with relevant authorities, the Ministry of Human Resources and Social Security issued the Guidelines on Further Strengthening the Legal Aid to Labor Personnel Dispute Mediation and Arbitration. The Legal Aid Duty Lawyers' Work Methods were issued. Peer assessment rules for the quality of criminal and civil administrative legal aid cases were introduced. In 2020, a total of 1.4 million legal aid cases were handled, and 15 million legal consultations were provided to 2.16 million people from different sectors. The amendment to the Arbitration Law was promoted and the legal system of arbitration was improved. The development of an international commercial arbitration center was promoted. The reform of the internal governance structure of arbitration institutions was carried out. The establishment of the China Arbitration Association was promoted. The regulatory system combining administrative guidance and industry self-regulation was improved. In 2020, 263 arbitration institutions nationwide handled more than 400,000 civil and commercial cases, with a total case value of more than 700 billion yuan.

- People's mediation and judicial stations' work

Conflicts and disputes involving the Covid-19 epidemic were investigated and resolved. The National Standard for People's Mediation Work was issued. The development of the mediation platform and international commercial mediation organizations in the Guangdong-Hong Kong-Macao Greater Bay Area was promoted. By the end of 2020, there had been 708,000 people's mediation committees and 3.209 million people's mediators nationwide. In the year, 4.709 million disputes were investigated and 8.196 million disputes were mediated. The work of judicial stations was coordinated in the new era. Real work was done to effectively improve the work network and enrich the workforce, and judicial stations continued to improve their work capacity and service level, gave full play to their its functions, and played an important role in maintaining social harmony and stability, and promoting grassroots social governance. At present, there are 39,000 judicial stations nationwide, with a staff of more than 140,000 people.

- The unified national legal qualification examination

Continued efforts were made to reform and improve the content and manner of legal professional qualification examinations, in order to make examination-based personnel promotions more scientific and effective. Conscientious work was done to organize the legal professional qualification examination while adhering to routine Covid-19 control measures, the Guidelines on Organizing the Unified National Legal Professional Qualification Examination While Adhering to Routine Covid-19 Control Measures. More than 708,000 people registered for the examination. The management behavior of legal professional qualification services was standardized by introducing the Measures for Legal Professional Qualification Management. Research was conducted to promote the establishment of a unified pre-job training system for legal professionals.

- Judicial appraisal work

Great efforts were made to promote the reform of the judicial appraisal management system. The Guidelines on Improving the Quality and Credibility of Judicial Appraisal were issued. Regulations on the classification of forensic, physical evidence and audio-visual data for judicial appraisals were introduced. A sound record and reporting system for interfering with judicial appraisals and a sound management system for appraisers to testify in court were established. By the end of 2020, there had been more than 3,100 judicial appraisal institutions registered with and managed by judicial administrative organs nationwide with more than 38,000 appraisers.

V. Legal Protection of Human Rights

In 2020, in the face of the sudden Covid-19 outbreak, China put the people and human life above all else. It took the strictest and most thorough possible measures to prevent and control the epidemic, made every effort to save and treat patients, coordinated epidemic prevention and control and economic and social development, comprehensively protected the rights and interests of the people, and promoted the development of China's human rights.

1. Safeguarding the right to life

- Reducing poverty

Poverty eradication is the top priority in China's human rights protection, and China has always attached great importance to poverty reduction. In February 2020, the CPC Central Committee and the State Council issued the Guidelines on Grasping the Key Work related to, Agriculture, Rural Areas, and Farmers to Ensure the Achievement of Moderate Prosperity in All Respects on Schedule, setting the two major goals of completing a moderately prosperous society and winning the battle against poverty. The State Council Leading Group for Poverty Alleviation and Development singled out for poverty alleviation the 52 counties nationwide that had not emerged out of poverty by the end of 2019 and the 1,113 poverty-stricken villages with more 1,000 impoverished people each or with a poverty rate of more than 10%. The outstanding problems, which restricted poverty alleviation efforts, were solved in a timely manner to ensure that all the remaining impoverished people and counties are lifted out poverty. In June, the General Office of the Ministry of Human Resources and Social Security issued the Circular on Doing Poverty Alleviation Work through Improving Skills While Adhering to Routine Covid-19 Control Measures, guiding all localities in taking stronger and more targeted policy measures, actively overcoming the difficulties and problems faced, and effectively doing a good job in poverty alleviation through improving skills. In July, the Supreme People's Court, the Supreme People's Procuratorate and the Ministry of Public Security jointly issued the Regulations on the Rapid Return of Poverty-Related Property in Criminal Cases in Accordance with the Law to regulate the rapid return of property in the field of poverty alleviation, improve the efficiency of the use of poverty alleviation funds and promote the implementation of national policies for the benefit of the people. In August, the All-China Federation of Trade Unions (ACFTU) issued the Circular on the Allocation and Use of Central Government's Special Assistance Funds for 2020, allocating special assistance funds of 554 million yuan to support registered poor workers to relieve their hardship.

• Improving the social assistance system

In February, the Ministry of Civil Affairs and the State Council's Poverty Alleviation Office issued the Action Plan for Social Assistance to Alleviate Poverty, which requires that "no household is left out and no one is left behind." The Ministry of Civil Affairs, in conjunction with 10 departments including the Central Judicial and Law Enforcement Commission, jointly launched a special campaign to improve the quality of assistance and services for vagrants and beggars without any source of income, and to provide timely settlement procedures for eligible vagrants and beggars to escape their plight. In August, the General Office of the CPC Central Committee and the General Office of the State Council issued the Guidelines on Reforming and Improving the Social Assistance System. The guidelines are a top-level design for reforming and improving the social assistance system with a focus meeting the people's basic needs and achieving high-quality development of social assistance. The guidelines are designed to coordinate development of the social assistance system and promote the development of a new pattern of social assistance.

2. Protecting of the right to life and health

- Actively fighting against the epidemic

In the face of the once-in-a-century Covid-19 epidemic, China put the people and human life before everything else. It promptly set up a central leading group to deal with the epidemic, dispatched a central steering group, established a joint prevention and control mechanism under the State Council, and quickly formed a unified command, comprehensive deployment and multifaceted prevention and control strategic layout nationwide. The country took the strictest and most thorough possible epidemic prevention and control measures and made every effort to treat patients. It took more than one month to initially contain the epidemic, about two months to keep the daily number of new cases in China to within single digits, and about three months to achieve decisive results in the defense of Wuhan and the rest of Hubei. And then the country fought several localized epidemic wipeouts in succession to protect people's lives and health to the maximum extent.

- Improving the food and drug systems

In January, the State Administration of Market Regulation, the Ministry of Education, the National Health Commission, and the Ministry of Public Security jointly issued the Guidelines on the Implementation of the Main Responsibility to Strengthen School Food Safety Management to protect school food safety. In March, the CPC Central Committee and the State Council issued guidelines on deepening the reform of the medical insurance system, putting forward guidelines on solving the problem of unbalanced and insufficient development of medical insurance. In July, the General Office of the State Council issued the Key Tasks for Deepening the Reform of the Medical and Health System in the Second Half of 2020, requiring the strengthening of the concept of greater health, effectively strengthening the planning and organization and leadership of efforts to deepen medical reform, coordinating the work of adhering to routine Covid-19 control measures and deepening medical reform. In December, the Amendment to the Criminal Law (XI), adopted at the 24th Meeting of the NPC Standing Committee, improved the relevant provisions on drug-related crimes, stipulating that where the personnel of the drug-using units knowingly provide others with counterfeit or substandard drugs, produce or sell drugs prohibited for use by the drug regulatory department under the State Council in violation of the drug administration laws and regulations, produce or import drugs without obtaining relevant drug approval documents, or sell the above-mentioned drugs knowingly, and whoever provides false certificates, data, materials or samples, or adopts other deceptive means, or fabricates production or inspection records during drug application registration shall bear criminal responsibility in accordance with the law.

3. Protecting labor and employment rights and interests

- Protecting migrant workers' labor rights and interests

In 2020, the procuratorial organs combatted the "malicious non-payment of wages" and other crimes of refusal to pay labor remuneration as one of the important measures to serve and safeguard efforts to fight the "three major battles." In August, 15 departments including the Ministry of Human Resources and Social Security and the National Development and Reform Commission issued the Guidelines on the Current Employment and Startup of Migrant Workers, proposing measures to improve the employment and startup of migrant workers, such as widening employment channels, promoting local employment, strengthening equal employment services and protecting rights and interests, and giving priority to ensuring stable employment of poor laborers.

• Supporting employment and promoting the realization of the right to work through multiple channels

In July, in accordance with the requirements of the executive meeting of the State Council on promoting the employment of college graduates, the central government allocated 9.45 billion yuan to support the special posting program for rural teachers. In the same monitor, three departments including the General Office of the Ministry of Education jointly issued the Report on the Employment of College Graduate from 52 Poor Counties That Have Not Emerged from Poverty, further clarifying the focus of work and comprehensively enhancing the precision and effectiveness of employment assistance for graduates from poor families. Also in July, the General Office of the State Council issued the Guidelines of the General Office of the State Council on Supporting Multi-Channel Flexible Employment, which put forward specific policies and measures in three aspects: employment development channels, the business environment and employment guarantees.

4. Protecting of the right to education

In June, the Ministry of Education issued the Guidelines on Strengthening the Work of Ensuring Children with Disabilities in Accept Compulsory Education Together with Their Peers, putting forward guidelines on further strengthening the work ensuring children with disabilities attending classes together with their peers in the new era and improving the work mechanism of those children studying together with their peers to promote the fair and quality development of special education. Also in June, 10 departments including the Ministry of Education jointly issued the Guidelines on Further Strengthening the Work of Controlling School Dropouts and Improving the Long-Term Mechanism for Ensuring Compulsory Education, requiring all localities to strengthen the organization and guarantee to better protect the rights of school-age children to accept compulsory education. In July, the Ministry of Finance allocated 29.35 billion yuan of subsidies for improving the weak links and enhancing the capacity of compulsory education in 2020, and continued to support localities in largely eliminating the problem of excessively large class sizes in urban schools, and basically strengthening the areas of weakness of small-scale rural schools and township boarding schools. In August, five departments including the Ministry of Education issued the Guidelines on Further Strengthening and Regulating the Management of Education Fees, requiring further improvement of the policies, systems and regulation of education fees, continued consolidation of the achievements in the management of education fees, and the promotion of the fair and quality development of education. In December, the Ministry of Education promulgated the Rules on Educational Discipline in Primary and Secondary Schools (for Trial Implementation), which for the first time provide for educational discipline in the form of departmental regulations, aiming to bring educational discipline into the rule of law and better ensure schools fully implement the Party's education policy and the fundamental task of establishing moral education.

5. Protecting the rights and interests of veterans

In January, 20 departments including the State Council and the Ministry of Veterans Affairs jointly issued the Guidelines on Strengthening the Preferential Treatment of Military Personnel and Their Families, Veterans and Others Entitled to Preferential Treatment, requiring efforts to standardize the content of preferential treatment, improve the management mechanism, establish a preferential treatment certificate system, clarify the catalogue of preferential treatment, improve incentives and punishments, and strive to ensure that those entitled to preferential treatment are respected in the whole of society and make military service a profession respected in the whole of society. In October, the General Office of the Ministry of Education issued the Circular on Further Improving the Recruitment, Training and Management of Ex-Servicemen Students in Higher Vocational Schools, requiring the enhancement of technical skills and employment and startup abilities of ex-servicemen to promote their full and stable employment. In November, the 23rd Meeting of the Standing Committee of the 13th NPC adopted the Law of the People's Republic of China on the Protection of Veterans, which systematically provides for veterans' transfer and acceptance of veterans, retirement and resettlement, education and training, employment and startup, preferential treatment and pensions, and commendation and incentive, strengthens the protection of veterans and safeguards their legitimate rights and interests.

6. Protecting of the rights and interests of specific groups

- Protecting the rights and interests of women and children

In January, the Supreme People's Procuratorate and the All-China Women's Federation jointly issued the Circular on Establishing Cooperation Mechanisms to Promote the Protection of Women's and Children's Rights and Interests, which called for strengthening the punishment and combating of crimes against women and children's rights and interests, promoting the development of a social support system for the judicial protection of minors, and promoting the improvement of the legal system for the protection of women and children. In March, the Joint Prevention and Control Mechanism of the State Council issued the Work Plan for the Relief and Protection of Children without Guardianship due to the Covid-19 Epidemic to make arrangements for the further improvement of the relief and protection of children without guardianship due to the Covid-19 epidemic. The General Office of the Ministry of Civil Affairs and the General Office of the Ministry of Education issued the Circular on Coordinating the Work Related to the Prevention and Control of the Covid-19 Epidemic and the Resumption of Work and Schooling in the

Field of Children's Welfare. The circular requires localities to promptly identify, report and classify and deal with children without guardianship due to the Covid-19 epidemic, and ensure that the basic livelihood and care of this group of children is basically guaranteed. In May, the Supreme People's Procuratorate issued the Guidelines of the Supreme People's Procuratorate on Strengthening the Procuratorial Work for Minors in the New Era, which provide guidance on strengthening the procuratorial work for minors in the new era. Also in May, nine departments including the Supreme People's Procuratorate jointly issued the Guidelines on Establishing a Compulsory Reporting System for Cases of Infringement on Minors (for Trial Implementation) to effectively strengthen comprehensive and integrated judicial protection for minors and punish crimes against minors promptly and effectively. In May, the Civil Code adopted by vote at the Third Session of the 13th NPC focused on safeguarding the rights and interests of women and minors, clarifying the obligation of the two parties to inform each other of major diseases before marriage and establishing a cooling-off period for divorce and improving the legal system related to adoption to strengthen the protection of women and minors. In June, the Supreme People's Procuratorate released the White

Paper on the Prosecution of Minors (2014-2019), which comprehensively summarizes the judicial protection work for minors by procuratorial organs nationwide from 2014 to 2019 and demonstrates the specific practices and prominent results in the procuratorial work for minors. In October, the 22nd Meeting of the Standing Committee of the 13th NPC revised and adopted the Law on the Protection of Minors, improving protection from six major sources: the family, the school, societies, networks, the government, and the judiciary, and enhancing the level of legal protection of minors. In December, the 24th Meeting of the Standing Committee of the 13th NPC revised and revised and adopted the Law on the Prevention of Juvenile Delinquency, which clarifies the principles and mechanisms for preventing juvenile delinquency. The meeting also adopted the Amendment to the Criminal Law (XI). The amendment stipulates that, "Where a person has sex with a young girl under the age of 14, he shall be considered to have raped her and shall be punished with a heavier penalty." It adds the crime of sexual assault by persons with special duties. The crime of sexual assault, providing that, "A person who has special responsibilities for the guardianship, adoption, care, education, medical treatment of a female minor, who has reached the age of fourteen but is less than sixteen years old, has sexual relations with the female minor" shall be given criminal penalties. The amendment further clarifies the circumstances of applying heavier penalties to the crime of child molestation.

- Protecting the rights and interests of the elderly

In May, many provisions of the Civil Code adopted with a vote at the Third Session of the 13th NPC protect the rights and interests of the elderly. First, it adds the right of residence provisions to provide legal support for the "house pension." Second, it establishes adult guardianship system, giving the maximum respect for the will of the elderly. Third, it expands the scope of bequest supporters. In November, the General Office of the State Council issued the Plan on Effectively Solving the Difficulties of the Elderly in Using Intelligent Technology. To further promote the solution of the difficulties encountered by the elderly in using intelligent technology, the plan proposes to ensure that both traditional service methods and intelligent service innovation are available at the same time, and provides more comprehensive, more intimate and more direct facilitation services for the elderly. In December, nine departments including the Ministry of Civil Affairs issued the Guidelines on Accelerating the Implementation of the Project to for Retrofitting Homes for Aging for the Elderly, aiming to promote the improvement of home living care conditions for the elderly around the country, make home living facilities safer and more convenient and comfortable, and improve the quality of home elderly care services.

• Protecting the rights and interests of people with disabilities

In the battle against poverty, China has always included the poverty eradication of poor people with disabilities, constantly strengthening the top-level design and improving special support measures. By the end of 2020, China has steadily achieved the goal of ensuring poor people with disabilities and their families have their basic needs met and have access to compulsory education, basic medical care and safe housing. Over the past five years, more than 7 million registered poor people with disabilities have been lifted out of poverty as scheduled, with an annual average more than 1 million people emerging from private, creating a miracle in the history of human poverty reduction for people with disabilities.

In May, more than 30 articles of the Civil Code adopted with a vote at the Third Session of the 13th NPC protect directly provide for protecting the rights and interests of people with disabilities. The Civil Code has built the institutions and mechanisms for protecting the civil rights of persons with disabilities in China by giving them equal protection of civil rights and interests, civil capacity correction and support, inclined protection of civil rights and introduction of social responsibility, in order to ensure that persons with disabilities equally enjoy and exercise civil rights. In September, the Call to Action: Empowering Women and Girls with Disabilities for the Future We Want, initiated by China Disabled Persons' Federation and jointly supported by UN ESCAP, UN Women, UNFPA and Rehabilitation International, was released, urging governments and the international community to further integrate guaranteeing equal rights for women and girls with disabilities and promoting inclusive development into the Convention on the Elimination of All Forms of Discrimination against Women (CEDAW), the Convention on the Rights of Persons with Disabilities and the United Nations 2030 Agenda for Sustainable Development and all other relevant international instruments, and put forward specific recommendations for implementation in terms of life security, social security, medical care and health, education and employment, home and family, participation in public affairs and international cooperation for women and girls with disabilities. In September, the Ministry of Industry and Information Technology and the

China Disabled Persons' Federation issued the Guidelines on Promoting Information Accessibility. In October, the 22nd Meeting of the Standing Committee of the 13th NPC revised and adopted the Law on the Protection of Minors, which provides for the protection of the rights and interests of minors in need of special care, including minors with disabilities, and the right to education of minors with disabilities. In September, the Guidelines on Protecting Persons with Disabilities from Major Infectious Disease Outbreaks (for Trial Implementation) were issued. In November, the Guidelines on Social Support Services for the Protection of Persons with Disabilities from Major Infectious Disease Outbreaks (for Trial Implementation) was released, filling the gap in the guidelines on protecting persons with disabilities from major infectious disease outbreaks at the national level. In November, the National Sign Language Program of the National Anthem of the People's Republic of China (GF0024-2020) was released. This is the latest achievements in standardizing the national sign language mainly for sign language users with hearing disabilities and effectively satisfies the desire of sign language users with hearing disabilities to use the national anthem in a standard, uniform and serious manner on occasions when the national anthem is played and sung for many years.

7. Judicial protection of human rights

In January, the Supreme People's Court issued the Guidelines on Further Strengthening the Concept of Goodwilled and Appropriate Execution in Execution Work, requiring the people's courts to strengthen the concept of goodwilled and appropriate execution in the execution process, strictly regulate and fairly protect the legitimate rights and interests of all parties, and protect the legitimate rights and interests of successful parties in accordance with the law while minimizing the impact on the rights and interests of the executees. In May, the Ministry of Justice had the "Legal Aid for People's Livelihood and Poverty Alleviation" campaign carried out nationwide, putting forward 10 legal aid measures for the benefit of the people in three major areas: helping reopening, promoting the fight against poverty, and enhancing the people's sense of gain. In June, the Supreme People's Court issued the Regulations on Issues concerning the Appearance of Leaders of Administrative Organs in Court in Response to Lawsuits to further regulate the appearance of leaders of administrative organs in court in response to lawsuits and effectively protect the legitimate rights and interests of the people.

VI. Protection of Intellectual Property Rights

In 2020, China has made positive progress in solidly promoting the protection of intellectual property rights.

1. Institution building

The Patent Law of the People's Republic of China, the Copyright Law of the People's Republic of China, and the Amendment to the Criminal Law of the People's Republic of China (XI) were reviewed and adopted. The Regulations on the Transfer of Suspected Crime Cases by Administrative Law Enforcement Organs were promulgated and implemented. Revisions were made to the Rules for the Implementation of the Patent Law of the People's Republic of China and the Regulations of the People's Republic of China on the Protection of New Varieties of Plants. The General Office of the CPC Central Committee and the General Office of the State Council issued the Plan for Implementing the Guidelines on Strengthening the Protection of Intellectual Property Rights from 2020 to 2021. The Office of the Inter-Ministerial Joint Conference on the Implementation of the Intellectual Property Strategy of the State Council issued the Plan for Further Implementing the National Intellectual Property Strategy and Accelerate the Development of Intellectual Property Rights in 2020. The Office of the National Leading Group for Combating Intellectual Property Rights Infringement and the Manufacture and Sale of Counterfeit and Shoddy Goods, the Central Publicity Department, the Supreme People's Court, the Supreme People's Procuratorate, the Ministry of Public Security, the Ministry of Ecology and Environment, the Ministry of Culture and Tourism, the General Administration of Customs and the State Administration of Market Regulations jointly issued the Guidelines on Strengthening the Destruction of Infringing and Counterfeit Goods.

2. Audit and Registration

- Patents

In 2020, 530,000 invention patents were granted in China, representing a year-on-year increase of 17.1%, 2.377 million utility model patents were granted, up 50.2% year-on-year, and 732,000 design patents were granted, an increase of 31.5% year-on-year. By the end of 2020, the effective number of China's invention patents had been 3.058 million, an increase of 14.5% year-on-year. Among them, the effective number of domestic (excluding Hong Kong, Macao and Taiwan) invention patents was 2.213 million, and the number of invention patents per 10,000 people reached 15.8. The number of valid utility model patents was 6.948 million, an increase of 32.0% year-on-year. The number of valid design patents was 2.187 million, an increase of 22.2% year-on-year. The patent examination cycle remained stable, and the examination cycle for high-value patents was compressed to 14 months. In 2020, 72,000 international patent applications under the Patent Cooperation Treaty were accepted, an increase of 18.6% year-on-year; among them, 67,000 were from domestic sources, an increase of 17.9% year-on-year.

- Trade marks

In 2020, 5.761 million trademarks were registered in China, down 10.1% year-on-year. By the end of 2020, the cumulative number of trademark registrations had reached 34.475 million, and the average examination period for trademark registration was compressed to four months. In 2020, 7,553 applications for international registration of Madrid trademarks were submitted by domestic applicants, an increase of 16.4%

year-on-year, ranking third in the Madrid Union. By the end of 2020, the cumulative number of effective registrations had reached 44,223. In 2020, 24,524 Madrid territorial extension applications (converted by multiple categories of one trademark) were designated by foreign applicants to China, and the substantive examination of 62,651 categories of Madrid territorial extension applications was completed, with the examination cycle shortened to four months.

- Copyright

The total number of copyright registrations in 2020 was 5.039 million, representing a year-on-year increase of 20.37%. Among them, the registration volume of works was 3.316 million pieces, up 22.75% year-on-year; the registration volume of computer software copyright was 1.723 million pieces, up 16.06% year-on-year. The total registration volume of copyright pledges for the year was 384, involving a main debt amount of 4.06 billion yuan.

- Geographical indications, special signs and official signs

By the end of 2020, a total of 2,391 geographical indication products had been approved, 9,479 enterprises using special marks had been approved and recorded, and a total of 6,085 geographical indications had been registered as collective trademarks and certification trademarks. Ten applications for protection of geographical indication products were accepted in 2020, 6 geographical indication products were approved for protection, 765 geographical indications were registered as collective trademarks and certification trademarks, and 1,052 enterprises were approved to use special geographical indication marks. The filing of official marks related to the China International Development Cooperation Agency and the National Healthcare Security Administration was completed, and 37 special marks for the 19th Asian Games and the 4th Asian Para Games in in 2022 were approved. The 2022 Winter Olympic Games and the Winter Paralympic Games mascot, volunteer logo and seven other Olympic symbols were promulgated for protection.

- Integrated circuit layout designs

In 2020, a total of 14,375 applications for registration of IC layout designs were accepted, an increase of 72.8% year-on-year; 11,727 applications were registered and promulgated and were issued certificates, an increase of 77.3% year-on-year. By the end of 2020, a total of 46,000 applications for IC layout design registration had been accepted, and a total of 39,000 applications were registered and promulgated and were issued certificates.

3. Judicial protection

In 2020, China's courts concluded 466,000 intellectual property cases in the first instance, and introduced 10 sets of judicial interpretations and normative documents such as regulations on the evidence in civil intellectual property litigation. The Supreme People's Procuratorate set up the Intellectual Property Procuratorial Office, integrated criminal, civil and administrative procuratorial functions, and coordinated and strengthened the design and research guidance of the intellectual property protection system of the procuratorial organs.

- Strengthening intellectual property trials

In 2020, the Supreme People's Court accepted 3,470 new civil intellectual property cases and concluded 3,260 such cases. Local people's courts nationwide accepted 443,326 new civil first-instance intellectual property cases and concluded 442,722 such cases. Local people's courts nationwide accepted 42,975 new civil second-instance intellectual property cases and concluded 442,975 such cases. In 2020, the Supreme People's Court accepted 1,909 new intellectual property administrative cases and concluded 1,735 such cases; local people's courts nationwide accepted 18,464 new intellectual property administrative cases of first instance and concluded 17,942 school cases; local people's courts nationwide accepted 6,092 new intellectual property administrative cases of second instance and concluded 6,183 such cases. In 2020, local people's courts nationwide accepted a total of 5,544 new criminal cases of first instance involving intellectual property rights and concluded 5,520 such cases; local people's courts nationwide accepted 869 new criminal cases of second instance involving intellectual property rights and concluded 854 such cases.

- Increasing efforts to combat criminal intellectual property crimes

In 2020, the Kunlun 2020 special campaign was carried out to as an important part of the efforts to combat intellectual property crime. Also in 2020, more than 21,000 cases of infringement of intellectual property rights and the manufacture and sale of counterfeit and shoddy goods were detected, with more than 32,000 suspects arrested and a total value of more than 18 billion yuan involved. More than 41,000 execution actions were conducted against physical markets and more than 260 activities were organized to destroy infringing and counterfeit goods.

- Strictly approving the arrest of suspects of intellectual property crimes in accordance with the law

In 2020, procuratorial authorities nationwide approved the arrest of 7,174 suspects of 3,930 IPR-related crimes, and prosecuted 12,152 persons in 5,848 cases. To break up, 2,879 persons were arrested in 1,509 cases of counterfeit of registered trademarks, and 4,891 others were prosecuted in 2,290 similar cases; persons were prosecuted; 2,970 persons were arrested in 1,745 cases of selling counterfeit registered trademarks and 4,947 others persons were prosecuted in 2,496 similar cases; 498 persons were arrested in 270 cases of illegally manufacturing and selling illegally manufactured registered trademarks and 972 others were prosecuted in 403 similar cases; 366 persons were arrested in 203 cases of copyright infringement and 653 others were prosecuted in 274 similar cases; 19 people were arrested in 12 cases of the crime of selling infringing copies and 26 others were prosecuted in similar cases; 52 people were arrested for in 30 cases of infringing trade secrets and 50 others were prosecuted in 30 similar cases; 390 people were arrested in 161 cases of several crimes or other crimes including infringement of intellectual property rights and 612 others were prosecuted in similar cases.

- Strengthening the supervision of criminal proceedings

The procuratorial organs promptly corrected the problems of not transferring cases, not filing cases, improperly filing cases, replacing imprisonment with fines, and unfair decisions regard crimes of infringement of intellectual property rights. In 2020, at the suggestion of the procuratorial organs, administrative law enforcement organs transfer 228 cases of suspected crimes of infringement of intellectual property rights involving 262 people; upon the supervision of the procuratorial organs, the public security organs filed 181 cases involving 230 people and supervised the withdrawal of 243 cases for 304 people. Trial supervision was conducted and erroneous criminal verdicts were reversed in accordance with the law, second instance protests and trial supervision protests were lodged in a total of 57 cases, and the courts changed the sentences of 15 cases for 18 persons.

4. Administrative law enforcement

- Strengthening the administrative protection of patents

A special law enforcement and protection campaign was carried out to severely investigate and deal with patent infringement and counterfeiting violations. In 2020, the market regulation authorities network nationwide investigated and handled 7,100 million cases of patent counterfeiting. The intellectual property management authorities handled more than 42,000 cases of administrative adjudication of patent infringement disputes, an increase of 9.9% year-on-year.

● Strengthened trademark administrative law enforcement protection

In 2020, the market regulation authorities investigated and handled 31,300 trademark violation cases, with a value of 790 million yuan and a confiscation amount of 700 million yuan. This included 29,600 cases of trademark infringement and counterfeiting, with a case value of 765 million yuan and a confiscation amount of 67,800 yuan. In 2020, 811 cases of suspected trademark infringement crimes were transferred to judicial organs in accordance with the law.

● Strengthening administrative law enforcement of copyright protection

The "Swordnet 2020" special operation was launched to crack down on copyright infringement and piracy in the fields of audiovisual works, e-commerce platforms, social networking platforms and online education, and regulate the order of copyright dissemination on online platforms, and continuously consolidate the results of the special control program. A total of 3,239,400 infringing and pirated links were removed nationwide, 2,884 infringing and pirated websites (APPs) were shut down, and 724 cases of online infringement and piracy were investigated and handled, including 177 criminal cases involving 301 million yuan, and 925 cases of online copyright disputes were mediated.

- Strengthening the protection of administrative law enforcement against unfair competition

With a focus on people's lives and staying problem-oriented, a special law enforcement operation was launched against anti-unfair competition. The supervision and law enforcement of the Internet and other key areas were strengthened to combat counterfeit, false advertising, infringement of trade secrets and other unfair competition actions, to maintain a fair competitive market order in accordance with the law, and to protect the legitimate rights and interests of operators and consumers. In 2020, a total of 7,371 cases of unfair competition were investigated and handled during the special operation, with a value of 2.76 billion yuan and a confiscation of 416 million yuan.

- Strengthening the protection of administrative law enforcement for new varieties of plants

Actions were carried out against infringement of new plant variety rights, focusing on supervision of various seedlings, flower fairs and trade fairs, and crack down on the production or sale of propagation materials of forestry authorized varieties without the permission of the variety owners, counterfeit forestry authorized varieties, and the sale of forestry authorized varieties without using their registered names in accordance with the law. Special sampling inspection of seed market in spring, summer, autumn and winter was conducted to purify the market environment of the seed industry.

- Strengthening the protection of customs law enforcement

In 2020, IPR protection measures were taken 65,300 times, 61,900 batches of suspected import and export infringing goods were seized, representing a year-on-year increase of 20.11%, and the number of goods involved was 56,181,900, representing a year-on-year increase of 20.07%. This protected the legitimate rights and interests of nearly 1,000 IPR rights holders in 45 countries and regions.

- Strengthening the protection of administrative law enforcement of the network market

The online inspection working group for online performance market was established. The group conducted online enforcement inspection and reviewed online performance APPs 1,623 times. Centralized law enforcement inspection and special inspection were carried out, investigating and dealing with 42 illegal online performance platforms and seven online music websites in accordance with the law, finding and removed from the internet 940 illegal songs, and assisting relevant units in closing seven illegal online animation websites.

5. International cooperation

● Actively participating in multilateral and bilateral consultations and international rule-making

China deeply participated in global intellectual property governance under the framework of the World Intellectual Property Organization (WIPO). Efforts were made to bring into force on April 28, 2020, of the Beijing Treaty on Audiovisual Performances, the first international intellectual property treaty concluded in China and named after a Chinese city since the founding of the People's Republic of China. The negotiations on the intellectual property chapter of the Regional Comprehensive Economic Partnership Agreement (RCEP) were completed, promoting the formal signing of the agreement. President Xi Jinping and European leaders promulgated the official signing of the Agreement between the Government of the People's Republic of China and the European Union on Cooperation on, and Protection of,

Geographical Indications. China's procedures for ratification of the Marrakesh Treaty to Facilitate Access to Published Works for Persons who are Blind, Visually Impair were launched. Accession to the Hague Agreement concerning the International Registration of Industrial Designs was promoted. The negotiation process of the World Intellectual Property Organization's Treaty on the Protection of Broadcasting Organizations and the Treaty on the Protection of Traditional Cultural Expressions was advanced.

● Actively participating in international conferences and forums and contributing more Chinese solutions

Chinese representatives actively participated in conference of the World Trade Organization (WTO) Council on Trade-Related Aspects of Intellectual Property Rights (TRIPS) and related meetings, and introduced to WTO members China's IPR-related initiatives in response to the Covid-19 epidemic. At important meetings such as the Special Session of the World Intellectual Property Congress of the International Association for the Protection of Industrial Property (AIPPI) and the World Intellectual Property Challenge Forum of the Group of 20 (G20), Chinese representatives discussed with various parties on policies and remedies in response to the Covid-19 epidemic, and advocated the use of the unique advantages of intellectual property rights to promote global innovation and economic recovery. China hosted for the first time the 13th IP5 Heads of Office Meeting by video, and adopted the 2020 IP5 Joint Statement. Chinese representatives participated in TM5 and ID5 annual meetings. China hosted or co-hosted the 12th Meeting of BRICS Heads of Intellectual Property Offices, the 11th Meeting of China-ASEAN Heads of Intellectual Property Offices, the 20th China-Japan-South Korea IP Office Directors' Meeting, and the 8th China-Mongolia-Russia Intellectual Property Symposium.

- Strengthening judicial exchange and cooperation and joint law enforcement actions

The World Intellectual Property Organization (WIPO) Arbitration and Mediation Center provided arbitration and mediation services for foreign-related IPR disputes in the Lingang New Area of the Shanghai Pilot Free Trade Zone. China actively sent representatives to participate in the WIPO International Forum on Intellectual Property for Judges and the 2020 International IP Court Conference to publicize China's IP judicial protection achievements and enhance its international influence.

China co-organized the Forum on International Cooperation in Fighting against IPR Infringement and Counterfeiting with the World Intellectual Property Organization during the Third China International Import Expo in November 2020. China organized a China-Europe online seminar on Enforcement of Plant Variety Rights. China conducted multilevel law enforcement cooperation with law enforcement departments of relevant countries on 46 key cross-border cases about lead verification, evidence exchange, joint operations and judicial assistance. At the invitation of Interpol, China continued to participate in the Operation Eagle to combat intellectual property crimes on the internet, achieving positive results and winning the understanding and support of the international community.

VII. Building the Rule of Law in Ecological Civilization

In 2020, legislation, law enforcement and justice in China actively served the development of ecological civilization with new results.

1. Ecological civilization legislation

- Issuing a number of guiding documents

In March, the General Office of the CPC Central Committee and the General Office of the State Council issued the Guidelines on Building a Modern Environmental Governance System, which explicitly build a systematic modern environmental governance system led by the Party committee and dominated by the government and with the enterprises as the main players and with the participation of social organizations and the public. In April, the 13th meeting of the Central Commission for Comprehensively Deepening Reform reviewed and adopted six documents, including the Master Plan for Major Projects for the Protection and Restoration of National Important

Ecosystems (2021-2035), to promote ecological protection and restoration. Also in April, the General Office of the CPC Central Committee and the General Office of the State Council issued the Measures for Assessing the Effectiveness of in Pollution Prevention and Control Battles in Provinces, Autonomous Regions and Municipalities Directly under the Central Government, which make clear the contents of the assessment of the effectiveness of the battles against pollution by Party committees, people's congresses and governments in all provinces, autonomous regions, and municipalities directly under the central government. In October, the Fifth Plenary Session of the 19th CPC Central Committee considered and adopted the Recommendations of the CPC Central Committee on Formulating the 14th Five-Year Plan for Economic and Social Development and the Long-Range Objectives through 2035 (hereinafter referred to as the "Recommendations"), which pointed out that during the 14th Five-Year Plan period, China would take "making fresh progress in ecological civilization" as a principle that must be followed in promoting economic and social development, focus on building a system for promoting ecological progress, improve the mechanism for coordinating ecological progress, and establish sound various systems, laws and regulations for ecological civilization. In

November, the 16th meeting of the Central Commission for Comprehensively Deepening Reform considered and adopted the Guidelines on Comprehensively Implementing the Forest Chief System, further ascertaining the principal responsibility of local Party committees and governments at all levels to protect and develop forest and grassland resources.

- Formulating, amending and repealing a number of laws, regulations and rules related to environmental resources protection

At the legal level, in February, the NPC Standing Committee considered and adopted the Decision on a Complete Ban of Illegal Wildlife Trade and the Elimination of the Unhealthy Habit of Indiscriminate Wild Animal Meat Consumption for the Protection of Human Life and Health, which provides strong legislative safeguards to comprehensively ban wild animal meat consumption, crack down on illegal wildlife trade, and prevent and control public health and safety risks at source. In April, at the 17th Meeting of the Standing Committee of the 13th NPC, the Law of the People's Republic of China on the Prevention and Control of Environmental Pollution by Solid Waste was revised and passed, clarifying the state's implementation of the household waste classification system and establishing the principles of household waste classification. The law strengthened environmental supervision over industrial solid waste and hazardous waste, improved the systems for preventing and controlling environmental pollution such as construction waste and agricultural solid waste, and strengthened the legal responsibility for illegal acts. In May, the Civil Code of the People's Republic of China was adopted at the Third Session of the 13th NPC, clarifying the green principle that "When conducting a civil activity, a person of the civil law shall act in a manner that facilitates conservation of resources and protection of the ecological environment" as well as stipulating the obligations and legal responsibilities for environmental protection that persons of the civil law shall undertake when engaging in civil activities. In October, the 22nd Meeting of the Standing Committee of the 13th NPC adopted the Biosafety Law of the People's Republic of China, which is a basic, comprehensive, systematic and overarching law in the field of biosafety, systematically sorting out and comprehensively regulating various types of biosafety risks, clarifying the institutional mechanism and basic system of biosafety risk prevention and control, and filling the gap of basic laws in the field of biosafety. In December, the 24th Meeting of the Standing Committee of the 13th National People's Congress adopted the

Amendment to the Criminal Law (XI), which increased the penalties for the crime of polluting the environment and raised the statutory penalties, criminalized the acts of "falsifying" environmental assessments and environmental monitoring, destroying nature reserves, illegally introducing, releasing and discarding invasive alien species, and added the crimes of illegal hunting, harvesting, transporting and selling of terrestrial species. The Law of the People's Republic of China on the Protection of the Yangtze River, the first special law to protect the entire Yangtze River basin ecosystem and promote the green and high-quality development of the Yangtze River Economic Belt, was passed to address the major issues of regional coordination, and provide comprehensive regulations on planning and control, resource protection, water pollution prevention and control, ecological and environmental restoration, green development, protection and supervision.

At the level of government regulations and departmental rules, in March, the 86th Executive Meeting of the State Council adopted the Regulations on Crop Pest Control, providing a legal basis for pest control. In December, the 117th Executive Meeting of the State Council adopted the Regulations on Emission Permit Management, regulating the application and approval procedures for emission permits, requiring emission units to establish a ledger system and strengthen ongoing and ex-post supervision, and providing a legal basis for ensuring fixed sources of pollution discharge emissions in accordance with the permit and regulate them in accordance with the permit. In April, the Ministry of Ecology and Environment promulgated the Measures for the Registration of Environmental Management of New Chemical Substances, which regulates the conduct of environmental management registration of new chemical substances and scientific and effective assessment and control of environmental risks of new chemical substances, focusing on new chemical substances that may pose greater risks to the environment and health; the Measures for the Environmental Management of New Chemical Substances issued by the former Ministry of Environmental Protection was repealed. In May, the Ministry of Transportation promulgated the Measures for the Management of High-speed Railway Safety Protection, highlighting the responsibility of strengthening the inspection and supervision of the authorities of ecology and environment for production activities engaged in the emission of dust, smoke and corrosive gases near high-speed railroads. In July, the Ministry of Agriculture and Rural Affairs promulgated the Measures for the Management of Agricultural Films, establishing a sound management system of agricultural films and building a full-chain regulatory system. In August, the Ministry of Agriculture and Rural Affairs and the Ministry of Ecology and Environment promulgated the Measures for the Management of Pesticide Packaging Waste Recycling, which aims to prevent pesticide packaging waste pollution, protect public health and safeguard the ecological environment. In November, the Ministry of Ecology and Environment promulgated the Regulations of the Ministry of Ecology and Environment on the Approval Process of Environmental Impact Reports (Forms) for Construction Projects to standardize the approval process of environmental impact reports and environmental impact forms for construction projects and to improve the efficiency and service level of the approval process. In December, the Ministry of Ecology and Environment promulgated the Measures for the Management of Ecological and Environmental Standards to clarify the formulation, implementation, filing and evaluation of ecological and environmental standards. In the same month, the Ministry of Ecology and Environment promulgated the Measures for the Management of Carbon Emissions Trading (for Trial Implementation) to regulate the national carbon emissions trading and related activities.

In 2020, positive results were also achieved in

environmental resources legislation across the country. The 13th Meeting of the Standing Committee of the 13th Jiangsu Provincial People's Congress adopted the Jiangsu Province Ecological and Environmental Monitoring Regulations, which are the first local regulations on ecological and environmental monitoring in China. The 20th Meeting of the Standing Committee of the Fifth Chongqing Municipal People's Congress adopted the Chongqing Municipal Water Pollution Prevention and Control Regulations. The 44th Meeting of the Sixth Standing Committee of the Shenzhen Municipal People's Congress adopted the Regulations on Ecological and Environmental Public Welfare Litigation in the Shenzhen Special Economic Zone.

• Developing and revising a number of technical specifications related to environmental resources

In 2020, China issued 184 environmental protection-related documents and 122 national environmental standards. In March, the State Forestry and Grassland Administration issued 52 forestry industry standards, including the Technical Specification for National Park Master Plan. Among them, the three national park industry standards—the National Park Master Plan Technical Specification, the National Park Resource Survey and Evaluation Specification, and the National Park Boundary Survey and Marking Specification, and the wo administrative license industry standards—the Forestry and Grassland Administrative License Implementation Specification and the Forestry and Grassland Administrative License Evaluation Specification were released for the first time. In August, the General Office of the Ministry of Natural Resources, the General Office of the Ministry of Finance and the General Office of the Ministry of Ecology and Environment jointly issued the Ecological Protection and Restoration Project for Mountains, Waters, Forests, Farmland, Lakes and Grassland. From September to December, the State Administration for Market Regulation (the National Standards Committee) approved the release of five national standards, namely the Specification for the Establishment of National Parks, the Technical Specification for the Master Plan of National Parks, the Specification for the Assessment and Evaluation of National Parks, the Specification for the Monitoring of National Parks, and the Specification for the Survey and Demarcation of Nature Reserves. In November, the Ministry of Ecology and Environment, the National Development and Reform Commission, the Ministry of Public Security, the Ministry of Transport, and the National Health Commission promulgated the National Hazardous Waste List (2021 Edition), and the Ministry of Ecology and Environment promulgated the

Construction Project Environmental Impact Assessment Classification Management List (2021 Edition).

2. Ecological civilization law enforcement

● Continuously promoting reforms in ecological civilization regulation

The Measures for the Management of Funds for Compensation for Ecological and Environmental Damage (for Trial Implementation) and the Guidelines on Several Specific Issues concerning the Reform of the Compensation System for Ecological and Environmental Damage to promote the reform of the compensation system for ecological and environmental damage, and 31 provinces, autonomous regions, and municipalities directly under the central government and the Xinjiang Production and Construction Corps nationwide issued provincial-level reform implementation plans. The Guidelines on the Implementation of the Reward System for Reporting Ecological and Environmental Violations, guiding the establishment and implementation of the reward systems for reporting ecological and environmental violations around the country, and promoting the reform of the ecological and environmental regulatory system. The reform of the forest chief system, forest rights collection and storage guarantee, and the integration of state-owned forest farms and the transfer of collective forest rights was carried out.

- Strengthening law enforcement in key areas

Oversight conducted through the random selection of both inspectors and inspection targets and the prompt release of results was implemented nationwide, 587,400 law enforcement inspections were carried out. Nationwide, 126,100 decisions on environmental administrative penalties were issued, with fines totaling 8.236 billion yuan. The Ministry of Ecology and Environment set up a leading group for addressing public complaints and proposals and reporting and its office to promote the reform of the mechanism for handling public complaints and proposals, integrate agencies for the management of public complaints and proposals and reporting, and focus on solving outstanding problems. In 2020, the office provided nearly 200,000 clues for various special operations. Also in 2020, the Ministry of Ecology and Environment responded to 157 environmental emergencies of all kinds, and supervised and handled 34 major and sensitive environmental emergencies. A total of 441,000 cases of problems reported by the public were received and handled nationwide, with a 100% completion rate on schedule.

- Promoting central and provincial-level supervision of eco-environmental protection

In August, the second round of the second batch of central and provincial-level supervision of eco-environmental protection was carried out, conducting pilot supervision of Beijing, Tianjin and Zhejiang Provinces, the two central government enterprises—Aluminum Corporation of China and China National Building Materials Group Co. Ltd, and the National Energy Administration and the State Forestry and Grassland Administration. This is the first time the relevant departments of the State Council were put under supervision and a total of more than 10,500 reports from the public were received and transferred for handling. All 31 provincial-level administrative areas and Xinjiang Production and Construction Corps set up provincial-level supervision agencies. The 2020 ecological and environmental warning film on the Yangtze River Economic Belt was completed, revealing a list of 169 problems. And 226 of the 315 problems disclosed in the 2018 and 2019 warning films were corrected.

- Solidly promoting ecological protection and development

The Guide to Ecological Protection and Restoration Projects for Mountains, Waters, Forests, Farmland, Lakes and Grassland (for Trial Implementation) to guide and regulate the implementation of ecological protection and restoration projects in various places, and integrate protection and restoration of mountains, waters, forests, farmland, lakes and grassland. The Special Action Plan for Mangrove Protection and Restoration (2020-2025) and the Coastal Zone Protection And Restoration Project Work Plan were issued (2019-2022) to support local mangrove ecological restoration. The national grassland protection and restoration and grass industry development plan was prepared, and the National Grassland Monitoring and Evaluation Work Guide was issued. The Grassland Acquisition and Occupation Audit and Approval Management Norms were introduced, specifying restrictions on the acquisition and occupation of grasslands within the ecological protection redline, and strictly limiting the acquisition and occupation of basic grasslands for development projects. The special action for mangrove protection and restoration was promoted. The ecological status of wetlands of international importance was monitored, and a white paper on the ecological status of wetlands of international importance in China was issued. The 2020 List of Wetlands of National Importance was released, adding 29 new wetlands of national importance. The system of national parks was promoted on a trial basis, the Spatial Layout Plan of National

Parks was prepared, and five national standards were developed, including the Specification for the Establishment of National Parks. The National Park Monitoring Indicators and Monitoring Technical System (for Trial Implementation) and four national park master plans (for trial implementation) were issued for the northeast tigers and leopards, giant panda, the Qilian Mountains and the Hainan tropical rainforest. The Green Shield 2020, Blue Sea 2020, the regulation of Yangtze River illegal docks and Yangtze River illegal fishing and other special operations were carried out to combat the destruction of nature reserves.

3. Ecological civilization justice

• Issuing a number of environmental resources judicial documents

In March, the Supreme People's Court issued the Style of Public Interest Litigation Instruments (for Trial Implementation) to standardize and unify the production of public interest litigation adjudication instruments. In June, the Supreme People's Court issued the Guidelines on Providing Judicial Services and Protection for the Ecological Protection and High-Quality Development of the Yellow River Basin and the Leading Cases of Judicial Protection of the Yellow River

Basin. In September, 10 departments including the Supreme People's Court, the Supreme People's Procuratorate, the Ministry of Ecology and the Environment jointly issued the Guidelines on Several Specific Issues concerning the Reform of the Compensation System for Ecological and Environmental Damage to clarify the procedural rules of compensation consultation, restoration responsibilities and fund management, and to strengthen the coordination of law enforcement and justice for ecological and environmental damage compensation. In December, the Supreme People's Court and the Supreme People's Procuratorate jointly revised the Interpretation of Issues on the Application of Law to Public Interest Litigation Cases, and the Supreme People's Court revised the Interpretation of Issues on the Application of Law to the Trial of Environmental Civil Public Interest Litigation Cases to bring the relevant provisions in line with the Civil Code.

- Trying environmental resources cases in accordance with the law

In 2020, the people's courts at all levels nationwide accepted 272,900 criminal, civil and administrative cases of environmental resources in the first instance, and concluded 253,300 such cases. A full play was given to the role of environmental public interest litigation and ecological and environmental damage compensation litigation in promoting environmental protection. People's courts at all levels nationwide accepted 4,679 cases of environmental public interest litigation and concluded 3,557 such cases; accepted 91 cases of ecological and environmental damage compensation (including judicial confirmation cases for ecological and environmental damage compensation and litigation cases) and concluded 62 such cases. The Yunnan Kunming Intermediate People's Court concluded the Green Peacock case and the Sichuan Garze Prefectural Intermediate People's Court concluded the Acer pentaphyllum Diels case, both being preventive civil public interest litigation case, strengthening the ecological protection of precious and endangered wildlife. The Lanzhou Intermediate People's Court in Gansu and the Yinchuan Intermediate People's Court in Ningxia heard the environmental civil public interest litigation cases involving abandoning wind power and light energy projects, strengthening the judicial response to climate change. Courts in Chongqing, Hubei, Jiangsu and other areas in the Yangtze River basin cracked down on illegal fishing in the Yangtze River basin and the industrial chain of acquisition, processing and sales, ensuring a smooth start of the 10-year fishing ban in the Yangtze River.

- Giving a full play to the guiding role of environmental resources judicial policy

In January, the Supreme People's Court held a conference on the judicial protection of the ecological environment of the Yangtze River Economic Belt and on the release of leading cases, reporting on the judicial service to safeguard the development of the Yangtze River Economic Belt and releasing the *Status of Judicial Protection of the Ecological Environment of the Yangtze River Basin* (White Paper). In May, the Supreme People's Court released *China Environmental Resources Trial (2019)* (White Paper), *Report on the Environmental Judicial Development in China (2019)* (Green Paper), and the 2019 People's Court Environmental Resources Leading Cases. In 2020, the Supreme People's Court released four batches of 80 leading cases of environmental resources protection, and the Supreme People's Procuratorate released three batches of 34 leading cases of environmental resources protection.

- Improving and innovating the mechanism of environmental resources trial

Continued efforts were made to promote the development of specialized institutions, and courts at all levels established environmental resources tribunals, environmental resources courts, circuit courts and other forms of specialized environmental resources trial institutions. By the end of 2020, courts nationwide had set up 1,993 specialized environmental resources trial institutions. Centralized jurisdictions and judicial collaboration areas were strengthened. Efforts were made to coordinate centralized jurisdictional courts and non-centralized jurisdictional courts of environmental resources, and promote centralized jurisdictional systematization within provincial-level administrative divisions. The collaborated cross-provincial ecological and environmental governance was strengthened. The high people's courts of the nine provinces and autonomous regions signed a framework agreement on collaboration in environmental resources trials, developing the basin judicial mechanism to promote collaborated eco-environment protection, and systemic governance in the Yellow River Basin. The coordination mechanism was improved. Courts strengthened their cooperation and exchange with the Ministry of Ecology and Environment, the National Forestry and Grassland Administration, improved the working mechanism, and jointly maintained the safety of environmental resources.

● Promoting international exchange and cooperation in environmental justice

Environmental law experts and senior judges from the

United States, the United Kingdom, Australia, Singapore and other countries to give lectures by video on soil pollution, climate change response, and biodiversity protection at the national court training course on environmental resources trials. Representatives were sent to participate in the Asia-Pacific Judicial Conference on Climate Change: Adjudication in the Time of Covid-19 co-organized by the United Nations Environment Program and the Asian Development Bank, as well as the China-Europe Seminar on Climate Change Legislation.

VIII. Legal Communication, Legal Education, and Legal Research

In 2020, China's research on legal publicity, legal education and jurisprudence focused closely on the major theoretical and practical issues in the development of the rule of law initiative in China, with remarkable results.

1. Legal publicity

- In-depth study, publicity, and implementation of Xi Jinping's thinking on the rule of law

In November, the Central Working Conference on Comprehensive Law-Based Governance was held, establishing the guiding position of Xi Jinping's thinking on the rule of law in comprehensive law-based governance, which is a major event of great practical significance and far-reaching historical significance in development of the rule of law initiative in China. In 2020, the Constitution Publicity Week conducted activities for in-depth study, publicity and implementation of Xi Jinping's thinking on the rule of law and the promotion of the guiding principles from the Constitution, integrating studying and publicizing Xi Jinping's thinking on the rule of law and publicizing and educating in the Constitution. The General Office of the NPC Standing Committee, together with the Central Publicity Department and the Ministry of Justice, held a symposium on in-depth study and publicity of Xi Jinping's thinking on the rule of law and improvement of the socialist legal system with the Constitution as the core to further deepen the study and publicity of Xi Jinping's thinking on the rule of law. Officials of the relevant central state organs were organized to study Xi Jinping's thinking on the rule of law, play the leading role of the central state organs, and ensure the world of society becomes more conscious ideologically, politically and in action to study, publicize and implement Xi Jinping's thinking on the rule of law. With a focus on studying and publicizing Xi Jinping's thinking on the rule of law, publicity activities were carried out to this thinking is embraced in enterprises, in rural areas, in Party and government organs, in schools, in the communities, in military barracks, in the internet, so that the grassroots people feel the great truth of the thinking. This was done to guide the whole of society in unswervingly following the socialist path of rule of law with Chinese characteristics.

- Popularizing the Civil Code

Eight departments including the Central Publicity Department jointly issued a circular on the study and publicity of the Civil Code. A series of 12 public lectures on the Civil Code was launched, which were watched more than 10 million times. The leaders the Legal Affairs Commission of the NPC Standing Committee and other units produced the Civil Code Open Class and got it online. In the form of cases and cartoons, the wall chart *The Civil Code and Life: The Law in the Form of a Chart* was produced, and the feature film *The Civil Code: The People's Code in the New Era* was made, which was widely popular. All regions and departments and industries widely carried out learning and publicity activities with a strong sense of target, wide social coverage, a high level of public participation and vivid and intuitive forms, forming encouraging multifaceted dissemination throughout the whole media.

- Carrying out special rule of law publicity for epidemic prevention and control

Six departments including the Central Office of Law-Based Governance and the Central Judicial and Law Enforcement Commission held a press conference with the theme of "legal safeguards for Covid-19 prevention and control", publicly releasing the developments concerning the implementation of General Secretary Xi Jinping's major speeches and the guiding principles from the Central Commission for Law-Based Governance, and the formulation and implementation of the Guidelines of the Supreme People's Court, the Supreme People's Procuratorate, the Ministry of Public Security and the Ministry of Justice on the Punishment of Crimes against Covid-19 Prevention and Control in Accordance with the Law. The State Council Information Office held a press conference on the developments concerning the Guidelines on the Judicial and Law Enforcement Organs Ensuring Reopening during Covid-19 Prevention and Control in Accordance with the Law. *Questions and Answers on Legal Knowledge* and *A Compilation of Laws and Regulations* on epidemic prevention and control were published. A special wall chart on Legal Protection for Covid-19 Prevention and Control, explaining the law in the form of Questions + Cases + Pictures + Legal Reviews + Knowledge Links. Public service messages were sent to more than 500 million cell phone users nationwide to prevent and control the epidemic in accordance with the law. Articles on Covid-19 prevention and control are published on the Legalinfo WeChat official account, which were read 120 million times. For acts such as price gouging, disrupting the order of epidemic prevention and control, endangering public safety and obstructing official duties, more than 300 leading cases in 29 groups were continuously released. All local departments combined the popularization of law on Covid-19 epidemic prevention and control with grassroots law-based governance, and actively give full play to the role of grassroots communities and rural legal popularization positions to guide the whole of society to act whether the framework of the law.

- Strengthening the development of rule of law cultural positions

At present, the country has more than 3,500 parks, more than 12,000 squares, more than 34,000 corridors featuring rule of law culture, and more than 30,000 youth rule of law education bases nationwide. The third batch of 47 national rule of law publicity and education bases were named and opened to the public for free. The promotion and protection of the red rule of law culture was strengthened and the red rule of law cultural traditions were passed on. The naming of the eighth batch of national democracy and rule of law demonstration villages (communities) was organized, and a number of advanced models were reviewed and promoted. New media technology was used to promote law, the number of fans of the Legalinfo WeChat official account exceeded 16 million, and the judicial and law enforcement new media became an important position for the promotion of law.

- Organizing the selection of the top ten national figures of the rule of law in 2020

The Guiding Principles from the Constitution, the Power of the Rule of Law: 2020 Annual Rule of Law Figures Special Program was produced and broadcast on CCTV 1 and 12 prime-time, reflecting achievements in fight against the Covid-19 epidemic in accordance with the law, developing the Civil Code, combatting organized crime and rooting out local criminal gangs, rule of law poverty alleviation, and implementing the seventh five-year plan for increasing public knowledge of the law in 2020. This further highlighted the faith of officials and members of the public, especially the frontline police officers, in the Constitution and adherence to the rule of law.

- Reviewing and accepting the implementation of the seventh five-year plan for increasing public knowledge of the law

The National Office for Increasing Public Knowledge of the Law issued the Plan for Reviewing and Accepting the Implementation Seventh Five-Year Plan for Increasing Public Knowledge of the Law, stipulating what is to be reviewed and accepted and by what criteria, methods and steps. It stressed the need to discover problems, help solve them, and avoid the practice of formalities for formalities' sake and going through the motions. Provinces, autonomous regions, and municipalities directly under the central government and Xinjiang Production and Construction Corps, and the relevant bodies of central Party and government departments reviewed and evaluated themselves in accordance with the Review, Acceptance, Assessment and Evaluation Index System of the Seventh Five-Year Plan. The Ministry of Justice and the National Office for Increasing Public Knowledge of the Law organized random surveys and research, and checked the popularization of law in grassroots villages, communities, schools and enterprises. Through individual talks, random online legal knowledge tests and online surveys, these accurately assessed the effectiveness of the popularization of law, and promoted the investigation of gaps and fill in the gaps around the country, which effectively promoted the implementation of the measures to review and accept the implementation of the seventh five-year plan for increasing public knowledge of the law.

- Organizing a series of activities for students nationwide to learn and abide by the Constitution

The fifth national initiative for students to learn and abide by the Constitution was carried out to ensure that the study and promotion of the Constitution becomes an important political task in schools around the country, and guide education officials, teachers and students in widely participating in the study and education of the Constitution and the law. As of December 30, 2020, more than 7.1 billion people had participated in the study of law through the Ministry of Education's website https://qspfw.moe.gov.cn, and more than 89 million Little Guardians of the Constitution had been selected through online learning assessments. On National Constitution Day, the Seventh Morning Reading of the Constitution was held in the education system, and more than 72 million teachers and students in more than 360,000 schools participated in the simultaneous reading of the Constitution.

- Continuing the initiative for "young legal literacy volunteers promoting rule of law culture at the grassroots level"

In 2020, during the initiative, more than 510,000 on-site legal literacy activities were organized, more than 51,000 online legal literacy activities were carried out, volunteers promoted the rule of law more than 930,000 times for more than 125 million people.

2. Legal education

● Widely carrying out professional teaching both online and offline, and coordinating the promotion of Covid-19 prevention and control and legal education

In 2020, in order to coordinate the promotion of Covid-19 prevention and control and legal education, the law schools actively explored the development of distance learning courses through the internet to ensure the smooth and orderly promotion of coursework. In February, China University of Political Science and Law, together with Southwest University of Political Science and Law and East China University of Political Science and Law, launched the project "Three Schools On the Law in Response to Covid-19". In the project, the legal talents of the three schools analyzed the real cases that happened during the Covid-19 outbreak, popularized legal knowledge, created a fresh, healthy and upward social environment, and performed the social service function of universities. In March, in order to meet the strong demand of law students for professional knowledge during the epidemic prevention and control period, and to help market players to correctly deal with the legal risks brought about by the epidemic and the sudden legal problems during the epidemic outbreak, 13 legal experts from Peking University, Tsinghua University, Renmin University of China, Southwest University of Political Science and Law, East China University of Political Science and Law, and Zhongnan University of Economics and Law jointly launched the project "Public Service Law Lectures", which were broadcast live for free through the Professor Plus platform.

- Deepening international exchange and cooperation

In October, the Third 21st Century International Forum of Law School Deans and Jurists was held, in which deans and experts from law schools of foreign universities such as Oxford University and Yale University and domestic law schools focused on. In October, the 4th China and Africa Law School Deans' Forum was held in online format with the theme of China-Africa Legal Education shared their views on legal education in the transition of civilization. In October, the Fourth China-Africa Forum of Law School Deans, with the theme of "Legal Education Exchange and Cooperation in the Context of One Belt, One Road", was held online, and the participants exchanged views on the hot issues of China-Africa legal education cooperation in the new situation of the epidemic.

- Creating a new platform for legal education

In June, Tianjin University held the first seminar on innovation of legal education in Chinese universities and the symposium on the fifth anniversary of the re-establishment of Tianjin University School of Law, and released the Initiative for the Establishment of Innovation Alliance of Legal Education, and the Innovation Alliance of Legal Education was officially established. The alliance was initiated by some famous law schools nationwide, and is open to all universities that are interested in promoting the reform and innovation of Chinese law higher education, aiming to build a platform for universities nationwide to discuss the opportunities and challenges of law education and share the experience of law education reform and innovation.

- Electing the ninth group of national outstanding young jurists

The election of the ninth group of national outstanding young jurists was organized by the China Law Society and launched in May 2019, receiving great attention and widespread concern from the legal profession and other sectors of society. The election was completed in November 2020, a total of 10 recipients of the title of "National Outstanding

Young Jurist" and 20 others were nominated for the award. In December, the Ninth Symposium of National Outstanding Young Jurists was held in Beijing, and 10 winners of the title of National Outstanding Young Jurists and 20 nominees were honored. The 10 National Outstanding Young Jurists and 20 nominees were honored. These 10 National Outstanding Young Jurists have all been active in China's jurisprudence in recent years and have made outstanding contributions to the study of the socialist theory of the rule of law with Chinese characteristics.

• Continuing the Lectures on Political Science and Law Practice in China

In 2020, these lectures were held in seven universities, including Tsinghua University, Peking University, Renmin University of China, China University of Political Science and Law, and Southwest University of Political Science and Law. Seven leaders at the vice ministerial level or above in the judicial and law enforcement system gave lectures on learning and implementing Xi Jinping's thinking on rule of law and the guiding principles from of the Fifth Plenary Session of the 19th Party Central Committee, to help ensure law school students are well-prepared to join the socialist cause and cultivate new-era legal talents.

3. Legal research

- Deepening research and interpretation of Xi Jinping's thinking on rule of law

In November, the Central Working Conference on Comprehensive Law-Based Governance established Xi Jinping's thinking on the rule of law as the guiding thought of comprehensive law-based governance. The legal circle studied and publicized Xi Jinping's thinking on the rule of law in depth, and the China Law Society set up a major special project on Xi Jinping's thinking on the rule of law. Renmin University of China, East China University of Political Science and Law and other universities established Xi Jinping's thinking on the rule of law research centers or institutes one after another. Important domestic law academic journals published academic interpretations of Xi Jinping's thinking on the rule of law, strongly promoting the theoretical interpretation of Xi Jinping's thinking on the rule of law.

- Fruitful results achieved in the research on civil law with the enactment and implementation of the Civil Code as an opportunity

In 2020, the study of civil law not only reached a new height, but also integrated many years of civil law research, which stems from the formulation and adoption of the Civil Code. On the basis of theoretical research on civil law also reaching a high level, many major theoretical innovations published in 2020 laid a solid theoretical foundation for the formulation and implementation of the Civil Code. The representative articles include "Reconstructing the Environmental Tort Relief System with the Theory of Ecological Restoration" and "The Civil Law Significance of Administrative License". In terms of the expansion of the problem domain, the issues of ecological protection, improvement of the business environment, right of residence and epidemic prevention and control gave rise to a large number of innovative results. In terms of theoretical objectives of research, to promote the implementation of the Civil Code, a large number of results were achieved in the research on shifting from the legislative theory to the judicial application level, especially on the relationship between the application and other legal departments such as the Constitution, administrative law, criminal law and economic law.

- New developments in the study of sectoral jurisprudence

The research on constitutional law focused on the review of constitutionality, constitutional principles, the basic scope of the Constitution, 30 years of the Hong Kong Basic Law, the Civil Code and the Constitution, the epidemic and the Constitution, science and technology and the Constitution. In jurisprudence, discussions were focused on comprehensive law-based governance and national governance modernization. The study of administrative law focused on the revision of the Administrative Penalty Law, the codification of administrative law, the development of law-based government, administrative agreements, the renewal of the rule of law system for public health and emergency response, the reform of the reconsideration system with administrative reconsideration as the main channel for resolving administrative disputes, and the improvement of the system for public interest litigation. Economic law studies focused on the revision of the Anti-Monopoly Law, prevention and control of systemic financial risks, legal regulation of the digital economy, utilization of foreign investment, and the basic theory of economic law. Criminal Law research focused on issues such as the Amendment to the Criminal Law (XI), criminal compliance and unit crimes, criminal law response to epidemic prevention and control, criminal law response to modern technology risks, personal information crimes, and crimes of mafia-like organizations. Criminal procedural jurisprudence research focused on such topics as the penal policy of severity tempered with mercy and strengthening the judicial protection of the private stipulate with enterprise compliance. Civil litigation jurisprudence studies focused on the Civil Code and the new civil evidence regulations. Administrative litigation jurisprudence studies focused on administrative public interest litigation and administrative agreements. International jurisprudence research was about the extraterritorial application of domestic law, international intellectual property protection, international investment, and global anti-epidemic. Legal history studies focused on the integration of traditional law resources in the codification of the Civil Code, traditional Chinese governance, and systematization of traditional law.

IX. International Exchanges and Cooperation

In 2020, China worked hard to promote international legal exchanges and cooperation in the fight against the Covid-19 epidemic, actively carried out judicial assistance and anti-corruption work in spite of the epidemic outbreak, deeply participated in relevant international legislative activities, continued in-depth legal exchanges pursuing the Belt and Road Initiative, continuously promoted international rule of law dialogues, and innovated forms of foreign jurisprudence exchanges with positive results.

1. Mutual legal assistance and international anti-corruption cooperation

- Mutual legal assistance contracting

In 2020, China ratified the extradition treaties with Turkey, Belgium and Cyprus, and the treaty on the transfer of sentenced persons with Pakistan.

- Judicial assistance in handling cases

In 2020, the country reviewed and handled 3,817 cases of service of judicial documents in civil and commercial matters, and 67 cases of investigation and evidence collection and legal ascertainment, and recognition and enforcement of judgments in civil and commercial matters.

- Special efforts to track down fugitives

In March, the Skynet 2020 campaign was launched. By the end of 2020, a total of 1,421 fugitives had been recovered, including 314 who were supervised and 28 for whom red notices had been issued, and the amount of stolen money had been about 2.95 billion yuan.

- Multilateral affairs

In October, the Chinese delegation took part in the first G20 Anti-Corruption Ministers Meeting and made a statement, exchanging views on ensuring G20 plays a leading role and promoting international cooperation against corruption. The meeting adopted the *G20 Anti*-Corruption Ministers Meeting Ministerial Communiqué, calling on all G20 members to deepen collaboration on international anti-corruption efforts, strengthen anti-corruption efforts in response to the epidemic, and work together to create a clean business environment. In October, the Chinese representative spoke at the general debate of the

75th session of the Legal Committee of the UN General Assembly on "the Rule of Law at the National and International Levels", focusing on China's comprehensive promotion of the rule of law and its anti-corruption efforts. In November, President Xi Jinping attended the 20th meeting of the Council of Heads of State of the SCO, the 12th BRICS Summit and the 15th summit of the Group of Twenty (G20) leaders via video link and delivered major speeches, in which the leaders reached an important consensus on strengthening international cooperation against corruption, which was written into the Moscow Declaration of the Council of Heads of State of the Shanghai Cooperation Organization, the XII BRICS Summit Moscow Declaration, and the Declaration of the Riyadh Summit of the G20 Leaders.

- Discussion

In November, the China Forum on International Legal Cooperation was held in Beijing. Experts and scholars from home and abroad attended the forum and discussed criminal in absentia trial and due process, confiscation and disposal of illegal proceeds, cooperation in extradition and its alternative measures, and corporate anti-corruption compliance.

2. Participation in international legislative activities

• International environmental protection and climate change

In June, the UNFCCC secretariat held a series of video conferences entitled June Momentum. Co-sponsored by the Chairs of the Subsidiary Body for Implementation (SBI) and the Subsidiary Body for Scientific and Technological Advice (SBSTA), the conferences covered a wide range of topics such as post-epidemic recovery, nationally determined contributions (NDCs), adaptation, finance, loss and damage, and transparency. The conferences were the first online exchange events held through the UNFCCC main channel to pay the way for the 26th UN Climate Change Conference to be held in Glasgow, UK, at the end of 2021. In September, President Xi Jinping delivered an important video message at the UN Summit on Biodiversity, advocating that all countries adhere to ecological civilization, uphold multilateralism, maintain green development and enhance responsibility, emphasizing China's efforts to build a modernization characterized with harmony between man and nature, and invites all parties to participate in the 15th Conference of the Parties to the Convention on Biological

Diversity to be held in Kunming in 2021. Also in September, the Ministry of Ecology and Environment and the Ministry of Foreign Affairs jointly organized an online ministerial roundtable on Biodiversity beyond 2020: Building a Shared Future for All Life on Earth, which focused on biodiversity and sustainable development, global governance of biodiversity beyond 2020. Ministerial representatives from 17 countries, including Brazil, Costa Rica and Egypt, as well as representatives of international organizations and NGOs, such as the United Nations Environment Program, participated in the meeting by video. In late November, President Xi Jinping attended the G20 Riyadh Summit by video, elaborating on issues such as economic recovery and sustainable development. The Summit adopted the G20 Leaders' Riyadh Summit Declaration. In his speech at the Riyadh Summit side event on the theme of "safeguarding the Earth", President Xi Jinping proposed to step up efforts to combat climate change, promote clean energy transition and build an ecosystem that respects nature. In December, President Xi Jinping attended the Climate Ambition Summit 2020 organized by the United Nations and other relevant countries to commemorate the fifth anniversary of the Paris Agreement, and delivered a major speech entitled "Building on Past Achievements and Launching a New

Journey for Global Climate Actions", announcing a series of new initiatives for China's nationally determined contributions.

- International maritime law

In February, the first part of its 26th session of the Council of the International Seabed Authority was held in Jamaica and reviewed the Draft Regulations on Exploitation of Mineral Resources in the Area. The Chinese delegation made statements on regional environmental management plans, international seabed resources and the formulation of regulations on exploitation. In December, under the topic of "Oceans and the Law of the Sea" at the 75th session of the General Assembly, China called on all parties to join hands to build a maritime community with a shared future and expressed its active support for the work of the International Tribunal for the Law of the Sea, the International Seabed Authority and the Commission on the Limits of the Continental Shelf established under the United Nations Convention on the Law of the Sea in global ocean governance.

- The internet

In July, the UN inter-governmental expert group on cybercrime held its sixth meeting, which focused on international cooperation and prevention of cybercrime and resulted in more than 70 specific recommendations on international cooperation and prevention. The Chinese delegation participated in the meeting and spoke in the panel discussion session, introducing the experience of carrying out international cooperation against cybercrime and enterprises helping to prevent cybercrime.

- International criminal justice cooperation

In September, the Chinese delegation video participated in the fifth meeting of the BRICS Counter-Terrorism Working Group, where the participating parties mainly exchanged views on the international regional counter-terrorism situation, national counter-terrorism initiatives and BRICS counter-terrorism cooperation. Before the meeting, the inaugural meeting of the BRICS Counter-Terrorism Working Group's sub-working group for counter radicalization had been held by video under the auspices of China, with Chinese representatives chairing the meeting and making speeches to comprehensively elaborate China's counter-terrorism and counter-radicalization policies. In October, the Chinese delegation participated in the 10th session of the Parties to the United Nations Convention against Transnational Organized Crime and stressed that the situation of transnational organized crime remains serious and complicated, and that China will always be a practitioner of multilateralism, firmly uphold the international system with the United Nations at its core, work with other countries to prevent and combat transnational crime, and promote the building of a human community with a shared future and universal security. In December, the Chinese delegation participated in the 29th and resumed sessions of the UN Commission on Crime Prevention and Criminal Justice and made statements under three agenda items, actively advocating the achievements of rule of law development and also expressing China's willingness to seriously participate in the preparatory work of the 14th United Nations Congress on Crime Prevention and Criminal Justice and actively take part in the relevant activities of the United Nations in the field of crime prevention and criminal justice.

- pace law

In October, the Chinese delegation participated in the 75th session of the UN General Assembly Committee on Disarmament and International Security, which voted for the Resolution on the "No first placement of weapons in space" and reaffirmed the need to study and take practical measures to reach a treaty on the prevention of an arms race in outer space. The concept of building a human community with a shared future was once again included in the UN's resolution on space.

- Human rights

In October, the Chinese delegation participated in the sixth session of the intergovernmental working group on transnational corporations and other business enterprises with respect to human rights (IGWG) under the UN Human Rights Council. The session discussed article by article. The revised text of the second edition of the legal instrument on transnational corporations and other business enterprises and human rights.

- Other areas

In February and November, The Hague Conference on Private International Law held its third and fourth meetings of the Experts' Group on Jurisdiction in The Hague, the Netherland. The meetings discussed issues related to rules of direct jurisdiction in international civil and commercial matters, in which the Chinese delegations participated by video. In August, the 30th Meeting of States Parties to the United Nations Convention on the Law of the Sea was held at the United Nations Headquarters in New York, and the participating States Parties voted to elect six members of the International Tribunal for the Law of the Sea, and the Chinese candidates were successfully elected. In November, the election of judges of the International Court of Justice (ICJ) was held at the UN headquarters in New York to elect five members of the Court, and the Chinese candidate, Judge Xue Hanqin, currently Vice-President of the ICJ, was successfully re-elected.

3. Intergovernmental dialogue on rule of law

- Dialogue under the UN framework

In September, President Xi Jinping attended the 75th anniversary summit of the United Nations and delivered a major speech, emphasizing that the UN should uphold justice, enforce the rule of law, promote cooperation and focus on action in the post-epidemic era, and reaffirming that China will always be a practitioner of multilateralism, actively participate in the reform and development of the global governance system, and promote the building of a human community with a shared future. In September, President Xi Jinping delivered a major speech at the general debate of the 75th session of the UN General Assembly, stressing that the global governance system needs urgent reform and improvement, and that it is necessary to adhere to the path of multilateralism, uphold the international system with the UN at its core, properly resolve differences among countries through dialogue and consultation, and guard the moral bottom line and international norms. In November, the Chinese representative spoke at the general debate on the report of the ICJ at the 75th session of the UN General Assembly, and positively evaluated the important role played by the ICJ in upholding multilateralism and safeguarding international justice and equity.

- Dialogue and cooperation under the framework of the SCO

In September, State Councilor and Minister of Public Security Zhao Kezhi took part in the 15th Meeting of Security Council Secretaries of SCO Member States and made five proposals to strengthen the SCO's security cooperation. Zhao exchanged views with other participants mainly on the current international and regional security situation, and on cooperation among SCO member states in combating the "three evil forces" of terrorism, separatism and extremism, drug trafficking and organized crime, and on maintaining information security. In October, the president of the Supreme People's Court, Zhou Qiang, participated in the 15th Meeting of the Supreme Courts of the SCO member states hosted by the Supreme Court of the Republic of Kazakhstan. He delivered opening and closing speeches and made a special speech. He proposed to widely gather consensus on judicial cooperation, continuously improve judicial cooperation mechanisms, and continuously enhance the level of judicial cooperation, and discussed with all parties on judicial exchanges and cooperation during the Covid-19 outbreak. The meeting adopted the Joint Statement of the 15th Meeting of the Presidents of the Supreme Courts of the SCO Member States. In October, Mr. Zhang Jun led a delegation of the Supreme People's Procuratorate to participate in the 18th Meeting of the Prosecutors General of the Shanghai Cooperation Organization and made a speech on the current practices and effective mechanisms in combating corruption, introducing the main measures and significant results of China in combating corruption and making suggestions on strengthening cooperation among countries in combating corruption.

- Dialogue and cooperation under the ASEAN framework

In January, the president of the Supreme People's Court, Zhou Qiang, met with the president of the Supreme Administrative Court of Thailand, Piya Patangta and his delegation that were in China to study court IT application. In November, the president of the Supreme People's Court, Zhou Qiang, held a working meeting with the chief justice of the Supreme Court of Singapore, Mr. Sundaresh Menon, and participated in the 4th China-Singapore Legal and Judicial Roundtable, delivering opening and closing speeches and making a special address. The representatives of the two sides jointly announced the official publication of *A Compendium of China-Singapore International Commercial Cases Curated for their Relevance to the Belt and Road Initiative*. Participants at the roundtable exchanged insights in the following areas:

a) Sharing the Courts' Best Practices in Dealing with Covid-19 / Challenges Covid-19 Posed to the Courts and the Profession,

b) How to Unify the Legal Application Standards Through Similar Cases and Precedents,

c) The Application and Limitation of General Legal Principles in International Commercial Disputes, and

d) Court Procedural Rules-Features Relevant to the Belt and Road Initiative.

- Dialogue and cooperation under the framework BRICS

In September, Yang Jiechi, member of the Political Bureau of the CPC Central Committee and director of the Office of the Central Foreign Affairs Commission, attended the 10th Meeting of the BRICS High Representatives on National Security via video link. Participants exchanged views on international and regional hotspot issues, biosecurity, counter-terrorism and cybersecurity, and agreed to strengthen communication, coordination and cooperation to jointly safeguard international law and multilateralism. In September, the president of the Supreme People's Court, Zhou Qiang, attended the BRICS Chief Justice Forum, delivered opening and closing speeches, and delivered a speech at the seminar on protecting economic actors' interests and the business environment through administrative litigation, introducing the efforts of Chinese courts to strengthen judicial protection of property rights and serve to improve the business environment. The forum adopted the Joint Statement of the BRICS Chief Justice Forum. In October, Chairman of the NPC Standing Committee Li Zhanshu attended the 6th BRICS Parliamentary Forum by video and delivered a speech, emphasizing the strengthening of cooperation among BRICS legislatures. Participants exchanged insights in the BRICS partnership in the interest of global stability, general safety and innovative growth: parliamentary dimension. The heads of legislative bodies of BRICS countries participated in the meeting by video, and the meeting adopted the Declaration of the 6th BRICS Inter-Parliamentary Forum. In November, President Xi Jinping attended the 12th BRICS Leaders' Meeting hosted by Russia and delivered a major speech titled Overcoming the Epidemic Together, Promoting Cooperation Together. In November, President Xi Jinping attended the 12th BRICS

Summit hosted by Russia and delivered a major speech titled "Fighting Covid-19 in Solidarity and Advancing BRICS Cooperation through Concerted Efforts". Xi emphasized the need to adhere to multilateralism, joint efforts to overcome the challenges of the epidemic, safeguard the multilateral trading system with the World Trade Organization as the core, and implement the Paris Agreement on Climate Change and the UN 2030 Agenda for Sustainable Development. The leaders exchanged views on the theme of "BRICS Partnership for Global Stability, Shared Security and Innovative Growth". The summit adopted the Moscow Declaration of the 12th BRICS Summit. In December, Procurator-General of the Supreme People's Procuratorate Zhang Jun participated in the 4th BRICS Attorneys General Meeting and made recommendations on combating crimes in the cyber and economic fields.

- Other areas

In April, Minister of Justice Fu Zhenghua attended in Beijing the opening ceremony of the international video-link forum on Covid-19 and legal system hosted by the Russian Ministry of Justice and delivered a speech, introducing China's efforts to provide quality and efficient legal services and rule of law safeguards for Covid-19 prevention and control and economic and social development. He also advocated strengthening international cooperation in the legal and judicial fields and building a human community with a shared future together.

4. Foreign legal exchanges

• Legal exchange under the ASEAN framework

In October, the 17th China-ASEAN Commercial Legal Cooperation Seminar was held in Guangxi. Delegates discussed in depth the cooperation between China and ASEAN in the field of commercial law around the theme of "The China-ASEAN FTA Diversified Dispute Resolution Mechanism: Research and Practice", with the participation of scholars from Cambodia, Malaysia, Myanmar, Singapore, Vietnam and other ASEAN countries.

• Legal exchanges with African countries

In August, the 7th Course of China-Africa Legal Professionals Exchange Program hosted by the China Law Society was held online in Beijing, focusing on the Civil Code, the pursuit of the Belt and Road Initiative, foreign investment protection, and China's international arbitration. More than 70 legal practitioners from 14 African countries attended the course.

- Legal exchanges with the Eurasian region

In September, the Belt and Road Eurasian Region Rule of Law Workshop sponsored by the China Law Society was held online in Beijing, focusing on topics such as Chinese criminal justice, Chinese commercial arbitration, the Chinese corporate legal system, Chinese international commercial courts, the Chinese foreign investment legal system, and the Belt and Road Initiative. Some 287 legal practitioners from 10 countries in the Eurasian region attended the workshop. In September and October, representatives of the China Law Society held video meetings with the leaders of the legislative bodies of Germany, Russia, Uzbekistan and Kazakhstan, and expressed that China will insist on mutual benefit and open cooperation with all parties, and provide good legal guarantees for the development of relations between China and other countries in various fields.

- In September, the Symposium on Legal Risks and Countermeasures for International Investment and Trade was held online in Beijing

The theme of the symposium was the Belt and Road Initiative and the China-Africa Joint Arbitration Mechanism, with four topics including the Rules of China-Africa Joint Arbitration Center and the Belt and Road Commercial Dispute

Resolution Mechanism. Representatives from Chinese and African jurisprudence participated in this conference.

• In September, the Ministry of Foreign Affairs of China and the National Institute for South China Sea Studies jointly held the virtual international symposium themed "The South China Sea: From the Perspective of Cooperation"

The conference focused on topics such as the origin and current situation of the South China Sea, peaceful settlement of disputes and the United Nations Convention on the Law of the Sea, implementation of the Declaration on the Conduct of Parties in the South China Sea and regional maritime cooperation.

• In November, the China Forum on International Legal Cooperation (2020), hosted by the China Law Society, was held in Beijing

President Xi Jinping sent a letter to the forum. Xi pointed out that pursuing the Belt and Road Initiative together requires a good legal business environment. China insists on openness, inclusiveness, and mutual benefit, and is willing to work with all parties to actively carry out international legal cooperation and provide legal support for building an open economy and promoting the recovery of the world economy. Xi said that China welcomes friends from the legal profession to attend the China Forum on International Legal Cooperation

(2020), and hopes that all the participants will have in-depth communication and consensus on "International Legal Cooperation in the Context of Covid-19", and contribute wisdom and strength to the use of legal means to promote the development of the Belt and Road Initiative and respond to global challenges more effectively. With the theme of "International Legal Cooperation in the Context of Covid-19", the forum issued Beijing Declaration of the China Forum on International Legal Cooperation. Representatives from 18 countries and relevant international organizations, including China, Russia and Brazil, participated in the forum by video.

• In December, the Seminar on Joint Response to Terrorism under the New Circumstances was held in Beijing, hosted by the China Institute of International Studies

The participants had in-depth discussions on the new circumstances and challenges of counter-terrorism and security on the international and regional spheres in the time of Covid-19, counter-terrorism concerns and experiences of various countries, and the right path to deepen international cooperation against terrorism. The conference was attended by government officials, heads of counter-terrorism research institutions and scholars from 12 countries, including Russia, France, Egypt and Pakistan via video link.

Conclusion

The year 2021 marks the centenary of the founding of the CPC and is the first year China implements the 14th Five-Year Plan and embarks on a new journey toward building a modern socialist country in all respects. The Fifth Plenary Session of the 19th CPC Central Committee drew a grand blueprint for the development of the Party and the country in the new period, and China has entered a new stage of legal development.

The CPC Central Committee issued the Plan for Building the Rule of Law in China (2020-2025) (hereinafter referred to as the Plan). The Plan points out that the development of the law-based China should achieve scientific and complete unity of legal norms and ensure that law enforcement and justice are fair, efficient and authoritative; that the operation of power is subject to effective constraints and supervision; that the legitimate rights and interests of the people are fully respected and protected; that the legal faith is generally established; and a law-based state, government, and society are built in all respects. The Plan is divided into nine parts: 1. Unswervingly take the socialist legal path with Chinese characteristics, and strive to build a law-based China with good law and good governance; 2. Fully implement of the Constitution and firmly uphold its dignity and authority; 3. Develop complete legal norms to promote the development of good law and protect good governance; 4. Develop an efficient system of legal implementation and promote strict law enforcement, impartial justice, and universal compliance with the law; 5. Develop a tight system of legal supervision and effectively strengthen the supervision of legislation, law enforcement and judicial work; 6. Develop a strong legal system and lay a solid foundation for the development a law-based China; 7. Develop a sound system of Party regulations and unswervingly promote rules-based Party governance; 8. Closely focus on the overall interest of the Party and the country in the new era and safeguard national sovereignty, security and development interests in accordance with the law; and 9. Strengthen the Party's centralized and unified leadership of the development a law-based China and give a full play to the role of the CPC exercising overall leadership and coordinating the efforts of all the actors. As the first special plan on the development of a law-based China since the founding of the People's Republic of China, the Plan is a programmatic document for promoting comprehensive law-based governance in the new era, charts the course and provides guidelines for the coordinated promotion of the development of a law-based China in the 14th Five-Year Plan period.

Having completed the first of the Two Centenary Goals[1] and having begun to work for the second, the Chinese people, under the strong leadership of the CPC, adhere to the guidance of Xi Jinping Thought on Socialism with Chinese Characteristics for a New Era, thoroughly implement Xi Jinping's thinking on the rule of law, unswervingly take the socialist legal path with Chinese characteristics, certainly promote the work of comprehensive law-based governance to make greater progress, to provide strong legal protection for the 14th Five-Year Plan to kick off to the good start, and to celebrate the centenary of the CPC with outstanding achievements.

---

1 The Two Centenary Goals are to complete the building of a moderately prosperous society in all respects by the centenary of the Communist Party of China in 2021 and to build China into a great modern socialist country that is prosperous, strong, democratic, culturally advanced, harmonious, and beautiful by the centenary of the People's Republic of China in 2049.

Appendixes

Ⅰ. Laws, legal interpretations, and decisions enacted or revised by the NPC and its Standing Committee in 2020

1. Law of the People's Republic of China on the Prevention and Control of Environmental Pollution by Solid Waste

2. Civil Code of the People's Republic of China

3. Law of the People's Republic of China on Administrative Action for Public Employees

4. Law of the People's Republic of China on Archives

5. Law of the People's Republic of China on the People's Armed Police

6. Law of the People's Republic of China on Safeguarding National Security in the Hong Kong Special Administrative Region

7. Law of the People's Republic of China on Urban Maintenance and Development Tax

8. Deed Transfer Tax Law of the People's Republic of China

9. Decision of the NPC Standing Committee on Amending the Patent Law of the People's Republic of China

10. Law of the People's Republic of China on Biosecurity

11. Law of the People's Republic of China on the Protection of Minors

12. Law of the People's Republic of China on Export Control

13. Decision of the NPC Standing Committee on Amending the National Flag Law of the People's Republic of China

14. Decision of the NPC Standing Committee on Amending the National Emblem Law of the People's Republic of China

15. Decision of the NPC Standing Committee on Amending the Law of the People's Republic of China on the Election of the NPC and Local People's Congresses at All Levels

16. Decision of the NPC Standing Committee on Amending the Copyright Law of the People's Republic of China

17. Law of the People's Republic of China on the Protection of Veterans

18. Law of the People's Republic of China on the Prevention of Juvenile Delinquency

19. Law of the People's Republic of China on the Protection of t Yangtze River

20. Amendment to the Criminal Law of the People's Republic of China (XI)

21. National Defense Law of the People's Republic of China

22. Decision on a Complete Ban of Illegal Wildlife Trade and the Elimination of the Unhealthy Habit of Indiscriminate Wild Animal Meat Consumption for the Protection of Human Life and Health

23. Decision of the NPC Standing Committee on the Postponement of the Third Session of the 13th NPC

24. Decision of the NPC Standing Committee on Authorizing the State Council to Temporarily Adjust the Application of Relevant Legal Provisions in the China (Hainan) Pilot Free Trade Zone

25. Decision of the NPC Standing Committee on the Timing of the Third Session of the 13th NPC

26. Decision of the NPC the Establishment of a Sound Legal System and Implementation Mechanism for Safeguarding National Security in the Hong Kong Special Administrative Region

27. Decision of the NPC Standing Committee on the

Addition of National Laws to Annex Ⅲ to the Basic Law of the Hong Kong Special Administrative Region of the People's Republic of China

28. Decision of the NPC Standing Committee on Awarding State Medals and National Honors to Persons Who Have Made Outstanding Contributions in the Struggle against the Covid-19 Epidemic

29. Decision of the NPC Standing Committee on the Continuation of the Duties of the Sixth Legislative Council of the Hong Kong Special Administrative Re

30. Decision of the NPC Standing Committee authorizing the State Council to carry out pilot projects in nine cities in the Guangdong-Hong Kong-Macao Bay Area for Hong Kong legal practitioners and Macao practicing lawyers to be qualified to practice in the Mainland and to engage in the legal profession

31. Decision of the NPC Standing Committee on the Qualifications of Members of the Legislative Council of the Hong Kong Special Administrative Region

32. Decision of the NPC Standing Committee on Strengthening Supervision over State-Owned Assets Administration

33. Decision of the NPC Standing Committee on the Establishment of the Intellectual Property Court of the Hainan Free Trade Port

II. Administrative regulations enacted or revised by the State Council

1. Regulations on the Control of Crop Pests and Diseases

2. Decision of the State Council on Revising and Repealing Government Regulations (State Council Decree No. 726)

3. Cosmetics Supervision and Management Regulations

4. Regulations on Safeguarding Payments to Small and Medium Enterprises

5. Regulations on the Implementation of the Budget Law of the People's Republic of China

6. Decision of the State Council on Revising the Regulations on the Transfer of Suspected Criminal Cases by Administrative Law Enforcement Agencies

7. Regulations on State Science and Technology Awards

8. Decision of the State Council on Revising and Repealing Government Regulations (State Council Decree No. 732)

9. Regulations on Government Inspection Work

10. Regulations on Enterprise Name Registration and Management

III. Judicial interpretations issued by the Supreme People's Court and the Supreme People's Procuratorate in 2020

1. Decision of the Supreme People's Court on Revising the Arrangement between the Mainland and the Macao Special Administrative Region on the Mutual Recognition and Enforcement of Civil and Commercial Judgments

2. Reply of the Supreme People's Court and the Supreme People's Procuratorate on the Issue of Denying the Recidivism of a Probationer Who Commits a Crime Punishable by a Fixed Term of Imprisonment or More within Five Years after The Expiration of the Probation Period

3. Reply of the Supreme People's Court and the Supreme People's Procuratorate on the Application of Article 344 of the Criminal Law of the People's Republic of China

4. Regulations of the Supreme People's Court on Issues concerning the Appearance of Leaders of Administrative Organs in Court to Answer Lawsuits

5. Regulations of the Supreme People's Court on the Judicial Police of the People's Courts Performing Their Functions in Accordance with the law

6. Regulations of the Supreme People's Court on Issues concerning Representative Proceedings in Securities Disputes

7. Decision of the Supreme People's Court on Amending the Provisions on Issues concerning the Application of Law in the Trial of Civilian Lending Cases

8. Regulations of the Supreme People's Court on Issues on the Application of Law in Civil Cases of Infringement of Commercial Secrets

9. Regulations of the Supreme People's Court on Issues on the Application of Law in Hearing Administrative Cases of Patent Authorization and Confirmation of Rights (Ⅰ)

10. Reply of the Supreme People's Court on Issues of Application of Law in Disputes Involving Network Intellectual Property Infringement

11. Interpretation of the Supreme People's Court and the Supreme People's Procuratorate on Issues concerning the Specific Application of Law in Handling Criminal Cases of Infringement of Intellectual Property Rights (Ⅲ)

12. Regulations of the Supreme People's Court on Issues concerning the Trial of Disputes Involving Crew Members

13. Regulations of the Supreme People's Court on Evidence in Civil Litigation on Intellectual Property Rights

14. Supplemental Arrangement concerning Mutual Enforcement of Arbitral Awards between the Mainland and the Hong Kong Special Administrative Region

15. Interpretation of the Supreme People's Court on Issues concerning the Application of Law in the Trial of Civil Disputes Relating to Food Safety (I)

16. Regulations of the Supreme People's Court on the Application of the Time Effect of the Civil Code of the People's Republic of China

17. Decision of the Supreme People's Court on Abolishing Judicial Interpretations and Related Normative Documents

18. Decision of the Supreme People's Court on Revising the Interpretation of the Supreme People's Court on Issues concerning the Application of the Trade Union Law of the People's Republic of China in the Work of Civil Trials and Other 27 Judicial Interpretations on Civil Matters

19. Decision of the Supreme People's Court on Revising 29 Judicial Interpretations in Commercial Matters, Including the Reply of the Supreme People's Court on the Question of Whether the State-Owned Land Use Rights of Bankrupt Enterprises Should Be Included in the Bankruptcy Property

20. Decision of the Supreme People's Court on Revising the Judicial Interpretation of the Supreme People's Court on Issues concerning the Application of Law in the Trial of Disputes on Infringement of Patent Rights (II) and 18 Other Judicial Interpretations on Intellectual Property Rights

21. Decision of the Supreme People's Court on Revising 19 Judicial Interpretations of the Supreme People's Court on Issues concerning Civil Mediation in the People's Courts and Other Judicial Interpretations of Civil Litigation

22. Decision of the Supreme People's Court on Revising the Judicial Interpretation of the Supreme People's Court on Issues concerning the Seizure of Goods Transported by Rail by the People's Courts and Other 18 Judicial Interpretations on Execution

23. Interpretation of the Supreme People's Court on the Application of the Book on Marriage and Family of the Civil Code of the People's Republic of China (Ⅰ)

24. Interpretation of the Supreme People's Court on the Application of the Book on Inheritance of the Civil Code of the People's Republic of China (Ⅰ)

25. Interpretation of the Supreme People's Court on the Application of the Book of Property of the Civil Code of the People's Republic of China (Ⅰ)

26. Interpretation of the Supreme People's Court on the Application of Law in the Trial of Construction Contract Disputes (Ⅰ)

27. Interpretation of the Supreme People's Court on the Application of Law in the Trial of Labor Dispute Cases (Ⅰ)

28. Reply of the Supreme People's Court on the Scope of Application of the New Judicial Interpretation of Private Lending

29. Interpretation of the Supreme People's Court on the Application of the Stipulations of the Guarantee System of the Civil Code of the People's Republic of China

30. Decision of the Supreme People's Procuratorate on the Abolishing the Interpretation of the Supreme People's Procuratorate on Issues concerning the Specific Application of Law in Handling Criminal Cases of Illegal Operation of Table Salt

31. Working Rules of the Procuratorial Committees of People's Procuratorate

32. Decision of the Supreme People's Procuratorate on Abolishing some Judicial Interpretations and Regulatory Documents

图书在版编目（CIP）数据

中国法治建设年度报告. 2020 / 中国法学会编. —北京：中国长安出版传媒有限公司，2021.9
ISBN 978-7-5107-1060-5

Ⅰ. ①中… Ⅱ. ①中… Ⅲ. ①社会主义法治–建设–研究报告–中国–2020 Ⅳ. ①D920.0

中国版本图书馆 CIP 数据核字（2021）第 151946 号

责任编辑：刘英雪　刘　爽

中国法治建设年度报告（2020）

中国法学会　编

出版：中国长安出版传媒有限公司
社址：北京市东城区北池子大街 14 号（100006）
网址：http://www.ccapress.com
邮箱：capress@163.com
发行：中国长安出版传媒有限公司
电话：（010）66529988-1319
印刷：天津鑫旭阳印刷有限公司
开本：710mm×1000mm　16 开
印张：24
字数：210 千字
版本：2021 年 9 月第 1 版　2021 年 9 月第 1 次印刷

书号：ISBN 978-7-5107-1060-5
定价：88.00 元